ANT

ANT

THE INCREDIBLE JOURNEY
OF NBA RISING STAR
ANTHONY EDWARDS

CHRIS HINE

HARPER
An Imprint of HarperCollins*Publishers*

HarperCollins books may be purchased for educational, business, or sales promotional use. For information, please email the Special Markets Department at SPsales@harpercollins.com.

FIRST EDITION

Designed by Bonni Leon-Berman

Library of Congress Cataloging-in-Publication Data has been applied for.

ISBN 978-0-06-343895-8

25 26 27 28 29 LBC 5 4 3 2 1

To Mom, Dad, Jennifer, Carolyn, and Matt.
Thank you for everything.

CONTENTS

ANT

INTRODUCTION

Anthony Edwards sat on the sidelines at the Delta Center in Utah, breathing hard after putting up several shots at the end of Timberwolves shootaround in March 2024. I had put in a request with the team's PR staff to interview Edwards this morning, something I only do on the road when I really need to speak with him for a story.

It may seem hard to believe, given the amount of media Edwards is in—commercials for Adidas and several other major corporations, viral sound bites from postgame interviews and press conferences—but Edwards doesn't always like it when microphones or cameras are in front of him. He can grow weary of their presence, especially as his fame rose through his first five NBA seasons. So as a beat reporter who has covered Edwards as long as he's been in the NBA, I know I have to pick my moments. This morning in Utah was the right moment. No other media was present. National outlets don't come to Utah, no other reporters travel regularly on the Wolves beat, and team-affiliated media was not going to horn in on my time with Edwards. I could have a rare chance of interviewing him one-on-one.

I needed to speak with Edwards for a feature I was writing about him for the newspaper I work for, the *Minnesota Star Tribune*. It revolved around how at twenty-two, he was the emotional fulcrum of a team that featured two older, All-NBA level players (Karl-Anthony Towns and Rudy Gobert) who had run-ins before with high-profile teammates earlier in their careers: Towns with Jimmy Butler in Minnesota and Gobert with Donovan Mitchell in Utah. The feature was a chance to highlight an aspect of Edwards's personality—how he is the ultimate positive teammate. How that is both a part of who he is and an intentional leadership tactic, that he knows his energy can have a ripple effect throughout a team.

His energy wasn't at full blast this morning, and when a team PR representative went over to inform Edwards he had been requested for media, a disappointed look came over his face. He didn't want to do it. Before he could say a word, the PR rep said, "It's just Chris." There were no cameras around, no need for Edwards to put on his usual mix of charm and humor. He looked at me standing about twenty feet away, and he waved me over.

We spoke for about five minutes, and I used some of the quotes in an article that ran the following month during the Wolves' playoff run to the Western Conference Finals. The headline: "Timberwolves' Positive Team Chemistry Cooked Up by All-Star Anthony Edwards." The two quotes I used from Edwards distilled who he has been as a teammate at every level of athletic competition, from his youth football days playing for the Atlanta Vikings until now.

First we spoke about Gobert, with the context being how Gobert, the four-time Defensive Player of the Year, faces a barrage of external criticism on social media from people who think his defense is overrated and that he looks clumsy on offense.

"You can't talk about his flaws," Edwards said. "You have to talk about what he great at. He's been doing a phenomenal job this entire season. I'm just not the type of guy that be like, 'Aw, he's trash.' I'm always trying to uplift my teammates."

Then we spoke about Towns, who also gets his share of social media criticism and whom Butler came to despise during his brief stint in Minnesota. Edwards took the opposite approach. He had always been Towns's ultimate hype man, the one who would pump him up by saying he could play at an MVP level, and he didn't let Towns's flaws obscure his relationship with him.

"The stuff he do, you accept him for who he is," Edwards said. "We got a team full of people that's like, we gonna tell you about yourself, but we also gonna embrace each other."

Then he said: "I just pride myself on always wanting to see my teammates, a smile on they face."

That's the ethos of Anthony Edwards. Later that night, Edwards put a smile on everyone's face, including his own. This was the same day Edwards created one of the most memorable highlights of his career: his posterizing dunk over Jazz forward John Collins. In seven seasons covering the NBA, I had never seen a road arena react in total shock as those fans did in Salt Lake City that night. Edwards didn't even dunk the ball. He threw it down at terminal velocity through the hoop, and it was so vicious, Collins went out of the game for concussion evaluation. Edwards's leaping ability was evident from his first year in the NBA; this was on another level.

I watched as Edwards did his postgame interview with local television and he saw the replay for the first time. He exclaimed, among other things, "Oh my God," elongating the vowel sound in "God" to make it sound like *gawd*. He said it with an inflection and pitch that you can recognize from a lot of people from Atlanta in his life, namely his "Uncle" Drew Banks. In the locker room, his teammates couldn't believe what had happened. It was like a roomful of schoolkids who had to share just where they were and what their reaction was when this extraordinary thing occurred. Kyle Anderson asked, "Y'all ever see a dead body?" Veteran Mike Conley said he nearly drew the first technical foul of his career coming off the bench. He then compared Edwards's leaping ability to a cat who just keeps rising. Nickeil Alexander-Walker said that one day he would tell his grandchildren he got the assist on the play.

Edwards came in and did his postgame media scrum: cameras around, multiple media members present. There was no need to force the wide smile on his face.

"Watching Vince Carter jump over somebody or like watching T-Mac [Tracy McGrady], I always dreamed of dunking on somebody like that, and that was like my favorite one of all time," Edwards said.

When the interview session was over, Edwards was watching the replays back on his phone, and just before I left the locker room, I heard him exclaim, "Got 'eeeeem!" loud enough for anyone outside to hear.

His energy permeated the locker room and that team after he arrived in 2020. His positivity, his jovial nature, and his ability to do special things on the court galvanized the Wolves squad. They are qualities he has always possessed, qualities coaches have always asked him to tap into not just for himself but for those around him.

Given his life story and the obstacles Edwards overcame to get where he is, it's remarkable he has that within him. His spirit never dimmed, and perhaps what happened in his youth growing up in the Oakland City section of Atlanta served to make it stronger when it might have kept others down. Those around him marvel at the obstacles he overcame and the lengths Edwards went to as a teenager to make his NBA dream come true. The viral clips, the highlights, and the commercials are what people see about Anthony Edwards. What they don't show is another side, a man who is wise beyond his years when it comes to emotional intelligence and his ability to read a person or a situation. The term "old soul" came up several times in interviews for this book.

In the fall of 2024, I asked Edwards if he wanted to sit down for an interview for this project. He initially agreed, but about ten days later, he changed his mind. Why? He was tired of doing extra interviews, longtime Edwards coach and business manager Justin Holland communicated to me. I must have caught him on a good day that morning in Utah. My request came on the heels of a bunch of commercial shoots. Besides, Edwards told Holland, dozens of people in his orbit had already spoken for the project, so he didn't need to (so he felt).

This book has eleven chapters, but in a way it is the first in the life story of Anthony Edwards. Most of this book was written and reported from August through November 2024. Upon publication, Edwards will be finishing his fifth NBA season at twenty-three years old. So much of his career and legacy is still ahead of him. This is the story of how Edwards got to this point, and how the personality and ability of one of the NBA's brightest stars came to be.

CHAPTER 1

THE ATLANTA VIKINGS

Mozley Park, about ten minutes north of where Anthony Edwards grew up in the Oakland City section of southwest Atlanta, has elevated hills surrounding its football field. When the Atlanta Vikings would practice on that field, the youths' parents could watch, but they couldn't come down from the hills. If they did, they had to make sure they remained a fair distance away.

No matter what the coaches were doing in practice, no matter how many hitting drills they were doing, no matter how many suicides the kids were running, it was understood nobody could come down from the hill to complain. The coaches had to coach, and parents had to understand what they were signing off on. As Kyle Sturdivant, one of Edwards's childhood friends and AAU basketball teammates, put it, "The Atlanta Vikings football program is like Alabama youth football." That might be a bit sacrilegious for Sturdivant to say in the same state with the University of Georgia Bulldogs, but the point is the same.

It was also on this hill that Yvette Edwards would cheer on her youngest child, Anthony. She would wear the Vikings purple and gold colors, accessories to match.

"She gonna put her makeup on, long eyelashes—them big long eyelashes, them throwbacks," said her cousin, Tommy Slaughter, who also coached Anthony on the Vikings when he was eight and nine. "She was gonna let you know who her baby was."

She had to be looking good as Ant Man, the team's running back, was going to be scoring a lot of touchdowns. She would make a lot of noise, though not just for her son—it was for everyone on the team. If the team's quarterback, Reign Watkins, did something special, Yvette would cheer just as loud for him too. That carried over to AAU basketball, where Yvette's energy and enthusiasm filled up the gym. She would make clothes or jewelry for the other moms to wear in support of their kids, like large hoop earrings individualized with each kid's number.

"Gregarious, fun, shit talking . . . crazy eyelashes, crazy outfits," said Dana Watkins, or Coach Dana to Edwards and his friends. He is Reign's father, the coach of Edwards's early AAU basketball teams, and someone who played a large role in Edwards's development. "You got to have your wild sisters, [as well as your] more conservative sisters. She was one of the wild ones. Just a fun-loving, energetic superfan. His number one cheerleader for sure, which is most important. I'm sure he hinges on that."

Yvette would drive to that hill in her white crossover SUV, with one window taped up, after she got off work around 8 p.m. Eleven-year-old Anthony would still be on that field running after practice, making up for being out of uniform, showing up late, or goofing off. Yvette would become anxious in the car, wondering just when Anthony would be done. Even though there was no complaining from the hill, she'd blow the horn and flash the lights at the coaching staff down on the field.

"She'd say, 'Coach, I don't mean to be rude, but I just got off work at Walmart and I'm trying to go home and cook for him to get him ready for school,'" coach Tim Wynn said. "And I could look and see it in her eyes."

"It" was the exasperation of being a single mother trying to keep her family of four kids together while holding down that job at Walmart.

Wynn, the Atlanta legend who runs the Vikings program, told Yvette she could go straight home from that moment onward. Don't bother coming to get Anthony. He and others would take care to see that he got home safe from practice. That favor also had a secondary effect.

"Momma ain't looking for him on that hill," Wynn said. "Momma can't bail you out."

The Vikings formed a significant portion of Edwards's youth. From the time he could play football, around age five, to the time he stopped playing in high school, his life was a constant toggle back and forth between football and basketball. June to December was football; December to June was basketball. Rinse and repeat until he was about fourteen years old. He was never not playing sports. Despite having three other kids to take care of (Antoine, Antony, and Antoinette, so named after their father, Anthony), and despite scraping by while living in Oakland City, one of the most dangerous areas of Atlanta, Yvette and her mother, Shirley, were there to cheer on their Ant Man, no matter if the game was in Atlanta or at an out-of-state tournament. Several people in Edwards's life refer to him as a momma's boy, and the two had a special bond. The sentiment from multiple people was *Yvette loved all her children, but . . .*

They wouldn't have to finish the sentence; it was understood Anthony had a special place in her heart.

"She was juggling, but it always seemed like Ant was the centerpiece," Dana said. "They slept in the same bed together . . . and with Ant's sports, it trumped everything."

His time with the Vikings was her time to show up and watch Edwards show out. No matter the stresses of day-to-day life or the rigid discipline of the practices during the week, there were always Ant Man's football games to look forward to on the weekends. It was a time for a lot of joy in their lives. On some of Edwards's highlights on YouTube, you can see Yvette cheering in the crowd. Those memories are a keepsake for Edwards and his family.

"I almost get teary-eyed," Slaughter said. "Those videos . . . Ant can always pull those up and see his mother running, cheering, yelling when he's doing something positive. And I don't know how many times at night, or when he's by himself, do he ever go back and pull that up and look at her?"

Practice?

Wynn can't remember how many games he's won—likely over 800, he says, with less than 30 losses. During a dinner of wings and fries in August 2024 at a J.R. Crickets in southwest Atlanta, he and a few others swapped stories about Edwards's time on the Vikings, with the details sometimes becoming exaggerated. Also strolling into the restaurant that night came a few of Wynn's alumni, and he stopped to catch up with each of them.

The towering but soft-spoken Wynn summed up his coaching style in a word: militant.

"What was the difference between then [when he played] and now, and what I gathered was preparation, fundamentals, discipline, structure," Wynn said. "That was my thing."

If a player was out of uniform, he ran. That included during games. In one game, Slaughter said, the Vikings' quarterback didn't show up with the right-color socks, so Wynn made him run around the track for the entire game—allowing for a break at halftime. Slaughter called this "the Tim" and would threaten some of his own players with it. Even if an assistant coach was out of uniform, Wynn would tell him to sit in the stands.

"If we're gonna be coaches, we got to set an example," Wynn said.

Everyone had to be in uniform, disciplined, and they were going to work in practice. If there was a limit on how often a team could practice during a week, the Vikings didn't care. They were still going to be out there as much as they felt was necessary, and each practice was going to be intense.

"They talkin' 'bout we couldn't practice but for two days, three days. We practiced every day," Slaughter said, scoffing at the idea that anyone would try to tell the Vikings what to do.

There was running, lots of it, up and down that hill, or suicides at the end of practice where coaches would line up at the twenty-yard line, the players on the goal line. Then the coaches would go back ten yards each time until they reached the opposite goal line.

"My brother came and witnessed one of our practices and had never seen anything like that," Dana said. "Never seen kids running the hills, sprinting up the hills, for apparently no reason at all."

Added Reign: "I don't think those type of practices would be allowed today."

But to those who were in the Vikings world, the high standards and rigid discipline were a part of the deal, beginning with the 6-and-under program and extended through 12-and-under. Rory Starkey, whose son Rory Jr. played in the Vikings program and went on to the NFL, said that when he was looking for a place for his son to play, he visited another program where the moms came down to the field in the middle of practice with juices and snacks.

"This was six-and-under, but this wasn't football as I understand it," Starkey said. "I asked people, Where are they playing real tough football? I was told Atlanta Vikings."

Reluctant as he was to practice—and Edwards wasn't alone in that sentiment—Edwards stuck it out with the Vikings every year until he graduated from the program. Each summer, Edwards and Reign Watkins would check in with each other to see if they were actually going to go through with football again, since neither wanted to go through conditioning again.

"He didn't want to come to practice," Dana said.

Edwards might goof around at home a little to miss conditioning at the start of practice, but he was going to run one way or the other, no matter how much he tried to get out of it.

Drew Banks, whose son Drew played with Edwards, and who became one of the most important people in Edwards's life then and now, witnessed the stall tactics Edwards would deploy to get out of this part of practice.

"Practice would be starting and he'll be getting dressed all slow because he didn't want to do the cardio, the actual running," Banks said.

He also knew that one way to get out of running after practice was to stall just long enough for his mother to arrive and convince the coaches it was time for him to go home.

"She gave us a little leeway, like five or ten minutes after, but then she'd say he gotta go," Banks said. "He knew that too. He used that to his advantage."

But the high standards yielded results. Vikings football was serious business, in more ways than one. Dana, who was the commissioner of

Mozley Park for a time, said when he first showed up to a 6-and-under game, parents and fans in the stands were betting on the result.

"This was my introduction to everybody putting money on it, people asking how much you got on it," Watkins said. "I'm like, 'What the hell y'all talking about? Six-and-under? This is what y'all doing?'"

When Edwards was ten, the Vikings welcomed a team from Detroit, Banks said, and a man associated with that program "bet the whole [Vikings] sideline" on the outcome.

"Mine might have been petty, like $150," Banks said. "But the guy came from Detroit, whatever you said, he was gonna bet. Some people sayin' $400, $500, $1,000. We don't know who the hell the guy was."

The Vikings got off to a slow start, and some nerves jittered through the crowd—until Edwards and Reign "figured it out." The Vikings won, and the man from Detroit paid everybody.

"People were betting on Ant way before now," Banks said with a laugh. "We *been* betting on him."

The betting was woven into the fabric of their games, and people were so prideful the Vikings could beat any team—across the city, the suburbs, or nationally—that they were more than happy to put their money on the line. That included some of Edwards's family members, like his uncle Chris, who knew Ant could single-handedly win games by himself.

When Edwards was ten, the Vikings were at a tournament that also featured Deion Sanders's Prime Prep Academy, with his son Shedeur, who was in Edwards's age group, Dana said. Prime Academy ended up not facing the Vikings, even though the Vikings were anxious for a matchup. At one point during the tournament, one of the Vikings coaches, Jermyn Wright, wasn't going to let it slide.

"He got on the mic, 'Hey, Prime Academy. You're ducking us!'" Dana said. "The whole crowd is listening to this. Called Deion out."

But the Vikings and Sanders's team still didn't play that day. As Reign said, the Vikings had played them in a previous year and "they ducked us after that."

Reign and Edwards were the team backbone during their years

playing together. Teams had trouble containing two athletes who could run circles around them or straight lines over them. Reign was a skilled, dynamic quarterback and also played tailback when Banks's son played quarterback. Edwards was an overpowering running back who looked like a youth version of Derrick Henry steamrolling or skating past helpless, tiny defensive backs.

"It was always Reign and Ant coming up, and if you put them two together, they can fight any team," Slaughter said.

The Vikings also had the best threads in the city. They had a seemingly unlimited uniform budget at every level. The older players got, the more uniforms they had, with Wynn's 12-and-under squad getting the most gear.

"Tim's team might have seven uniforms with five helmets," Slaughter said.

There was even one time the Vikings warmed up in one uniform, went into the woods near the field, changed, and reemerged in a different uniform.

"You can tell whoever was funding them knew they was nice because they had all the top stuff," Sturdivant said.

Dana, who handled the money as park commissioner, said with a laugh that the Vikings program was able to solicit donations from "the entrepreneurs of the area," as he put it. Some of those donations also came in from Vikings NFL alumni like Adam "Pacman" Jones and Jamal Lewis. One donor even gave $50,000 for two sets of 6-and-under uniforms and helmets.

"When I look back in hindsight, it was nonsense," he said. "It was such a waste of money."

Oakland City

On a Wednesday night in August 2024, the Vikings were going through another practice, and all age groups were feeling the pain. Some were doing crabwalks up the hill that Edwards and his teammates used to run on. The ground there is so worn on that section of the hill that there is no grass, only dirt.

To make matters worse, that hill is the last part of the park the sun hits as its setting. There isn't even a small reprieve of shade later in the day.

Once they were done on the hill, the players did laps around the field, with crabwalks in between. There would also be duckwalks, where a player would crouch and walk in that position. These were especially painful, and were something the team might do in the hotel the night before a road game.

"And when you do them right, it would kill you, especially a tall kid like Ant Man," Wynn said with a maniacal laugh.

One eight-year-old had to drag a pair of tires around the field after he said he wasn't doing his push-ups correctly. Parents sat off on the hills or in other remote parts of the park taking it all in, but not interfering.

Wynn sat nearby on his bucket, which was the same way he would watch Edwards's practices until something went wrong that caused him to come off his perch. That was a typical night of Vikings practice.

About a ten-minute drive northwest of the park on small Lockwood Drive, which is only about four blocks long, sat a man on his small front porch in front of a green and white house he has owned for over fifty years. In front of him on a driveway that extended up a small hill to the front door was a white 2004 Toyota Corolla, or as Ben Edwards, the grandfather of Anthony, pronounced it, "Tie-ota."

"Toyota, man," he said. "They don't make 'em too much more better. Got about 167,000 [miles] on it."

This was one of the cars that took Ben's four grandchildren around when they were younger and living in this house for a time with Yvette. The kids never went anywhere on public transportation, or what Atlanta calls MARTA (Metropolitan Atlanta Rapid Transit Authority). That was too fraught with peril.

"Their momma didn't like them to hang around in the streets. None of that stuff," Ben Edwards said. "When I tell you, they ain't never been on a MARTA bus, they don't know what that's like. That's true."

Ben only takes that Corolla out for a spin once a week, he said, just to go to the grocery store. Other than that, he just wants to sit on the porch and enjoy his peace. He's now alone in a home that once housed seven: him, his wife, Yvette, and her four kids.

"I don't want to go nowhere," he said. "I feel so much safer sitting on this porch and being at this house than anyplace else. You got to really watch yourself if you go out in these streets. Shooting and killing each other left and right like there ain't nothin' to it."

Off to the right of the house behind a metal fence is a basketball hoop with a backboard that's tilted. A log is on the back of it to weigh it down. Even though the boys have been out of the house a long time, the hoop remains, a relic to all the times Anthony played his brothers, in particular Antony (nicknamed Bubba), on that hoop.

"They had little fights, would come in the house and cry a little bit," Ben said. "Then next few minutes he'd go back out there, and see if he can beat him."

That applied to both of them, the inseparable Ant and Bubba, who was three years older than Anthony.

"Bubba and Ant Man like glue," Ben said. "Them two guys, man, they stuck together. They was together all the time. You seen one, you seen the other one."

That relationship endures, with Bubba sitting in seats at the Timberwolves home games across from the bench. He's typically seated next to Nick Maddox, one of Edwards's best friends since high school.

Going outside to play on that hoop was one of the only times the Edwards boys were let out of the house in Oakland City. On the walls of that house, Edwards used to write his life ambitions.

"It's still there," Ben Edwards said. "I don't bother with any of that stuff."

One of the walls says, "Future McDonald's All-American #GOAL."

If they weren't in the house or outside playing on the hoop, they were at school, at a gym, at football practice, or in the house eating, playing video games, or sleeping.

"They don't know what the streets is," Ben said.

Yvette made sure of that, and she made sure that she always knew where they were at any given moment.

"They couldn't do nothin'," Ben said. "She know every minute that they moved and was going somewhere, and she raised three good boys and a good girl."

In the summer of 2023, before it launched Edwards's signature shoe, the AE1, Adidas commissioned a custom mural of Edwards, Yvette, and Shirley in Atlanta. When he does get into his Toyota, Ben can drive a few minutes and see his grandson's face flanked by Yvette's and Shirley's, a testament to the pride Oakland City has in the Edwards family. Adidas held an event to unveil it that summer with a performance from fellow Oakland City native Lil Baby.

"The highlight of my offseason? Probably was the mural," Anthony said in September 2023. "I think that was more important than everything."

That night, in August 2024, Dana, who spent as much time around Edwards as anybody when Edwards was growing up, reintroduced himself to Ben. Ben wasn't frequently in attendance at Edwards's football and basketball games. Those were for Yvette, Shirley, Edwards's siblings, and his uncle Chris. Ben asked Dana and me that if they spoke to his grandson, "Tell him the house needs more paint." He enjoys keeping the house and enjoys his peace of mind when nobody is around. A much different scene than a decade prior.

The conversation Ben had with Dana that evening stirred something within him. Dana knew that Ben hadn't seen Anthony play any games since high school, and Dana offered to take Ben to see Anthony the next time the Wolves played in Atlanta. They swapped phone numbers. A few days later, Ben called Dana and said he wanted to go. They stayed in touch, and when that day came—December 23—Ben went with Dana to State Farm Arena to surprise Ant at a Hawks-Timberwolves game. Several times leading up to the game, Ben called Dana to confirm the logistics of the night, to make sure he knew what time to be ready and what to wear.

"Hey, man, it's about time," Ben said that night. "I have to go see him at least once."

Dana had made a hard sell in the months between that night on the porch and the Wolves's visit for Ben to come, that he should go see Anthony play in person while he still could.

"This man right here, talked to me like somebody who had some sense," Ben said of Dana. "I believe him, and he just does what he says he'll do."

"You're eighty-two years old, have a grandkid who's able to ascend where he's ascending, if you ain't going to see it now, when you gonna see it?" Dana said. "It's about the now. Life's about the now, taking advantage of it."

Anthony didn't know his grandfather was going to show up, and after he finished his pregame warm-ups, he turned around and saw Ben sitting under a basket. Anthony ran over to him, a big smile on his face, and bent down to give him a hug before chatting with him for a few minutes. They spent some time together after the game as well.

"Sad I ain't get the W for him, but I'm just happy he was here," Anthony told me in my capacity as beat writer for the *Star Tribune* following a Wolves loss. "My heart was warm when I seen him. That was great."

When asked if he got some of his swagger from his grandfather, Edwards laughed and said no, but he did get an important quality.

"I got my being down to earth. Just being cool under all circumstances," he said. "I think I got that from him. Like he never let any circumstance get him out of who he is and stuff like that. Just being cool, calm, and collected through everything."

Oh, and he got something else too—the desire to be a homebody.

"He just like me, man," Anthony said. "I wanna go to the house, be in my game room, play my [video] game. He wanna go sit on his couch, his little chair and watch his TV shows."

A ten-minute drive east of where Ben likes to sit on his porch is a boarded-up house and an even narrower street, now known as Andrew J. Hairston Place, where Yvette used to live before the family had to move in with Shirley and Ben. The house isn't much recognizable to Dana, who used to drop Edwards off there after football games and basketball tournaments. He had to confirm with Edwards via text that this was, in fact, the address of the old house.

"Ant has a softness to him," Dana said. "Nobody would ever confuse him with somebody being hard or street. That's not Ant. Ant is really a soft kid that's in a bigger body. He's not about that street life. He could . . . sound country, Atlanta, all that—but soft as all get-out, which is a good thing."

The light blue house looks a bit nicer, and seems to be a product of gradual gentrification that is creeping into Oakland City and surrounding neighborhoods near downtown Atlanta. Other lots appear as if they were condemned and abandoned for decades.

Oakland City is known for its violent crime rate and issues with drugs, especially heroin.

"You could almost know, okay, out of these fifty kids [on the team], some of them are gonna get in trouble. You can't save them all," Dana said. "Football is kind of their glue, but they go back out into the world, and I told Reign, be glad you know them, because if you're in the wrong place at the wrong time, one of these kids could save you."

Yvette never had an issue with the strict discipline the Vikings put in her son's life. With that, she was like several single mothers, Dana said, who sent their kids to the Vikings program for discipline and to have male authority figures in their lives. Infractions in school, like skipping class, could become grounds for discipline in football practice, even though the program wasn't affiliated with a school.

Sports were the vehicle to get Edwards out of their house in Oakland City and to keep him out of trouble. The same went for when they moved in with Shirley and Ben. It was better than hanging around outside. If Edwards wasn't playing sports somewhere away from the neighborhood, he was inside the house playing video games.

"He lucky he got video games," Slaughter said.

Anything besides being outside on the street. Edwards often talks about his love of video games, and back then he mostly played *Madden* or *NBA 2K* (usually with the teams of his favorite player, Kevin Durant). His love affair with gaming can often contribute to funny moments in interviews, like when he said he was unbeatable when he used to play *NBA 2K* as the "Grit n' Grind" Memphis Grizzlies, whose point guard, Mike Conley, became a teammate of Edwards's in 2023. The Netflix documentary *Starting 5* also played up Edwards's video game addiction, like showing him obsessing over a game as his family gathered for Thanksgiving, and how Edwards has a special suitcase for his system when traveling. His attachment to video games runs deep.

Video games became a part of who Edwards was, the way he and his family got through the day. They are still how he spends a significant amount of his free time. He's not one to go out a lot, his former college roommate Tye Fagan said, but he'd always be up late playing video games.

When Edwards joined the NBA, he purchased a luxury apartment with multiple bedrooms in Atlanta. But one room, according to Reed Ridder, a graduate assistant at Georgia who worked closely with Edwards, featured just a gaming chair and a TV on the floor when Ridder visited a few summers ago.

"He's got headphones in with his gaming chair and he's playing that," Ridder said. "And so I told him, 'You got millions of dollars, man.' And he's like, 'This is all I need right here, man, just the chair and the game.'"

An assistant coach who recruited Edwards to Georgia, Amir Abdur-Rahim, said he thought when Edwards entered the NBA, his penchant for video games stuck to him through the draft process, and it contributed to a perception that Edwards didn't love playing basketball when he spent so much time gaming.

"People laugh like, 'Man, why is this dude playing *Call of Duty* and *NBA 2K* for hours on hours. He need to get in the gym,'" Abdur-Rahim said.

Abdur-Rahim was an Atlanta native familiar with where Edwards grew up.

"He spent so much time on video games," he said. "But, so what, man? If you knew where he came from you would be in the house too."

Video games kept Edwards in those houses and out of trouble. He never displayed a desire to get caught in the dangers of the neighborhood.

"Ant didn't have that. Ant wasn't a street-type kid," Slaughter said. "You weren't gonna get that out of him. Ant gonna walk to the store and come back home. He ain't hanging out."

If Edwards was hanging out with friends, it was usually with some of his teammates who lived in other parts of Atlanta, and he'd often stay with families like the Watkinses because it would be convenient for him to get to tournaments or games with them. If those friends and their families entered Oakland City, they got in and out as quick as they could.

"That's one of the hardest parts," Sturdivant said. "Heroin, violence, robbing, prostitution, just to be candid. It's tough, and that's why I think he carries that shit on his shoulder to make it out of there."

Added Reign: "Definitely a place where it's not ideal to just be hanging out, especially as young kids. You see that growing up, their objective is to get out."

Edwards's uncle Chris played an important role in his childhood. Chris, who was Yvette's brother, would scoop the kids up to take them to a park, a gym, a field, anywhere they could to burn off energy and get out of the house.

"It was four bedrooms. It would get to the point where it would irk me because we were always crowded in the house," Chris Edwards said in a 2022 interview with the *Star Tribune*. "So I'd say, 'Let's go play, let's go to the gym. Let's go practice.' To get them out the house was to drop them off at the gym."

Those around Edwards credited Uncle Chris with being one of the prominent male figures in his life, since his father was not around much after Edwards was born.

"Chris did a lot," Slaughter said. "Chris did a ton, man."

Dana referred to Chris as a "protector" of Edwards, and it was Uncle Chris who knew how to keep his family out of trouble. He knew the streets of Oakland City, where to go and, more importantly, where not to go.

"Chris was Ant's surrogate guardian, provider, and consummate protector," Dana said. "Although Chris had a 'street edge' that was well documented with him, he was reluctant to expose Ant to any negative forces and assured that he was only left in the hands of trusted friends when he was unable to be present."

Chris would be right there with Yvette at Vikings games making sure everyone knew Edwards was his nephew, and he wasn't shy about putting a few dollars on Vikings games thanks to that confidence in his nephew to dominate the football field.

"Chris was one of those young uncles who got a stud nephew. Chris gonna let that be known," Slaughter said.

But that money wasn't always for himself; whatever costs were associated with Edwards's athletics, Uncle Chris was there if Edwards needed equipment or team fees.

"Yvette never had to worry about costs associated with any of the sports," Dana said. "If there were any gaps that needed to be filled, Chris most often was point person for Yvette."

Cousin Tommy

In early February 2024, Timberwolves head coach Chris Finch was in contention to coach the Western Conference at that season's All-Star Game. If the Wolves were able to win a few games before the All-Star break, Finch would lock up that honor (he eventually did).

At practice the day before a game against the Orlando Magic, Edwards was answering some questions about Finch's impact on the team and his coaching style. Finch has the reputation of being no-nonsense with his players and isn't afraid to call anyone out in a practice or film setting, and that includes Edwards and other big-name players.

"He don't kiss nobody's ass," Edwards said during that media scrum.

But when Edwards was asked just how hard Finch was on him, he flashed back to his days with the Vikings.

"That shit don't bother me, man," Edwards said. "I grew up playing football for my cousin and my mom gave permission for him to do whatever to me if I wasn't listening. What Finchy does to me is fuckin' nothin'."

Enter that cousin, Slaughter.

Throughout Edwards's life, there are people who think they are being hard on Edwards—from Finch to Tom Crean, his coach at Georgia, even his academic adviser in high school, Rachel Little. But nobody put Edwards through the hell he experienced when he began 8-and-under ball with the Vikings playing for his cousin Slaughter. And maybe it made Edwards better equipped to handle demanding coaches ever since.

The Vikings' methods were strict and harsh. Some might say they crossed a line, especially with kids that young. But there was a lot of pride in the results they produced and the men they cultivated, especially kids that came from tough neighborhoods. To Wynn, he was running a program to mold young men, and he was going to do it how he saw fit.

"Let me say this, when I got them kids, my thing was, one percent would probably go to . . . the NFL," Wynn said. "But what this is going to get you ready for . . . being a positive young man to go out here in society and be productive."

Starkey added, "Surviving."

Wynn continued: "This is what we were teaching them."

There was plenty of strict discipline when Edwards played 6-and-under ball, but it ramped up when he began playing for Slaughter, who was an assistant under head coach JP Jones. But Slaughter handled Ant. Slaughter first made his name around Atlanta as an AAU basketball coach. Javaris Crittenton, who went to Georgia Tech and played in the NBA, credited Slaughter with being one of the mentors who had a major influence on his career. The Vikings program didn't move Edwards up from his 6-and-under team even though he was dominating at the time. But Slaughter told his cousin Yvette when Edwards was done with that, "I got to get him right." Slaughter was going to coach him, and coach him hard.

"My thing was, this is my blood, I got to get him ready for ten-and-under and this man here," Slaughter said, pointing at Wynn, who coached the 12-and-under squad. "I'm considered a real tough seven-, eight-year-old coach. Real discipline, believe in aggressiveness."

That went double for Edwards when Slaughter was one of his

coaches. Slaughter saw a young Edwards as talented and gifted but also lazy. Yvette let her cousin discipline Edwards however he felt necessary.

"She can't save him, because we don't want to give him that," Slaughter said. "I could do things to Ant, discipline him, and other things that another coach couldn't get away with."

Said Edwards: "He used to grab my face mask, shake it, slap my helmet and shit."

This was all okay with Yvette.

"The only coach who could get away with grabbing him, shaking his face mask without him feeling some type of way or Momma complaining," Slaughter said. "I need to get all this in him right now before he get to [Wynn]. Because that man is going to teach him how to be a teenager, teach him responsibility."

During practices, Slaughter believed in doing a lot of hitting drills; this way his players understood how to play through pain.

"I probably hit more than any age group," Slaughter said. "I believed in coming off the ball, being aggressive, and being pain freaks, so when kids feel a shot, they can shake it off and be ready to roll."

For Reign, these were the worst drills the team went through. The running on the hills and the suicides were bad enough, but the copious hitting drills were what he couldn't take.

"The Oklahomas—they got started on that early," Reign said. "We had some hard hitters on our team. They not showing no mercy."

And because Slaughter was one of his coaches that year, there was no hiding for Edwards when he wanted to mess around and try to be late for practice or skip it altogether.

"Ant was my blood, so he couldn't miss practice," Slaughter said.

Not even when Yvette allowed him to miss one. When Yvette wanted to take Edwards to a local school's homecoming the night before a big game, Slaughter stepped in to say, "Ant comin' to practice." That's because in the upcoming game, Slaughter was planning to feed Edwards the ball a lot, and he didn't want anybody to think it was favoritism because they were related.

"I said why would you wanna put me in a situation where they say that's his blood, that's why he give him the ball every play? This and that," Slaughter said.

But Slaughter really didn't have to worry about that. All it takes is a few glances at YouTube clips of the Vikings to understand why they were so good. Edwards physically dominated almost everybody on the field. He had the size and agility to make anybody miss or regret hitting him. The Vikings faced complaints from other teams that Edwards had to be too old to be out there with his age group, but Yvette was only too happy to shout them down.

This was one of the benefits of Edwards's August 5 birthday; he just made the August 1 cutoff, but those extra months of growing he had on most of the other kids paid off at this point in his life. It also helped that Reign's birthday is the 11th.

"It just worked out to their benefit that this league had an August first cutoff, so time and time again, we would be accused of having kids that were too old, because not only were they skilled, they were tall," Dana said.

As Dana, Slaughter, Wynn, and Starkey reminisced about some of the best games the Vikings played, the details might have been fudged, games might have merged together. In one story, Slaughter claimed Edwards was dominating through a large snowstorm on the road:

"Goddamn, I never seen a kid run on ice," Slaughter said. "It started to snow, everybody there slippin' and fallin'. With those big ol' feet he had, he was gliding."

"They made us come way out there. It finna be a blizzard snowstorm coming."

Dana chimed in, "It was flurries."

Slaughter also said that was the same game the Vikings had to use three consecutive time-outs in the first half to allow Reign to throw up his breakfast before getting back under center. That was a separate game, the Watkins father-son duo said. But that did, in fact, happen.

"I normally don't eat breakfast before the game," Reign said. "This day [my mom] made breakfast. So I ate it. Got to the game, I remember it was like second quarter, all of it coming out."

His father was on the sideline trying to help Reign get through it as the coaching staff used one time-out after another to stall. Their other quarterback wasn't available for this game, so Slaughter was trying to milk every second he could.

"Dana come back around and tapped me on the back and said let's rock and roll, baby," Slaughter said.

"That's the kind of kids y'all made," Dana said.

The game plan after that was to give Edwards the ball as much as possible in an effort to conserve Reign's energy.

"Look at the kind of pressure I put on [Ant]," Slaughter said. "I used every time-out in the first quarter in a championship game with a team that's just as good. I said, 'Ant, you ready?' The more I ran Ant, the more Ant just became more of an animal."

The Vikings won that game, and it was a performance that let Slaughter and others around the program realize Edwards was "different," despite the reluctance to practice. There was nobody who could do what Edwards did on the field. The problem, sometimes, was that he knew it too, and that's where some of the hesitancy was when it came to practicing. From a young age, Edwards wanted to know the reasons behind what his coaches were doing with him. That has continued through his time in the NBA. If someone cannot give him a good reason, he won't buy in. But when Edwards was that young, he had no choice but to keep practicing.

"We would talk about not playing football in the upcoming season," Reign said. "It was about not wanting to go through it. I mean, the games, that's ultimately something that we enjoyed. The games were fun. Competition was fun, but practice? Man."

Edwards didn't have the power he would have later in life to walk away from a person or a situation he didn't like. Besides, Mom signed off on this, so he really didn't have a say.

Plus, he was too good. There was another game, with highlights available on YouTube, from when he was eight and the Vikings traveled to play a suburban school, McDonough. The Vikings had a roster full of Black players, while McDonough had plenty of white players, Dana said.

Edwards, wearing No. 44, dwarfed almost everyone on McDonough's team. This was one of the first times, Dana added, that opposing parents accused Edwards of being too old for this age bracket, because McDonough was not used to losing like this.

The highlights, from the company "Born to Compete," even slow down for a moment and drop out the crowd noise when Edwards delivers a punishing stiff-arm to a helpless defensive back. There was another moment where Edwards threw a block that ejected another, much smaller defender from his cleats into the air and onto his back.

In the second half, Edwards threw off a few defenders as he cut up the sideline and separated from the pack for his third touchdown of the game.

"You gotta see it, the speed differential, everything. He always had that," Slaughter said. "Most kids who had the size like that are not coordinated."

The Vikings won 40–7. This game was an encapsulation of who Edwards was as a youth football player. But it's significant for another reason. At the one-minute mark, the camera catches Yvette in what appears to be her outfit from Walmart clapping after the Vikings' first touchdown. It's only a brief moment where you can see her cheering, but there are a few videos like that online for Edwards and his family to see whenever they want.

"It's natural," Slaughter said. "If you can see something with your momma on there and every time they show him, they show him scoring and she's cheering and screaming with her work clothes on, coming right from work, tryna see about that boy."

As Edwards got older, Slaughter wished he could have been a larger part of his life, but for about twenty years, Slaughter has battled complications from colorectal cancer.

"They call it old-man disease," he said. "They didn't see this type of disease come to a young person; they always assumed you have to be old."

In the summer of 2024, he said he was going through TPN treatments to feed his body intravenously. This puts a lot of pressure on his kidneys, he said, and he also goes through dialysis as a result.

"And I don't even have bad kidneys," he said.

"You're on a machine fourteen hours a day, and you get fed through your veins, port in my chest," he added. "I get hooked up at night to be on a machine, make my medicine up every day. They bring me five days a week worth of medicine."

He said he had his first surgery in 2001 and has had over a dozen surgeries in his life. This type of life event isn't uncommon in their family, he said. Cancer claimed the lives of several family members going back generations, with colon cancer playing a big role.

"Hopefully it skips Ant," he said. "But it's a big part of my family. We've struggled."

Aunts and uncles, grandmothers and grandfathers all dying from it in their fifties and sixties, he said. He was diagnosed in his twenties but was still kicking in his forties.

Getting on a plane to spend a few days to see Edwards play in the NBA would be an ordeal. He asked what it was like to be at Timberwolves home games, and he grinned ear to ear when he heard how the crowd feeds off the energy Edwards brings, how he can command them with a wave of his arms and his megawatt smile.

"I wish that I was healthy enough to enjoy some of the small things, like going to watch him play in the US Olympics, going to some Minnesota games," Slaughter said. "I wouldn't even watch basketball like that the last few years because I was this great coach, and it was hard to sit and look at it.

"But I wanted Ant to do things great, and to watch him is just amazing. It's real amazing."

When Edwards made that comment in February 2024 about how hard Slaughter coached him back in the day, Slaughter said his phone began lighting up.

"He said, 'Basically I grew up with a fool coaching me,'" Slaughter said. "'Y'all talking about Finch? He's nothing. This MFer I grew up with, he'd grab my face mask, shake it up, threaten me—petrified of this motherfucker.'"

With that, Slaughter clapped his hands a couple times, sat back in his seat, and let out a few hearty laughs, the wheezing kind that make it sound like someone can barely breathe as they chuckle.

"Oh Lord," he said.

Uncle Drew, Playing for Wynn

From one perspective, Edwards wanting to escape the intensity of the Vikings practices didn't make him lazy; it just made him a normal kid. Who would want to go through all Edwards and his teammates had to go through? When Edwards was about to play under the self-described "militant" style of Wynn, he didn't feel much like playing football, Slaughter said, recalling a time he was taking Edwards to practice when he didn't want to go.

"Ant got one leg out the door," Slaughter said. "He's shaking his leg. *Take me home.* I said get your ass over here. Let me tell you somethin', this [Wynn] is who you gonna play for, for the next two years. I told 'Vette he needs this. If Ant gonna be what I think he is, he needs this right here."

From that point of view, the one shared by a lot of people in Edwards's life, the Vikings provided the structure and discipline Edwards would need to navigate his future. Especially early in his childhood and early teenage years, Edwards didn't thrive when left on his own without his people there. That applied to every facet of his life, from football to basketball to schoolwork. Nobody saw that more as Edwards was growing up than Banks, or Uncle Drew, as the Edwards circle knows him to this day.

"Made him who he is now," Banks said of the Vikings. "Ant was just naturally talented. Ant was one of them kids, he'd go through the motions unless you got a coach there that'll cuss him out and hold him accountable. Once you hold him accountable, he'll be totally different."

When Edwards played 12-and-under ball for Wynn, he would use his mother as a way to get out of doing those after-practice sprints and hill runs. But after a while, Wynn came up with a solution: he would just have Banks, who was an assistant on the team, take Edwards home. Yvette could return home straight from work and start on dinner, Edwards would get a ride home, and the coaches didn't have to cut short his postpractice running.

"After practice, we'd run his ass—forty-yard sprints," Wynn said.

"Everybody else is gone, he out there running forty yards. Come back, another one. He'd had to do like ten sets of them."

Added Banks: "Coach Tim wasn't having it."

Everybody won in this scenario except for Edwards, who then had to avoid his extra cardio the usual way—by practicing well, being on time, and being in uniform. The *Starting 5* documentary shows how much Edwards doesn't like packing his own bags for road trips. This usually falls to Banks. This tendency dates back to his Vikings days, when Edwards didn't want to properly pack for practice as a stall tactic to get out of running as practice began. Banks had to pack for him, and that continues to this day. Banks had already been helping Yvette with Edwards's transportation to and from practices and games, but now that he was on the coaching staff, this happened more frequently. As Banks put it, Edwards was always "my guy."

"No matter what it was," Banks said, "Momma did what she had to do. . . . So when I say he was my guy, like he needed this or if he needed that, or if I couldn't find him, I had to find him. The older he got I really had to track him down. Eleven and twelve? I probably could find him, because I knew there was only so many places he was gonna be. Somewhere playing something."

Wynn required the team go en masse to their games, which Banks likened to a "funeral" with about twenty cars showing up to a venue. Yvette would usually take Edwards to a meet-up spot, where he would then ride with Banks before going to the game herself. As he tended to do throughout his childhood, Edwards sat in the front seat on trips like this controlling the radio while other kids sat in the back.

"Nobody would say nothing to him. He was good," Banks said. "Whatever you wanna listen to. No issue. No disrespect."

Banks said when Edwards was eleven, the team lost some talent from 10-and-under ball, but that led to one of Edwards's best seasons "because he had to do more." That season also contained perhaps the most memorable football game Edwards ever played. Early in the season, the Vikings lost to the Cascade Wolverines but ended up facing them for that season's championship, with highlights still on YouTube.

"That was a game I didn't think we was gonna win," Banks said.

Banks's son Drew was injured, so Reign had to shift back to quarterback, with Edwards, wearing No. 3, playing primary tailback. On an early Vikings drive, they got near the goal line, and the person narrating the highlights for "Born to Compete" said, "As you see here, down on the goal line, they gonna go to No. 3. And you know this name. They call him Ant Man, one of the best players in the state for his age group. He gets to the end zone to give the Atlanta Vikings the lead."

Another Edwards touchdown gave the Vikings a 12–7 lead in the first half. But they were trailing 13–12 and needed to score late into the fourth quarter. This being 11-year-olds, a field goal wasn't an option. It was touchdown or bust on the final drive of the game.

With only a few plays left before time ran out, Wynn went into his bag for the winning play. The ball was on the right hash of the 14-yard-line, and the Vikings ran it right on a pitch to Edwards. Except Reign snuck out of the backfield to the left after making the toss. Edwards paused for a moment with the ball and got ready to throw. Cascade realized what was happening a little too late, and Reign had a step on the nearest defender. Edwards threw a perfect arching pass. Reign caught it at the 4-yard line and crossed the goal line as a defender tackled him for the winning score, 18–13.

"I told them two, 'That might've been one of your best games,'" Banks said.

When Edwards was in his second year of 12-and-under ball, Banks said Edwards dealt with a lot of "knickknack" injuries, as he called them. That resulted in an up-and-down year for him, even as the Vikings were still a juggernaut. He was healthy later that season when the Vikings welcomed a team from Tennessee that was older than they were, a team filled with 13- and 14-year-olds.

"Of course when they show up, they say, 'We ain't playing them,'" Dana said.

In the Vikings program, the age groups were used to scrimmaging against each other, so it was nothing for teams to match up against older competition. While the team from Tennessee balked at the idea of facing the Vikings, they eventually found a reason to stick around and take the game.

"Everybody put some money on it," Dana said.

Wynn made an agreement with the other team's head coach that the loser would make a donation to the other's program. Wynn was confident the Vikings could win straight up, but he at least wanted to negotiate a line for some added insurance.

"He said, 'We'll break your kids,'" Wynn said. "So I had to draw him up a waiver, sign it and date it, and I said give me six points."

Dana said Edwards was "acting a fool" early in the game and got benched. When he came back in, he went out to receive a pass and landed awkwardly on one of his ankles. When he came off to the sideline, the coaching staff thought he was just milking one of his many injuries that season. This one turned out to be more severe—he had broken it. This was the last game Edwards played for the Vikings program.

"Almost messed up Coach Tim's money," Dana said.

But the Vikings ended up winning a close game anyway. Afterward, Wynn and his opposing coach met to settle their agreement.

"He paid the guy he needed to pay for the money," Wynn said. "I told him, 'We'll feed y'all.' But he didn't even shake our hand. They went straight to the van and they left."

Edwards used to dream about playing football. Despite how rigorous the Vikings program was, in a 2022 interview with the *Star Tribune* Edwards called his experience "the best thing in the world that happened to me during that time in my life. . . . It was my pride and joy." Everyone in his life thought he was on a track to play college football and maybe make it in the NFL. He had the talent, he had the size and the physicality, and with the right prodding, he had the work ethic. He already had the reputation as one of the best players in the state. But that broken ankle was emblematic of how Edwards would feel moving forward in his football career. When he got to high school at Daniel McLaughlin Therrell High School, he still played football, but after sustaining more injuries, he gave it up.

"As I grew older, I'm like, I ain't trying to get hit like that," Edwards said in 2022.

This would have seemed unfathomable when Edwards was playing for the Vikings. Especially because when he played AAU basketball for Dana during this time, he really wasn't all that special.

"That was the mindset everybody had—football. He just played basketball to have fun. . . . We was straight thinking football," Banks said. "Basketball? Boy, stop."

CHAPTER 2

BASKETBALL, ANT'S OTHER SPORT

In the 2024 NBA playoffs, the Timberwolves faced the Phoenix Suns, which meant Edwards was set to square off against his childhood hero—Kevin Durant. Late in the third quarter of Game 1 at the Target Center in Minneapolis, Durant was guarding Edwards, and Edwards made his life miserable for a few minutes. First, Edwards pulled a series of moves in isolation on Durant to hit an open stepback midrange jumper. Then on Minnesota's next possession, Edwards forced Durant to navigate through consecutive Rudy Gobert screens on the perimeter. This gave Edwards enough room to drain a stepback three-pointer for a 16-point Minnesota lead. The energy coursed through the crowd, which hadn't experienced a playoff feeling like this since Kevin Garnett was with the Wolves twenty years earlier.

On his way down the floor, Edwards was feeling it too. He hopped backward, pounded his chest, and had more than a few words for Durant. Durant, who would say after that series that he loved "everything" about Edwards, could only laugh in the moment, even in such a big game. Following the Wolves blowout win, Edwards was asked about that exchange with Durant, since he had mentioned on several occasions that Durant was his favorite player.

"That was probably one of the best feelings ever in my whole life, for sure," Edwards said.

The spring and summer of 2024 was one long, full-circle moment for Edwards, who not only knocked off his hero in the playoffs; he also won a gold medal playing with him on Team USA. Think of the infinitesimal chances of something like this ever happening to anyone in life. What are the odds of making it to the NBA in the first place? Of Edwards's favorite player, who's thirteen years older than he is, having a long enough career that he's in the league at the same time? Of their respective teams just happening to meet in the playoffs? Of both getting selected to Team USA, being healthy enough to participate, and of their games complementing each other well enough that head coach Steve Kerr thought they'd be a good fit playing together off the bench?

It becomes even more improbable for Edwards considering the following: He was not a basketball prodigy from a young age. He was good enough to play high-level AAU basketball, but he actually came off the bench at times when he played many years under Dana and his assistant Jermaine Thompson.

"Ant was the sixth man, and it wasn't right," said Christopher Hinton Jr., a friend and former AAU teammate of Edwards who went on to play football at Michigan and in the NFL. "Everybody knew he should've been starting." (For the remainder of the book, we'll refer to the younger Hinton as Christopher and the older one as Chris.)

But he wasn't a set-it-and-forget starter as the team's best player, and that spoke to where he was during this time of his basketball life. Edwards didn't take off as a hooper until he hit high school, and the trajectory of his life at that time likely played a part in that. But from when he was a kid until the time he was about fourteen, he could only dream like everyone else of days in the NBA and of playing with or against his favorite player.

"That whole him and KD thing is a real thing," said Sturdivant, who was on a number of Edwards's AAU teams growing up.

He wore No. 35 when he was younger because of Durant, bought his shoes to wear, and friends said he would play with Durant's team on *NBA 2K*, whether with the Oklahoma City Thunder or later the Golden State Warriors.

Before the Olympics in July 2024, Edwards said his fandom of Durant began when he attended a game between the Thunder and Atlanta Hawks.

"That was the first player I liked on the court," Edwards said then.

To his friends, he even resembled Durant's play style, from the way he shot to the way he looked. His former teammates even used to tease him that he was Durant's son.

"'Bro, you look like Kevin Durant.' We'll always joke about it," Reign Watkins said. "He'll get on the game, start playing with Kevin Durant. So seeing it now is crazy."

To Christopher, there was a specific way Edwards resembled Durant, and everybody saw it.

"When he had his hair low, they had the same type of head," Christopher said. "Everybody thought that was KD's son."

So when he saw Edwards trash-talking Durant in the middle of a playoff game, Christopher said, "That gave me chills."

That's because when they all played together as kids, nobody could see this coming from Edwards. At that time, he was a member of very good AAU programs, first with Worldwide and then Southern Stampede, both of which were under Dana as coach. But he wasn't a standout. As Dana said, "Always an integral part of our team, but he wasn't *Ant*." Not the way he was in football.

"That was the mindset everybody had—football," Banks said. "He just played basketball to have fun, have something to do. When the [football] season started, he'd start football practice late. . . . The football coaches were like, 'Ant need to be here.' He was wasting time playing basketball. The whole city knew of Ant for football. Basketball? Stop it. Stop it."

Getting Started

The Vikings and the Atlanta youth football scene turned out to be a good recruiting ground for Dana to assemble a fairly good AAU team. Worldwide was one of the most renowned programs in the nation and Dana was able to recruit Christopher and Sturdivant (who jumped around a little bit but played multiple years with them), along with

Edwards, Messiah Thompson, and his son Reign to form an 8-and-under team affiliated with the Worldwide program under the direction of Dez "The General" Eastmond. Other Worldwide alumni include JJ Hickson, Collin Sexton, and Jaylen Brown. At the time, the only irreplaceable one on the floor for Edwards's squad was Christopher, because he was a dominant low-post presence.

"Big Chris was like a rock," Dana said. "Big body and he damn near 5'11", 215 pounds at nine, ten years old. You get him on the block and until the [defense] do something different, we're gonna keep doing that."

He said Edwards would have "lapses" on the floor and he'd remind Edwards that the only person who couldn't be replaced was Christopher. Edwards was excellent defensively while being "above average" offensively, Dana said, which was basically how the whole team was. He was also not that tall yet; he wouldn't hit some larger growth spurts until he was in middle school and high school.

"Ant was nice, but we just had a lot of nice players on the team," Reign said.

"We got ten other people that can do what you do . . . and Ant would just do stupid shit sometimes," Dana said.

Like in one tournament when Edwards took a game-winning shot, only he decided he was going to try out something he had been working on in practice at the worst possible moment.

"He goes in and does this little left-handed runner. It rimmed out," said Chris Hinton Sr., father of Christopher Jr. "After the game, I was taking the boys to get something to eat, and he said, 'Yeah, Mr. Chris, that was the first time I ever tried that.' I'm like, why would you pick that to do now? . . . Who does that? So years later, I'm retelling the story and he's like, 'Yeah, Mr. Chris, but I make them now.'"

Edwards's keys to playing time back then were his ability and desire to guard the other team's best player. This fed a love of on-ball defense Edwards had that traveled with him to the NBA. With the Wolves, Edwards has so many offensive responsibilities that the team doesn't ask him to guard the opponent's best player all game—that assignment goes to Jaden McDaniels. When they need him to for key stretches,

Edwards shows he can be one of the best perimeter defenders in the NBA if that's what he does on a regular basis. If there's one basketball trait of Edwards that has been a throughline from his early days on a court, it's on-ball defense. His off-ball defense has been a constant work in progress since early in his career, but when Edwards locks in on-ball, he can be tough to beat.

"He used to be the dude who used to be like, 'That's the best player?' Then he'd go pick them up full court," Sturdivant said. "He used to do that in practice. If you crossed over anytime, he's picking it."

In practices, Edwards was much the same way he was with the Vikings. Dana would have to light a fire under him to motivate him and keep him from being lazy. While Dana's practices weren't quite at the level of the Vikings, they weren't a cakewalk.

"We were the best conditioned AAU team in America," said Sturdivant, who went on to play in college at the University of Southern California and Georgia Tech.

Specifically, Sturdivant said Dana and Thompson would make the team run a "champion."

"So it's a suicide, right? But it's a long suicide," Sturdivant said. "You go full court, free-throw line, half-court, free throw, and now you do what, ten? You had to do like ten sprints."

"And they were timed," Reign said.

"We were doing that every day—losers got a champion," Sturdivant said. "That type of stuff. Ant always used to come in last."

That would be just the thing Dana would need to get on Edwards. If Edwards came in last, he'd watch as Edwards finished, then announce to the rest of the group that they had to go again because Edwards felt like taking his time. Then he'd come in first. Dana would tell Edwards he had to stop smoking. When Edwards would say he didn't smoke, Dana would shoot back, "Then stop running like you do."

Their practices ran long—and Edwards often controlled when they were done. As Sturdivant said, it felt like those practices were on "demon time." They'd scrimmage for two hours and then maybe go for another hour after.

"We never had a continuous day off," Sturdivant said.

But if Edwards hustled at the end, they could get done earlier than if he didn't. Just like with his football coaches, Edwards eventually saw the purpose behind the strict discipline. He knew how important Dana was at this point in his life.

"He was just like a godfather, for real," Edwards said of "Coach Dana" in a 2022 interview. "He just helped take care of me, made sure I was straight. He would take me all the way to the crib, to practice, all that. He was just a great dude."

Sturdivant said Dana was like a "father figure" to a lot of the kids who played for him, and he could see years later how Edwards benefited from having that kind of structure in his life when he wasn't playing football.

"Someone you could count on, showed him a lot of the distinct details that go around with being an all-around good man," Sturdivant said. "His discipline, from the games to the practices, to even us cleaning up our rooms [when they stayed at his house], everything had to be on point."

And they all stayed at the home of either Dana or Hinton Sr.—a lot.

"I Ain't Never Had a Bagel"

After a night of basketball and video games, a nine-year-old Edwards and his friend Christopher were finally tired out and ready for bed. Edwards was staying the night with the Hintons for the first time, and the first of countless nights he would spend there until he was about fifteen.

The Hinton family—Chris Sr., Mya, and their two sons, Christopher and Myles—lived in Johns Creek, Georgia, which was forty or so minutes north of Oakland City without traffic. With traffic? Easily over an hour. It seemed even farther than that. Their home was 12,000 square feet situated on three and a half acres. There was an in-ground pool in the backyard and plenty of room for the kids to run around and cause damage to the home while playing Nerf basketball.

"At one point, there was a hole, literally the size of a body, through the drywall," Mya said in a July 2024 interview from her and Chris's current home, a high-rise condo in downtown Chicago. Mya Hinton (née Whitmore) is a former Northwestern basketball player who grew up in Minnesota and was the *Minneapolis Star Tribune*'s Metro Player of the Year in 1987.

The rambunctiousness of the kids was the only worry they had in the neighborhood. Their home, along with Dana's, became a hub for teammates and friends to come and hang out. Then when everyone else went home, Edwards would stay. That first night, Christopher got up to turn off the lights.

"I'd cut them off. He'd say, 'Whatchu doing?'" Christopher said. "I'd say, 'Bruh, I'm about to turn the lights off. It's time to go to sleep.'"

Edwards answered: "Nah, you got to at least keep the bathroom light on."

Edwards couldn't sleep unless at least one light was in view. So Christopher, whom Edwards and others called "Big Chris," had to learn to sleep with the lights on when Edwards was staying at their place.

"I'd lose some sleep because that light used to mess with me," Christopher said.

Mya and Chris Sr. told him just to deal with it and don't ask too many questions.

"Don't push it," Mya said. "Just put a pillow over your head or something. It'll work out."

Looking back on those days, Christopher can now see why Edwards wanted the lights on—it deterred people from breaking in when he was home in Oakland City.

"If you didn't know Ant and where he's from—I started to understand the reason why he did certain things," he said. "At first I didn't understand, but the older I got and the more I matured, the more I was around him, I said okay, I understand X, Y, and Z."

The elder Chris Hinton is a former All-Pro NFL offensive lineman who spent thirteen seasons playing for the Colts, Falcons, and Vikings.

He spent some of his youth on the South Side of Chicago, and so he knew what a young Edwards might be facing when he was back home.

"In some ways I was that kid," Chris Sr. said.

So he was only too happy to have Edwards come around to hang with his son. Edwards was constant motion and energy in the house but at least all that space allowed the kids to run around without crashing into Mya and Chris that much.

"Our house was like a jungle gym," Mya said.

They'd play basketball outside, then come inside to play *Madden* or *NBA 2K*, or just run around playing tag or other games inside.

"Imagine ten dudes in a playroom," Sturdivant said.

"I won't lie, when it came to *2K*, he'd probably get me, but when it came to *Madden*, I used to get him," Christopher said.

Edwards and Chris have birthdays just five days apart, and a memory that almost brings a tear to Chris's eyes is when they had a joint birthday party at the house. Edwards's family—Yvette, Uncle Chris, Shirley, and his siblings—all came up. They grilled out, hung out by the pool, and played games on a picturesque summer day.

"The one thing I take away from it, whether it was Yvette or Grandma or Uncle Chris, they were appreciative. They didn't feel like we were trying to replace them, which we weren't," Chris said. "Because people don't know, he wasn't *the guy*. It wasn't like the people who were eventually reaching out."

"He didn't become *Ant* until high school," Mya added.

"It was more like we were a part of the village," Chris said.

The "village" being the connection and camaraderie their basketball team had, parents and kids included. Reign and Sturdivant compared their experience playing for the elder Watkins to be like that of family.

"We were just brothers," Reign said. "I didn't even think about it if he was staying at my house a particular weekend. I wouldn't even think of it as like, 'Oh, one of my friends is coming over.'"

"At that point, he was like my second brother," Christopher said. "Dana always joked, 'Ant, when are you gonna get in their family Christmas pictures?' That was our guy every summer. It was just like me and him, him and me."

When Edwards was younger, there weren't a lot of people trying to get their claws into him and get a piece of his eventual success. Such is the way for all potential NBA prospects in the AAU circuits when they start making a name for themselves. That wasn't the case as much before Edwards hit high school. He was just Ant Man. He could exist in this idyllic world at Dana's or the Hintons' house, playing games, messing with his friends.

The months of basketball season were much different for Edwards from the life he lived during football season. Then he lived at home or with his grandparents when Yvette moved the family there when Edwards was about eleven or twelve. Banks, Watkins, Slaughter, Uncle Chris, or whoever else was available could take him to and from practices to help Yvette with her work schedule.

But basketball season was different. Practices were on the northern end of town and near where Watkins lived in the northwest suburb of Smyrna. Basketball season also took place for the bulk of the summer, so for long stretches, Edwards didn't have to worry about being in school and he could stay with the Watkinses or the Hintons. They would practice during the week; he'd stay with them and then travel on the weekends to out-of-state tournaments. Edwards's family always made these weekend trips to the tournaments, and then would take him home. Yvette never missed a tournament, even with the amount of traveling she and her family had to do to make it.

"Even when we traveled to Florida, North Carolina, they all load up the car and they're all down there, even when they were stretching a dime," Watkins said.

During the week, nobody would have to take him back and forth through the traffic. Even if he was always moving in their houses, and that occasionally led to some damaged drywall, everybody loved having Edwards around.

"I miss those times," Christopher said. "Those were good times."

"I'mma get emotional, so just bear with me," Mya said. "But he was just a really cool kid. The conversations I heard him having with Chris, and his bond with our kids, just like to the core, he's just a good person."

Some of the fondest memories the Hintons had with Edwards tended to revolve around Edwards and his diet. Chris Sr. likes to tell a story of how Edwards would order a "double cheeseburger hold the cheese" when ordering burgers. Then when the restaurant workers would give him a burger with cheese on it, he'd say that was not what he ordered, and then they'd give him another one. He'd then eat both.

"Worked every time," Chris said.

Whenever Edwards would interact with Mya and Chris, food was usually in front of them. One of the first times they bonded with him was during a tournament in New Orleans, and Edwards came knocking on their door.

"Ms. Mya, I'm hungry. Whatchu got to eat?" Edwards said.

"We got bagels," she replied.

Edwards: "I ain't never had a bagel."

Mya: "Here's half a bagel, try it and you'll like it."

Mya gave him the half bagel with butter and Edwards went back to his room. Five minutes later, she said, came another *knock, knock, knock*.

Edwards: "Hey, Ms. Mya, can I get the other half of that bagel?"

A wide smile came across Mya's face as she retold that story in the summer of 2024.

"I was like, 'This kid.' I think he had me right there," Mya said.

Edwards was a notoriously slow eater, and while the other kids would wolf down their food at the Hinton house, Edwards stayed at the table to finish.

"One of the things I would always grill was boneless chicken thighs," Chris said. "He'd just take a chicken thigh and peel strands, like he was eating string cheese."

Their dinners with Edwards were their window into seeing his personality for those years. These moments at the table were their first indications Edwards had an "old soul," they said.

"Some of the conversations he had with you were just conversations that you wouldn't expect to come out of a younger person's mouth," Mya said. "Very inquisitive, asking questions about how things work. Issues that ten-, eleven-year-olds don't typically talk about."

"He would ask about, 'So what was it like playing football?'" Chris Sr. said. "We had a house full of boys and he'd just be sitting with me, talking."

As Edwards got older, some of the conversations turned to money, and how to handle that sort of success. Edwards loved his time at the Hinton house; this was an inspiration for him. He saw what his life could be if he became a professional athlete like Chris.

"I want to live like this," Edwards said to the *Star Tribune* in 2022. "That was a lot of motivation. I tried to stay there as long as I could."

"I remember getting a phone call from Uncle Chris one time, and it was just a random call," Chris said. "He was just calling and saying thank you. Thank you for y'all keeping Ant and just showing him another side."

The Tournaments

The Edwards family would usually travel wherever the team was playing on a given weekend, and Yvette was just like she was at the Vikings games—she was going to be a cheerleader for the rest of the team, and she was going to let everyone know who her child was.

"Yvette, that was her baby. She loved all her children. She loved all her kids, but . . ." Mya let the sentence linger with a laugh. "They were very supportive and they did whatever they could to get him where he needed to be. Her mother was right there with them. It was always a big family affair."

For one tournament, Yvette made oversize disc earrings with the names of all the kids on the team for their mothers to wear. They all did.

"She was good people," Mya said. "She was very high energy, very vocal at the games. I'd say [she and Edwards] were a good match."

Added Christopher, "He wouldn't let nobody mess with his mom and his grandma. You can tell he was a real momma's boy. He loved his mom and his momma loved Ant. She would do anything to protect Ant."

When Edwards rode with Banks to football, Edwards often sat in the front seat and didn't much care what was happening in the back seat. This was the same when he went to a tournament in the car with the Hintons. These were multi-hour car rides, with Edwards and the elder Hinton often having long conversations while the other kids were sleeping or were doing their own thing behind them.

"Not too many ten-year-olds want to sit up front when all the guys are in the back messing around," Chris Sr. said. "He'd jump up front, rides shotgun, and he wants to help me with directions."

They continued some of the conversations they'd have over those chicken thighs at the kitchen table. Of course, for every moment Edwards displayed maturity beyond his years, there were moments where he certainly showed his age. A legendary story about Edwards in the Hinton family includes a stop in Mobile, Alabama, en route to New Orleans. The family decided to stop at a nice seafood restaurant with some of the boys. Edwards was wearing a white undershirt tank top, colloquially known by a not politically correct nickname. They didn't have another shirt for him to wear, since the Hinton boys were all much bigger than Edwards. The restaurant was on the fancier side, and Edwards was in one of his talkative moods.

When Edwards re-creates a basketball memory of his, he doesn't just talk out the story, he has to act it out as well. On this day, Edwards was up in the walkways of the restaurant multiple times, making waiters and waitresses dodge him as he was talking about beating a few defenders in a recent tournament.

"He keeps getting up in the middle of the restaurant: 'Yo, Big Chris, remember when I crossed him up?' And waiters are coming by and he's like in the aisle doing all this," Chris said. "I'm like, 'Man, sit down. You got to sit down.'"

"I'm like, 'Just tell your story in your seat,'" Mya said. "He'd say, 'Okay, Ms. Mya. My bad, my bad.' He's got to move and talk."

Since Edwards's family made the trips, he'd get to stay with them once the car rides were done with Chris Sr. or Dana. One particular tournament when Edwards was nine happened around his birthday at

Disney World, and so he stayed with Shirley on the trip. Dana had a rule for travel tournaments—nobody goes in the pool until they were done playing on the final day. But Edwards had an affinity for swimming, and Shirley wasn't going to keep her grandson from the pool, especially not on his birthday.

"Don't let there be a pool around," Sturdivant said.

During the opening game on one of the days, Edwards got the ball off the tip and had a wide-open layup—he missed it. That set the tone for a scoreless day and for the team to tumble out of contention. On a car ride later that day, Dana grilled him about why that happened.

Dana: "Hey, Ant, how many points you score today?"

Edwards: "None."

Dana: "How did you enjoy swimming yesterday?"

Edwards: "Well, I didn't get into the pool that long."

Busted.

"Grandma is gonna let Ant do what he wants to do," Dana said. "I'm like, 'Ant, you don't get it dude. Bro, we're here for a short period of time.' Then he finally got it. You'd go to the loser's bracket and nobody cares about you. You're playing for twelfth place when you should've been in the final four.

"Always skilled, and he could coast and get by so much depending on where he was playing, until he got to the elite talent. Then he just blended in. . . . I can do whatever I wanna do and I could make mistakes or whatever, but when you're being held accountable—it changed around eleven, twelve."

Watkins said that even though Edwards didn't stand out at that point, he still had an inkling Edwards could develop into a player. The reason: Edwards was renowned throughout his youth for his big feet. Football and basketball coaches would always remember his big feet and big calves.

"I told Ant this predraft that if we lined all you guys up at eleven or twelve and someone asked, Who would you bet who would be in the NBA? Chris was dominating [in the post], but you're not gonna be six ten doing that, and you damn sure can't do it at six three," Dana said.

"I only saw Ant's father a couple of times. I know him enough to know his father is tall. Ant had some big-ass feet. That's gonna be a big dude right there. I'd say Ant's gonna be the kid who makes it."

The growth spurts didn't start coming for Edwards until high school, Dana said, and that's also when Edwards got more serious about his basketball potential. When Edwards was thirteen, they were no longer affiliated with Worldwide, and some players, like Christopher Hinton, dispersed to other teams, even though they remained close friends. Dana took Edwards, Reign, and others from their team and merged a team called Top Notch.

"A bunch of white suburban rich kids," Dana said. "But I loved the way the coach was coaching the team. He was a brother. I said we'll bring them over there and we ain't got to deal with all the parents and all the nonsense and bring our best players with some of their best players. That coach couldn't wait to hear that."

The program had significantly more money than what Dana was dealing with at Worldwide. He said some of the parents had connections to members of the Hunt family (the multibillion-dollar family who owns the Kansas City Chiefs, among other sports franchises and businesses). Through those connections, they got part of the Hunt family to invest in the team, Dana said. They had every member of the team fill out a questionnaire with questions like "What's your shoe size?" when they first came aboard.

"Jordans," Dana said. "That was our introduction."

The team got to swing by the house of the family members who were sponsoring them, and Reign reported back to his father that there were multiple maids and outside tennis and basketball courts. Dana and Chris may have introduced Edwards to a different lifestyle—this was on another planet. Dana added that this team was significant to Edwards for another reason—it was probably the first time in Edwards's life that he had white teammates.

"That team was learning for all of us," Watkins said. "They were forced to be with their teammates. It came natural to accept people for who they are. They're all pretty much chameleons."

This experience would help set up Edwards for what he would eventually encounter in high school—teammates and friends from all different backgrounds and economic strata. But that time was still a few years away, not until he was about sixteen. At this time in his life, he was thirteen, wrapping up his time with the Atlanta Vikings, still playing AAU basketball with Dana. His life had the same routine for about seven years. A lot of the same people were there. His mother, his grandmother, his siblings, Uncle Chris. Ben and Shirley took in the family when they had some financial trouble around the time Edwards was eleven or twelve. All seven of them living in Ben and Shirley's white and green house with the 100,000-mile-plus Toyota in the driveway and the hoop in the backyard.

It was in this house that Edwards wrote his dreams for his future on the wall. They weren't about the NFL. They were about basketball. Even though he wasn't a star yet, or even one of the best in the age group, there was always an affinity for basketball that outweighed his love of football. He was still growing, and had no idea what it might take to accomplish those goals. But his life was about to get a severe wake-up call. He was about to acquire the motivation, the competitiveness, and the work ethic that would make him one of the best teenage basketball players in the country. Maybe these came because of what would happen next in his life. Maybe they would have come anyway. If he could go back and change the course of events, maybe he'd take that gamble.

CHAPTER 3

UNCERTAIN TIMES

Shirley Edwards didn't always make the trips to her grandson's football games or AAU tournaments. There were times she would be away, and everyone knew that if she couldn't be there, it was likely because she wasn't feeling well or going through chemotherapy. For several years, Shirley had on-again, off-again battles with cancer. Whenever she would be able to be in attendance, it was a jolt of positive energy for those that knew what she was going through.

As Dana put it, she was like a "walking miracle" any time he saw her in the gym.

"Always had the best spirits," Dana said. "She had a wig on her head, shuffling into the game. 'How you doin', Grandma?' 'I'm all right!' Never complained about nothing, and there were periods of time she was going through chemo and all the hell associated with it.

"Now Grandma is a typical grandma. That's her grandbaby and she gonna be in the building. She was the rock of the family in a way."

If there's a throughline in Edwards's personality from his grand-mother through his mother that lives in him, it's his positive attitude. In a 2022 interview with the *Star Tribune*, Edwards's brother Bubba said his mother and grandmother were always beacons of positive energy, especially around him and his siblings.

"I ain't never seen them with low energy or bad vibes," Bubba said. "They were always in a happy place. Especially my grandma. She was the base of the whole family. She's always happy. She'll cheer you up if you're having a bad day or something like that. She's always easy to talk to, easygoing. Happiest person to be around."

Throughout his life, this has been one of the defining qualities of

Edwards. He can radiate infectious, positive energy, and it's one way in which he has had an effect on every team of which he was a part. Even in his Vikings and early AAU basketball days, his energy lifted his teammates. But it's not artificial. It is who he is. From his high school and AAU coaches to teammates and coaches on the Timberwolves, all said that energy is one of the biggest ways Edwards makes an impact off the court. In the grind of an NBA season, his smile and his joy of being around his teammates lift the collective mood any time he enters the facility or the locker room.

"All leaders have exactly one thing in common, that's that people follow them," Wolves coach Chris Finch said. "Doesn't matter how. . . . When you have Ant's personality, which is joyful, playful, magnanimous, roots for his teammates, genuine, all these things, people are naturally drawn to him. I've told him this from the beginning, people are naturally drawn to you. The way you use that is important."

Players at all levels would come to follow Edwards, whether he was intending that or not. If there's a reason for that, it is how his mother and grandmother were around him.

When Yvette fell on some harder times financially, she and her children moved in with her mother and father. By that time, Shirley had retired from a career in the post office. Edwards's father was not around much as he grew up, and some of that may have been because Yvette didn't want him to be. Multiple people who spent a lot of time around Edwards then either did not see his father at all, or did so only a few times. Slaughter said he might have come around "in spurts."

"I knew him from the neighborhood. His dad always been quiet," Slaughter said. "When you see his daddy, his daddy got the same posture like Ant, the hands, big-ass feet."

There was one time he showed up at one of Edwards's football games, Dana said, only for Yvette to pretend like he wasn't there. But she also made sure everyone around her knew what she thought of his presence.

"Talking around him, but right in front of him, 'I can't believe this man comin' around,'" Dana said. "And pacing back and forth. That struck a chord with her."

He added: "The way that Yvette got on him, if I was him, I wouldn't come back to another football game. 'I can't believe this motherfucker comin' around here.' He's on the other side of the fence just quiet."

Yvette was a fighter, and she wasn't one to hold back how she was feeling, especially when it came to her kids. As Bubba put it, "She's like our backbone. Any problem we had, anything we needed taken care of, she was there. She had our back. If we was one hundred percent wrong, she had our back."

Of all the terms people from this part of Edwards's life use to describe him, "momma's boy" comes up as frequently as any, and Yvette certainly loved her youngest.

"She was a momma's girl, and 'Vette, she loved her kids, man," Slaughter said. "Over in Oakland City, she did what she could do for them, but that baby boy, he was different. He was the one you could tell was gonna be different. His brothers, they knew it. . . . It was always Ant Man this, Ant Man that. Ant, they would do anything they can for him to achieve.

"Ant may have went through issues and had a tough road to a certain extent, but Ant still comes from a situation where he was protected."

There's an unflappable bravado about Edwards that rarely teeters into arrogance. It is one of his most charming and endearing characteristics. He has the swagger and the confidence to think he's the best in the world, and he has a smile to disarm anyone who thinks he's being overly boastful. This is one of the lasting legacies his mother gave to him. There was nothing he couldn't do in her eyes. Anything he wanted, he could accomplish, no matter the odds, no matter the family's finances. She imbued him with the confidence he would need when she wasn't around anymore.

"Ant has that engine in his back because his mom," Reign said. "She gave all of us confidence. I don't care if he's one-for-twenty or twenty-for-twenty, he still gonna feel like he's the best. That comes from his mom."

When Edwards was thirteen, people around the Vikings noticed that Yvette was starting to look different, but she was still coming to the games. Then she got testing as she began feeling sick—cervical cancer. Given all that Shirley had gone through, Dana said everyone assumed she too would be able to fend off the disease.

"To hear that Yvette had cancer, it wasn't like a big 'Oh, wow' moment," Dana said. "It's kind of like, she's gonna fight the fight, as long as you can fight it."

But by the time doctors discovered it, the cancer was already fairly advanced.

"They always assume you have to be old," Slaughter said.

But in Edwards's family, as Slaughter said, cancer can hit at younger ages, and it hit Yvette. Dana had to spend some months in California around the time Yvette was fighting the cancer, and it didn't go well. The cancer progressed quickly.

"It just hit, man. It hit," Slaughter said.

As Edwards told Netflix: "My mom was in a lot of pain, but she wouldn't show it."

Dana and Yvette had a conversation before she died, and they had made some plans for Edwards to live with him in the event she passed, he said. Banks also told Yvette he would do whatever he could to help. But there wasn't a lot of time to discuss and get ready.

"It seemed like it happened real fast for her," Dana said. "I heard she had cancer. Then six months later, I'm sitting in a room, and here she is sick on the bed."

He added: "I never knew her situation was dire until I heard she went to hospice. That was never communicated to me. I heard the word 'hospice,' and I was like, what?"

Said Slaughter: "She got sick and they didn't give her a chance. She was gone in months. Checked into the hospital and that was it."

On January 5, 2015, Chrisha Yvette Edwards died at forty-two in hospice care. That day, Edwards, Dana, and Edwards's father were among those there. Edwards mostly stayed silent. There was hardly any crying, any emotion from him at all. Dana theorized that because Edwards had that old soul, he knew deep down his mother wasn't suffering anymore.

"Ant, he's composed. As a thirteen-year-old, you just wonder what's going through his mind," he said. "For him to be as close as he was to her, she was his protector, number one cheerleader, and everything that you'd want an ideal mother to be, she was that to him. I think losing her probably gave him an additional sense of drive in some ways. I can only just speculate on that . . . but he was forced to mature a little bit. He was forced to lean on his siblings a lot more."

The funeral came a few days later. The Vikings team showed up wearing their jackets, and they adopted a phrase for the rest of that season, "Do It for Yvette," Reign said. Banks recalled several people coming up to Edwards and the family, pledging to help in any way they could.

"Shit got an expiration date. Seventy-two hours," Banks said. "Everybody go back to they own problems, they own lives. That's just how it is. . . . When the game ain't being played no more, and you got to deal with life, that's when it get tricky and sticky. When it comes to competing in sports, people are there. But when it comes to life, everybody got their own situation, own kids, own girlfriend, own family—who feeling sorry for you?"

Banks wasn't going to be one of those people. At the funeral, he kept checking in on Edwards throughout most of the hour-plus service.

"I was just watching," he said.

Just like in the hospice room—little to no emotion. Maybe Edwards showed emotion before or after, but in that church, he was stone-faced.

"He might have shed a small tear, but he didn't boo-hoo break down," Banks said. "He walked in there like a big boy, sat through the service. I was like, 'Damn, he made it through.' I don't know what's on the inside. I don't know if he had a talk with hisself."

Yvette had always been grateful for Banks's help and would send him text messages from time to time thanking him for all he did for her son. There was no way he was going to let Edwards down. As he sat, that pledge crystallized in his mind. Whatever he had to do to make sure Edwards was okay, he was going to do.

"I knew it was gonna be a long haul," Banks said. "I was sitting in church that day like, 'It's all good. He ain't got nothing to worry about.'

I ain't tell him that. But in the back of my mind, I knew he ain't got nothing to worry about. I already had my mind set. I knew how it was gonna go."

Edwards always had an innate ability to trust people, to let the right people into his life and keep the wrong ones out. Those around him marvel at this. Perhaps it was heightened survival instincts. Yvette wasn't there anymore to be the gatekeeper, and so Edwards had to learn the world quickly. Banks was always one of the people he could trust, and so when Edwards eventually went to high school in the Buckhead area of northern Atlanta, he ended up staying with his uncle Drew for close to two years.

But before that, there was still more turbulence. Shirley's cancer came roaring back. Like before, everyone hoped she would again beat it. This was different. She had just buried her daughter, and perhaps the grief for her was too much to overcome. With all this happening in Edwards's life, Reign said he, Edwards, and some friends took a trip to Florida for the Fourth of July. While Edwards was in Florida, Shirley died on July 5. Edwards wears the No. 5 because his birthday falls on the fifth of August, and his mother and grandmother both died on the fifth of the month. Those that were on the trip found out about Shirley's passing, but they decided to not tell Edwards right away. They wanted to let the thirteen-year-old have a few more hours of getaway before telling him the news, which came less than five months after Yvette died.

"They wanted to wait to tell him when he got back—and then he found out," Reign said.

Maybe there was crying in private, or around his siblings, after his mother passed. But this time, around Reign and some others, he let it out.

"I remember he broke down like I've never seen," Reign said. "This is the most I've seen Ant—probably the only time I've seen Ant cry. I remember he broke down, and all of us, we surrounded him, cheering him up. Like, 'Bro, we got you for life. Anything you need, we gonna be here.'"

After that came a lot of "blank" moments, Bubba said. The only answer the family had was to keep moving: Don't let the depressing thoughts creep in. Get to a gym, work it out on the court or on the football field.

"Just blank moments where it was just like, you got to deal with it," Bubba told the *Star Tribune* in 2022. "Because at some point you got to realize it's your mom, it's your grandmom, you're never going to see them again. You definitely have moments you feel down, like you're alone."

Edwards has touched on the deaths of his mother and grandmother previously, but he has never gone in depth. When the subject occasionally gets brought up in interviews during his NBA career, he will deflect or politely decline to answer the question. At All-Star weekend in 2024, when Edwards was asked a question about a cause he was taking up in honor of his mother, he said he didn't feel much like talking about it.

When asked in a 2022 interview with the *Star Tribune* how he got through that time in his life, Edwards said: "I was young, man. I was just—sports. I just played sports."

As Bubba put it: "Basketball really helped us stay focused with our futures and keep our head on the right track and not get too caught up in the pain. Basketball really was the answer to helping us cope with it."

One of the qualities Edwards admires about his brother Bubba is his dedication to making music. During the 2024 playoffs, Edwards said he'll often see his brother stay up recording songs until 5 or 6 a.m., and that inspires him to stay dedicated to his craft.

"When I wake up, he'll still be up making music," Edwards said in May 2024. "So him just working to get himself out there and be the best that he can be makes me get up every morning and be the best that I want to be and just showcasing to the world what I can do."

Bubba launched a rap career under the moniker "bdifferent," and as Dana put it, "In Bubba's lyrics, you hear a lot of stuff" related to their family's journey.

In the video for the song "Pain Birthed Me," Bubba is dressed in a suit at an outdoor podium that makes it appear as if he's speaking at a burial service. There are two empty chairs with roses on them. The lyrics discuss how much their deaths affected Bubba, how much he cried and how broken his heart was.

But toward the end of a song that deals with a lot pain, he says, "I know my momma smilin' and I know my granny do her dance when I make music. . . . It's a part of me, I can't lose it."

The song ends on a hopeful note because Bubba is now a grown man doing what he loves, and Yvette and Shirley wouldn't want anything more than that. If only they could see Yvette's baby do his thing.

"A Kid Confused"

At the time, Dana marveled at how unchanged Edwards seemed to be. Looking back on it, he realized Edwards might have been internalizing their deaths, perhaps a bit too much.

"I think therapy is good, but the burden that he's carrying, he probably doesn't feel that he could benefit from it," Dana said. "I've never had therapy, but I know it's good, and we can't even—we have no idea of the kind of pressure he can be under."

The next stage in Edwards's life was the one that defined him, that set him on his path to the NBA. The way he channeled his grief was by getting in the gym, a lot. It didn't matter whom he was living with—and Edwards moved around a lot during his teenage years—he always got to the gym even when he wasn't practicing or at a game. But in the immediate aftermath of their deaths, there was a lot to figure out.

"I saw a kid confused," Slaughter said.

"Seeing him and his siblings, just knowing you got all these kids motherless, it was a lot," Mya Hinton said.

Following their deaths, the Hintons had another important dinner-table conversation with Edwards: Would he come live with them permanently?

"He was at the house when we floated it with him," Chris Sr. said. "And it was like, okay . . ."

Then Chris imitated Edwards peeling his chicken thighs like it was string cheese—to signify that was something he would have to think about. The Hintons had everything set up; Edwards would attend Greater Atlanta Christian with Christopher even as Christopher focused more on football and Edwards was more focused on basketball.

"I wish we had went to high school together and kept growing up together and stuff like that," Christopher said. "But obviously I'm not gonna sit here and hold that against nobody. He has to do what's good for him and his family and he made the best decision. Even if things didn't turn out how it was, he'd always be Ant to us. I still would do anything for him."

There were a lot of dynamics in Edwards's situation. Dana had conversations with Yvette about Edwards coming to live with him after she passed, but Dana wasn't sure that Edwards's sister, Antoinette, was aware of those talks. What ended up happening was eventually Antoinette took charge. With the help of someone who played a big part in Edwards's life around this time, Winfred Jordan, who ran Ant's eventual AAU program Atlanta Xpress, she got an apartment. This is where Edwards ended up staying for a while.

"My sister, I love her to death, she's kind of the backbone of all of it," Edwards told Netflix for *Starting 5*. "She knew we had to all be together. We was going through some tough times and we didn't really have nowhere to stay. So she pretty much just went and got a job, forgot about college, and took care of us."

As much as Edwards had close relationships with other families, they weren't his own family. The Edwards siblings needed each other more than ever. Now was not the time for the family to break apart, and despite everyone else's best intentions, Edwards stayed with his family.

"Basically we'd have to get guardianship of him," Mya Hinton said. "You'd be giving up everything, and that's a big decision."

Dana said the family that funded Edwards's AAU program with Top Notch offered to pay for his education to a private school, and he had everything set up.

"But Ant just didn't want to do it," he said.

The main reason for this was that Edwards wanted to go to high school with Bubba, who was a senior at the public Daniel McLaughlin Therrell High School. Off he went to Therrell—and those that knew and cared for Edwards held their collective breath.

"I worried about him being a teenager, the environment and not having nobody like, 'Get your ass to school. Get your homework. Let me see your report card.' That's what I worried about," Banks said. "He wasn't a bad kid. I wasn't worried about him hanging with the wrong kids, getting in trouble, breaking in cars. I wasn't worried about that. I was worried about getting to school on time, not flunking out."

False Start

When Banks heard Edwards was insistent on going to Therrell, he had immediate concern. This likely wasn't going to work. Edwards always had a good head on his shoulders and a sense of whom he should hang with and whom he shouldn't. But Edwards needed guiding hands in his life to provide guardrails and discipline. He wasn't going to get that at Therrell, Banks thought.

"When you go from a little kid to a preteenager, when you get around young men, you know how life can get in the way, they can go left quick," Banks said. "At Therrell, I thought it was gonna be an issue because Therrell gonna let him get away with whatever. No structure."

Therrell is a predominantly Black public school about a ten-minute drive southwest of where Edwards grew up. It had an enrollment of around one thousand kids total from grades nine through twelve.

"If they have one white kid in that school, I'd be surprised," Dana said.

Having Bubba there his freshman year helped Edwards stay on track, and he played football and basketball. But Bubba graduated after that first year, and when Edwards entered his sophomore year, Banks's fears were realized.

"Bubba is gone now. So now Ant has to be mature enough, to get to school, do homework," Banks said. "Ant is one of those people that if you don't hold his feet to the fire with structure, Ant gonna be a typical kid. . . . Ant ain't no dummy, he just didn't like school, which a lot of athletes don't."

Banks said he kept his "ear to the street" since he knew some people who worked at Therrell, and when basketball season was over during Edwards's sophomore year, things hit a crisis point for Edwards's education.

While going there made sense on paper, given its proximity to where Edwards lived, those around Edwards quickly realized this was not where he should be long term. Edwards's attention to his education was lacking, to put it lightly, and there was nobody there to push him to get decent grades.

"Therrell couldn't do anything for him over there, letting him not go to class," Dana said. "He was telling me how [one of his teachers] was on the basketball staff. 'I'm taking jump shots during class. I ain't got to go to class.' It's like, 'We got to get him out of that.'"

"You're dealing with kids that are in, like, survival mode," said Kierre Jordan, Edwards's skills trainer and Winfred Jordan's son. "[At Therrell] they may be around a whole other lifestyle."

Where Edwards eventually ended up for high school was a whole other lifestyle from Therrell. Halfway through his sophomore year, Edwards wasn't going to school there anymore. He wasn't going to school at all for multiple months. Meanwhile, he decided his football days were over. After he suffered the serious ankle injury at thirteen with the Vikings, Edwards got hurt again and decided basketball was going to be his primary focus.

Edwards had given up football, the sport that was supposed to be his future. He was in peril from an academic standpoint. If there was a saving grace in his life at this time, it was what he was doing on the basketball court. That happened because starting at fourteen, just after Yvette and Shirley died, Edwards met someone who would help set him on the path to becoming an NBA prospect.

"I'll Be Unguardable"

Before Edwards began going to Therrell, his uncle Chris took him to a gym to work out with a coach named Justin Holland, whom he had heard about through a mutual friend of theirs. Holland is a former point guard who went to Liberty and returned to his native Atlanta to enter the coaching and training world. He was working with some prospects like M. J. Walker and Michael Durr the day Edwards walked into the gym at College Park Rec Center.

"He was about 6'2", I don't even think he had a haircut," Holland said. "Workouts are already going on, so I just kind of look at him, I say, 'Young fella, hop in the drill.' That was pretty much how it started, that simple."

When he started watching Edwards work out, Holland wasn't sure if Edwards would play in college, let alone the NBA. That mutual friend, Eric, had briefed Holland that Edwards had just lost his mother and grandmother, and Eric told Chris that Holland, who is fifteen years older than Edwards, would be a positive influence on him. Holland had experience in coaching players who had similar obstacles growing up as Edwards. What he didn't know was that the relationship between him and Edwards would keep growing, and it would change Holland's life as much as Edwards's. Holland would become Edwards's right hand, his business manager who now attends almost every home game and several road games during a Timberwolves season.

"We ended up being that way because I didn't have an angle," Holland said. "My whole goal was what I told Eric and his uncle, I would make sure he was good any way I can help, and I'll develop him on the court. So however I can be additive to whatever he has going on in life, I'll be there if it's anything that I could do to develop him as a basketball player . . . wasn't trying to sell myself to him anything like that. It was always just, 'Hey, man, let's work.'"

To Abdur-Rahim, who helped recruit Edwards to play at Georgia, Holland's ability to be no-nonsense with Edwards was what bonded them together. Edwards respects those who gave it to him straight, whether or not he wants to hear what they have to say in the moment. That became ingrained when he played for the Vikings and AAU under Dana. Holland found success getting through to Edwards with that way of coaching.

"Justin wasn't just telling them how awesome he was, but also I think

[Edwards] can see himself in Justin," Abdur-Rahim said. "Justin being from Atlanta himself, playing college ball at Liberty—Justin can talk a certain way to him and relate to him in a certain way that some people can't. Justin tells him the truth. But he also allows Ant to be who he is as well. He's not trying to change him."

A trait that was perhaps Edwards's most important back then was his ability to figure out who was good for him and who wasn't. He was naturally wary of people, and that was an important quality to have at this point in his life. When he was younger, he tended to be quiet until he got to know somebody, especially adults. Then his gregarious personality would shine through. As he got older and more personable, Edwards could work a room. He would smile and greet people, but that didn't mean he was going to let them into his life. In his future home, that's called being "Minnesota nice." He had already adopted that quality from the time he was a teenager.

"He's a politician," Holland said.

Edwards began working out with Holland on a regular basis, and Uncle Chris would take him to and from the workouts. But at this time, Uncle Chris was driving Uber to make money, Holland said, and there were times he would be late picking Edwards up, so Holland offered to take Edwards home.

"Me taking him home and seeing my relationships that I had with my other guys, I think that opened him up to just being able to let his guard down more and more," Holland said. "But it was never a point where I was trying to get close to him. It just kind of happened by happenstance."

When he did, he said he was taking Edwards all over the city. He wouldn't always stay at the apartment Antoinette had. He'd stay with other friends or classmates. Holland said on one of those rides to wherever it was Edwards was calling home that particular night, Holland got on him after Edwards wasn't competing in one-on-one competitions against some of the older players. That was a break-through moment in their relationship and in Edwards's development.

"'We don't respect people on the court, like, they have to earn your respect,'" Holland said he told him. "'Don't give it to them just [because] they're older. Make them earn your respect. Go out there and compete.' If you compete every day, you're gonna find yourself getting better. From there, he internalized it. Didn't really give me much of a response, verbally, but those following workouts, he started competing."

Over the next several months, Edwards could feel himself catching up to everyone else in the gym, Holland said. Once that started to happen, Edwards never wanted to leave. He was there night and day. The improvement just fed on itself, and the more Edwards got better, the more he wanted to keep getting better.

"He started understanding the intensity level, how hard you got to work, how many days you got to work," Holland said. "He saw those guys excelling, and then he felt himself getting better. That's when the light switch clicked on, and I think he just got addicted to it."

His personality started to come out more and more around Holland to the point that he said to him: *If you teach me how to shoot, I'll be unguardable.* Edwards always had the athleticism, but developing a consistent shot was going to take a lot of work, for a long time. Even when he got to the NBA, it was still a work in progress. But becoming a respected shooter has been a thread in Edwards's career from this time in his life.

"When I came to the league, the main thing was 'He can get downhill, but he can't shoot,'" Edwards said in December 2024. "He can't shoot, he can't shoot. So I've been trying to knock that off my name for a long time."

It irks him when people don't think he's a good shooter, that all he can do well is go to the rim. That determination to prove doubters wrong has fueled a burning passion to perfect his shot for a decade.

"If you give that shot-making ability to somebody like Anthony, who has the God-given natural ability to jump over cars and seven-foot people, you got a player that's gonna skyrocket up the charts," Holland said. "So when he told me if I learn how to shoot, I'll be unguardable, that might be one of the realest things he told me."

Because there would be no way for people to guard him if he could score from any spot on the floor, and if someone played too far up on him, he'd take him off the dribble. They were working out seven days a week. They'd work so late into the night sometimes that Edwards would call Holland's wife, Janene, to let her know it was his fault Holland wasn't home yet.

"He's a perfectionist," Holland said. "He won't leave the gym unless he ends on a win. 'Let me make the last shot, two in a row, three in a row.' I'd say, 'Ant, we gotta go. It's midnight. My wife is gonna leave me.' He'd then call and say, 'Ms. Janene, he's with me right now, we're leaving the gym.' . . . I have the most understanding wife."

In January 2025, a reporter asked Edwards after a win over the Wizards what advice he would give to younger kids who are trying to make a name for themselves in basketball. He thought back to these times with Holland.

"Playing basketball, I didn't start taking it seriously until I was about fifteen, sixteen," Edwards said. "But when you decide you wanna lock in on one thing, you got to really lock in. Me and my trainer Justin Holland, we was in the gym every day. . . . You got to find somebody that's willing and they got the time, and family is willing to sacrifice their time. Justin, his wife sacrificed their time together. He had a son, sacrificed his time. You got to find somebody that really loves you for who you are and then love the game, that's willing to put it together, and then it'll come out. Justin made sure I put in the work every night."

Those who knew Edwards then say the gym appeared to be the way Edwards dealt with the aftermath of his mother's and grandmother's deaths. There was a latent drive inside him that was now coming to the forefront. He wasn't a "lazy" kid anymore trying to avoid extra sprints in football practice. He welcomed the work, and he wanted to keep moving.

"It definitely motivated him, in my opinion," Sturdivant said. "He definitely would have been successful. But I don't know if he makes it to the point he does if everybody's still here. Once that happened, Ant had to be a grown individual for a long time, just in making decisions."

"Losing them probably gave him an additional sense of drive," Dana said. "I can only just speculate on that, because obviously he was a talented kid already. At fourteen, fifteen, he definitely started becoming the Ant Man we know."

There was also the likely burden he was placing on himself to help his family make it. That started to become more of a reality as he kept working and ascending the recruiting rankings. By the time he was a sophomore, the national attention was growing. Edwards started making a name for himself, and the kid who Holland thought might not even play in college was getting Division I programs coming to see his workouts.

Not only was Edwards working with Holland at this time, but Winfred Jordan also had Edwards working with his son, Kierre. Their relationship extends into Edwards's NBA days. When Edwards isn't working out in Minnesota in the summer, he'll spend stretches training with Kierre in Atlanta. Edwards regularly incorporates things he and Kierre work on in his repertoire, and he frequently references Kierre in interviews when those moves come up. For instance, four years into his NBA career, Edwards incorporated a subtle step after he shoots free throws to ensure he has the right amount of power generating from his legs. That was something Kierre and he practiced prior to that season. Edwards improved his free-throw shooting that season from 75.6 percent to 83.6 percent.

"You have to earn his trust for sure," Kierre said. "I'm going to help you get better, but then I'm also going to develop a friendship with you as well. How are you doing? How's life? How's school? Personal talks about women, whatever it may be. To just make sure that we can trust each other outside of just on the court."

When Edwards was sixteen, there was one session in particular with Kierre that was emblematic of the progress Edwards was making. Edwards was working out with Jordan McRae, who was in the middle of playing four seasons in the NBA with five different teams.

"When they played one-on-one, Ant wins every spot. Like Jordan may have won one spot," Kierre said. "And this one particular play, and I have this shit in my phone too, Ant gives him a head fake from the right wing, one, two dribble down the middle of the lane. Jordan jumps, and Ant dunks the ball."

It left McRae, who Kierre said could be "cocky," nearly speechless. When the workout was over, McRae called Kierre with one question—how old was that guy?

"'Like, bro, he's sixteen.' He was like, 'No fucking way he's sixteen,'" Kierre said.

Edwards's defense on McRae was what really impressed Kierre in that workout, and it was an eye-opening moment for him that Edwards could excel as a two-way player. When Kierre first met Edwards, he had hated doing cardio workouts, which made him initially skeptical Edwards would embrace the defensive end. But that's what he did prior to his teenage years, and it was still in him.

"I didn't think that he would be this dominant yet," Kierre said.

Kierre said he recorded the workout but assured McRae he would never post it to social media.

"It was so dominating from Ant, and I don't know if I can put my friend out there like that," Kierre said. "It was bad. Oh my God, it was bad."

Others weren't so fortunate to have the footage stay offline. In 2018, Edwards was at an Under Armor Pangos event, and he went viral for two dunks he had in that tournament—an authoritative one over another player and then one where he went between his legs. This was the start of Anthony Edwards: viral sensation.

"My phone just goes ding, ding, ding," Holland said. "And he's making shots, finishing. That's when he shot up there."

He shot up in the recruiting rankings, to the point he became the top-ranked player in his class. The following summer, Edwards attended the camp of Stephen and Seth Curry, and the way Edwards carried himself throughout the camp caught Steph's attention.

"You never want to get on a soapbox and be like, he's gonna be the next greatest player of all time type thing, but he was clearly the best player of that camp, clearly the number one pick for a reason. We saw all that," Steph Curry said. "It's a talent thing, but it's also his will.

He wanted to win every drill, every pickup five-on-five game we had during camp. That spoke to more than just his skill set. . . . He had that 'it' factor. I knew he was going to be great. Just a matter of how it was going to play out."

Also at the Curry camp that weekend was Omar Wilkes, who worked at Klutch Sports Group. He was having a conversation with Steph and Seth and asked them who the best player at the camp was.

"I kid you not, within four seconds of me asking that, Ant drives through the middle, pretty much knocks a kid over, and two-hand flushes through traffic, and they're like, 'Him,'" Wilkes said.

That prompted Wilkes to inquire more about Edwards, and he had a mutual friend that played basketball with Holland at Liberty. That began a relationship with Holland and eventually that led to Edwards signing with Klutch as his first agency coming out of Georgia. Wilkes, Holland, and Steph Curry would all be in the same place at the same time for another significant moment in Edwards's career about six years later, to watch Edwards receive a gold medal at the 2024 Paris Olympics standing next to Curry on the podium.

Edwards's former AAU teammates prior to the Xpress would go to his games and they couldn't believe what they were seeing.

"For me, seeing the progress that he made over the time we weren't playing together, I was blown away, honestly," Reign said. "Like, damn."

"I swear to you I texted my dad and said, 'Yo, Ant is a pro.' He said to get out of here," Christopher Hinton said. "I think he was fifteen years old, that's when he knew it himself. He's a confident guy, as you all know, but I think that's when he truly was like, 'Okay, I'm about to do this.' After that, he started getting notoriety and things really started to pick up."

Sturdivant squared off against Edwards when both were in high school and there was a play where Edwards had a "LeBron-like" block.

"I was like, yeah, it's getting different," Sturdivant said. "He was just doing stuff like that. He got a chance to really do it."

Sturdivant said that took place during the time "Atlanta knew [about Edwards] but the nation didn't know yet." Some people around

Atlanta were going to try their best to take advantage of Edwards's rising fame.

"When he was young, nobody really had time for Ant, because everybody had their own life," Banks said. "Nobody seen a lottery ticket . . ."

He let the sentence trail off. This was a formative time in Edwards's life, and he seemed to have a natural intuition to not let his circle get too large. There would be people coming at him, and he knew he had to keep a lot of them at arm's length. Edwards also didn't tend to hang around with a lot of people his own age. Naturally, there were some teammates and classmates he became close friends with, but he spent just as much time around some of the older adults he trusted at that time. Again, that "old soul" showed up, Holland said, a "true spirit of discernment" to read someone's character.

"He honestly didn't really hang out with a lot of kids," Holland said. "He was kind of always with adults, whether it was his AAU coach Winfred, being with me, Drew. He always stayed around older people and stayed away from the nonsense. I feel like it was a point where he knew he had a goal and he knew what he wanted to accomplish, and when he saw that, he was no-nonsense."

Mya Hinton remembered a time she had to break up a meeting between Edwards and a wannabe hanger-on. They were sitting in the stands with Edwards at a tournament when Edwards got a call to meet someone in the lobby. That didn't sit right with her.

"I went out there and I stood in the corner and the guy looked at me, and I just didn't look at him back," Mya said. "I said, 'You're on the clock, bro, and we're gonna wrap this up.' My momma bear claws came out. With Ant that time, there were so many people coming at him, I stood there and I made sure that guy saw me. At one point I called Ant and said, 'We're done.'"

But there was only so much protection people could offer him. At some point, Edwards had to make it in the world on his own. Looking back on it now, the Hintons are proud and almost relieved Edwards is the kind of person he is. That innate sense of what was right and wrong, who was good and who was bad. Because somehow, despite the obstacles in his way, he still got to where he should be. When Edwards played a game in Chicago in November 2024, the Hintons and Dana were there to greet him afterward. It was the first time the Hintons had seen him in a while. There were wide smiles and hugs all around. Edwards asked how their son Myles was doing playing football at Michigan. He showed them pictures of his daughter and told them they had to get to Minnesota for a game. He gave them his jersey from that night with the written message: "Love y'all. My family 4 ever."

"At the time, it was emotionally draining. . . . I worried about him, but he figured it out," Mya said. "Based on his history, this wasn't supposed to happen."

As Chris Sr. put it, with his perspective growing up on Chicago's South Side: "Some of the best basketball players that I ever saw, you never heard of. It could've gone horribly wrong, and you'd be writing a different story."

CHAPTER 4

MS. LITTLE AND THE CHAOS OF HOLY SPIRIT

In the Anthony Edwards universe, Rachel Little occupies a rare space and has a special title that Edwards bestowed upon her in a 2022 interview with the *Star Tribune*.

"She's probably the best white person I ever met in my life," Edwards said then. "My favorite white person. . . . I can't describe her, she's just a great person."

Ms. Little, as Edwards and those close to him still call her, now lives thirty miles north of Atlanta. She has a couch draped in a blanket with Taylor Swift album titles and a doormat that reads, "In this house, we listen to Taylor's Version." Without this millennial die-hard Swiftie, Edwards likely doesn't graduate from Holy Spirit Preparatory School, and who knows where his basketball and life trajectory would have ended up if he couldn't attend the University of Georgia, went to another school, or had to go overseas.

Holy Spirit is located in the upscale part of northern Atlanta known as Buckhead, which couldn't be much farther from Oakland City in terms of both physical distance (an hour-long commute, give or take, thanks to Atlanta traffic) and lifestyle. Here Edwards transferred from Therrell and entered a small, predominantly white Catholic school where most students attended its two campuses from kindergarten through twelfth grade. The dress code, which quickly became Edwards's nemesis, just like it was with the Vikings, was 1950s Catholic school chic: blazers, dress shirts, blue or black socks, belts and ties. Edwards racked up countless demerits for being out of dress code, to the point that his former coach Tysor Anderson kept socks and belts in his office specifically so Edwards would not get in trouble.

When Edwards arrived, the school was attempting to morph into a prestigious athletic institution. Edwards came in part because the relationship between his AAU coach Winfred Jordan and Holy Spirit coach Greg McClaire, but McClaire was fired during Edwards's first season before Anderson, the grandson of legendary college coach Charles "Lefty" Driesell, came aboard.

For a few years prior to Edwards's arrival in 2017, the basketball program began recruiting and funding the education for high-level athletes, including some from overseas. A lot of the responsibility for their well-being, and even their livelihoods, ended up falling to Little, who already housed three of those international students. She was about to get another basketball player as a regular houseguest.

Little was registrar at Holy Spirit (HSP for short), but her job title extended beyond that. For Edwards and her other students, she was a caretaker, chauffeur, cook, and Chick-fil-A buyer, and was constantly checking to make sure the kids did their homework. In Edwards's two years there, Little was in the academic trenches, making sure he was passing his classes and getting enough credits so he could eventually attend Georgia. She couldn't rest until the actual day Edwards got his diploma. Even when exams were over and graduation was near, there were a few fires she had to extinguish.

"Now I work in nuclear fuel and it's much less stressful," Little said.

She was like a mother, though she took great care to make it clear that she actually was not. Perhaps this was why Edwards ended up trusting her. There were others who may have wanted to be a mother to him. But he could use people who genuinely wanted to help him, and who didn't ask for anything in return. This was where he and Little got along great.

"He had tried to stay with some other basketball families at HSP . . . and they wanted to be his mom," Little said. "He was very much like, 'I don't need a mom. I have a mom, I have my sister. I don't need you to be my mom.' It was this delicate balance for me of how can I provide structure that I know is beneficial to him without making him feel suffocated?"

Little already had the three boys in her house, so she knew how to thread that line between being strict and giving freedom for Edwards to do what he wanted. She estimated that she spent about $14,000 on food to feed all the boys. She also did things like take Edwards to the dentist. When she did, he had so many cavities that he had to come back three more times to fill them all.

"It was crazy town," Little said. "But it also built a super special relationship with all of the kids."

She allowed a lot of autonomy for the students under her roof. If Edwards wanted to stay up late playing video games until 3 or 4 a.m., that was his choice. She wasn't going to make him turn it off. He at least had to do his homework and study for tests first.

"What people don't understand about Anthony is he thrives under a structure of a schedule," Little said. "But you just have to convince him that the structure is his idea, and then it's a win. But if he thinks the structure is what you try to impose—it just has to be on his terms, or at least him thinking it's on his terms."

Little has been to Minnesota for multiple games, tries to see Edwards when the Timberwolves come to Atlanta once a season, and stays in regular contact with him. It's surreal for her to think the Edwards who signed a contract for hundreds of millions of dollars and became one of the fastest-rising stars in the NBA was the same teenager whom she had to bribe with Chick-fil-A (chicken sandwich plus an extra-large sweet tea) so he would go to Saturday detentions.

"The most impressive thing to me was his resiliency and his emotional maturity," Little said. "When I think about if the people that raised me had passed away within six months of each other at thirteen, I would have been a hot freaking mess. . . . I would have been super depressed, not able to go to school. He just had this grand plan for his life, and this is what he was gonna do."

It's also ironic for Little to see all of Edwards's success, considering she and the school's principal at the time, Jocelyn Sotomayor, didn't want to admit Edwards at first.

Headed to the North Side

The story of Anthony Edwards's time in high school is filled with a few different and confusing twists and turns. Because of his August 5 birthday, Edwards was among the oldest players on his youth football teams, but he was always one of the youngest members of classes in school.

So he was set to graduate from high school at seventeen, and then turn eighteen that following August.

But after his freshman year when he attended school with his brother Bubba, then a senior, Edwards was falling through the cracks academically his sophomore year. Halfway through that year, Edwards sought to transfer to Holy Spirit, with Winfred Jordan helping make the connection with McClaire.

"I felt like he needed a change," Winfred said in an interview with journalist Chip Towers in 2019. "I was looking for a better situation for the young man, something that would make him better for the next twenty years of life and prepare him for college. He needed something a little more structured, something that would make him a little more polished as a young man. He needed more diversity in his life and more structure academically."

Holy Spirit certainly was different from Therrell in many ways. There was that structure that pushed him, teachers who wouldn't let up on him, and some other perks as well.

"There was warm cookie breaks," Dana Watkins said. "That gives you the extreme dichotomy of Therrell and Holy Spirit. Therrell it's like, 'Okay, we got to shut the school down because there's a gun on premises somewhere,' to warm cookie breaks."

Those cookie breaks came when he was in Little's office throughout the day. They were another "bargaining chip" Little said she used to get Edwards to do things he didn't want to do. Edwards preferred Grandma's Mini Sandwich Cremes, which they sold in a store across the street from Holy Spirit.

"I'd say, 'If you're on time to your next class, I'll go across the street at lunch and I'll get you [cookies],'" Little said. "It was always about food. Always about food."

Getting into Holy Spirit

Shortly after the calendar turned to 2017, Holy Spirit got a call from Edwards's people, Little said, asking if he could transfer there immediately. Little and the school's principal, Sotomayor, looked at Edwards's transcripts, and they saw a Bs and Cs student.

"Which, when we look at a public school student's transcript versus HSP, you basically take one letter grade off," Little said. "So him coming in, he would have been a C, D student. And we're like, ugh. . . . We're not touching this with a ten-foot pole. So we said no."

Added Sotomayor: "Anthony had so much support in terms of sports, but nobody really cared that much about academics. So when he came to us, he was behind. Sports were the most important, but without a high school degree, his prospects would have been diminished."

Here was one of the sticking points: HSP was a hard place for any student to assimilate into its culture, even if they started at the beginning of an academic year, Little said. That goes double for a midyear transfer.

"You were at a disadvantage if you were coming in as a transfer because you were starting at zero where everybody else has been raised on it," Little said.

A midyear transfer would be almost impossible in Edwards's case, because he wasn't even in school by the winter of his sophomore year.

To the administration at Holy Spirit, there was no way they could admit him midstream, especially after being out of school several weeks. Holy Spirit would revisit the conversation at the end of the school year, which meant Edwards would have to take online courses to keep up with where he should be academically. Little gave Edwards a curriculum he should take online. But when May came around, Edwards didn't complete the classes.

"I completely don't fault the siblings for that. It was a very complex situation," Little said. "They had so much freaking stuff going on. . . . I don't fault them for that at all. That was the one thing that had to fall behind on the wayside. It is what it is. So May comes around, and we're like, oh, wow, this is definitely not great.

"Again, it's going to be a no. We can't handle this right now. We don't have the capacity to do this."

But at no point throughout this process did Little or Sotomayor actually meet or speak with Edwards. Edwards's personality and charm was the ace in the hole. His family and friends persisted in telling the school it should at least meet with Edwards before making a final decision. After this several-month back-and-forth, Little and Sotomayor agreed to meet with Edwards.

"Thank God we didn't meet him [in February]," Sotomayor said.

Because they would have been tempted to go against their better judgment and admit Edwards immediately.

"Smiley, Bubbly, Happy Self"

The day Edwards met with Little, she had her approach prepared. First, she was expecting Edwards to be quiet and not say much, as someone who has just experienced a heavy amount of grief might be. But that wasn't going to sway her from her tactic of trying to scare the ever-living shit out of Edwards over what he was about to face academically at Holy Spirit.

"If you're going to be here, this is going to be the hardest thing you've ever done," Little said she told him. "You're not going to get any special treatment. You're going to have to be in study halls with me to make sure you're not falling behind, and so on.

"I'm laying it all out on what it's going to look like. And he was like, 'Okay. Sounds great!' He was just like, his smiley, bubbly, happy self."

Edwards's reaction puzzled Little, since he seemed so unbothered. They left her office and walked down the hallway to Sotomayor's. On the walk over, Little suggested that Edwards, who had dressed in the school's uniform for the interview (dress shirt and khakis), take out the earrings he was wearing since those were against dress code. It would be a nice gesture to show Sotomayor he was taking the uniform policy seriously, even if almost every day afterward he didn't.

"He said, 'See, you're already looking out for me.' And he like, bumped me, as we're walking, like we were longtime friends," Little said.

That was it. There was no way Little was going to let Edwards get away. Edwards walked into Sotomayor's office and she shut the door to have a quick word with Little in the hallway.

"I was like, we're screwed," Little said. "Because it's like, you can't not want to help this kid."

Sotomayor walked back into her office and noticed that Edwards's shirt looked like he had just taken it out of the bag and put it on five minutes before showing up at Holy Spirit.

"You could see the folds," Sotomayor said. "If he would have taken that shirt off, you could have folded it exactly as it was in the packet."

That, in its own way, was endearing to Sotomayor, and it gave Edwards some "brownie points," she said. Then during the meeting Sotomayor laid on the same spiel that Little did, that this would be a really hard process for Edwards, and he would have to work harder than he ever has in his life.

"He said, 'I'm used to working really hard,'" Sotomayor said. "At that time, I didn't know what that meant."

Edwards's charm and eagerness to take on those challenges won Sotomayor over.

"I will never forget that first meeting," Sotomayor said. "It was Anthony humble and just happy, smiling."

Holy Spirit agreed Edwards could come there, but on one condition—he would start the 2017–18 academic year as a sophomore, not as a junior. Holy Spirit had to course-correct for the time he missed at Therrell and the classes he didn't take online previous to that meeting. So Edwards was entering his third August attending high school, but he was reclassing as a sophomore.

Little began making sure Edwards had what he needed. She helped him get books from a used-book sale and clothes from a used-uniform sale. Right away Edwards and his peers on the basketball team experienced the culture shock of being at Holy Spirit. This came with the territory of the school trying to recruit high-profile athletes. They were bringing in kids who were different from the mostly white and Catholic core demographic into small classes—about forty or so in each. Not only that, but most of the students had been there since kindergarten. Now here came a bunch of new students of different backgrounds crashing those dynamics.

"These kids have other interests and live very different lives," Sotomayor said. "I think, for both sides, it was just a very different experience. I was excited, because I'm a minority myself [Sotomayor is Puerto Rican]. So I was like, we're gonna make the school diverse one way or another. But for some of the other kids, it was more difficult."

Edwards fared better than some of his teammates, not all of whom made it through to graduation, Sotomayor said. But his natural charisma to get along with people, no matter their background, not to mention his basketball prowess, made it an easier fit for him socially than others.

"Now you know how to interact with other races," Kierre Jordan said. "You can see it in his charisma. He can talk and laugh with and joke with everybody."

There wasn't an issue with Edwards personally, but there was an undercurrent of tension that existed at the school because the new athletes had come in. According to Anderson, who was only at the school for one year, the basketball players were watched a little more closely by some people at the school.

"We joke about the dress code and everything, but there were people at that school who had a more, uh, watchful eye over our basketball players," Anderson said. "Who were constantly on the lookout for them breaking any rules. Who were constantly on the lookout for them breaking dress code. I would get emails and texts about basketball players sleeping in Mass—they weren't the only ones sleeping in Mass. So they were a little more strict with those kids to the point it felt like resentment."

From Sotomayor's vantage point, there were students (mostly white) who had been on the basketball team their whole lives at Holy Spirit. Now Edwards and his teammates were replacing them, and there are only so many spots to go around on a varsity squad. That caused the resentment.

"I think the community was not ready to fully embrace kids coming from different backgrounds," Sotomayor said.

The administration was hearing—a lot—from the parents of kids Edwards and his teammates had displaced on the team.

"So many complaints from parents: 'My kid was on the team for four years. And all of a sudden, now he can't even make the team.' I felt for them. I did, I felt for them," Sotomayor said.

Demerits and Detentions

When Edwards first started attending Holy Spirit, he needed a ride one morning, so he called Banks. Banks drove from his house near the Atlanta airport, picked up Edwards, and dropped him off at the school in Buckhead. Given the traffic in Atlanta, that is a certifiably insane commute. It's a little over thirty minutes with no traffic, but in reality it was over an hour on some days, with some time to stop for McDonald's breakfast included.

"When I took him, I was like, 'Damn, whoever gonna get him to school, they got their work cut out for him,'" Banks said. "I thought it was just a onetime thing."

A few days later, Edwards called him again. *I need a ride to school.*

"It didn't take me long to figure out, oh, this all on me," Banks said. "If I don't get him to school, he ain't going. It took me two times to take him that it clicked in my mind that this a permanent job right here. I knew it. I read the room. . . . But the traffic? Oh my gosh. Like man, this ain't gonna work.

"That shit was bru-tal," he said, breaking up the two syllables in "brutal" for full effect. "I don't miss none of them days."

To cut down on time and make everyone's life at least a little easier, Edwards moved in with Banks for a good portion of the next two years. When he wasn't staying with Banks, the odds were he was at Little's place, especially in his second year at Holy Spirit. When Yvette was still alive, Banks pushed back when Edwards said he wanted to stay with Banks for a while, kind of like he would stay for stretches with the Watkins or Hinton families. Banks said no because he knew how "nasty" Edwards could be, always staying up late and eating bad food. It would have been a lot to take care of him on top of his own kids. But this was different. Yvette and Shirley were gone, and Banks had told himself when they died that he wasn't going to let Edwards down. That if nobody else would have his back, he would. So Edwards moved in with him.

"I'm telling you, like me and Justin, we talk now, like, 'Bro, I don't know how we got here, man,'" Banks said. "That school shit was so crazy. Because you got to understand, I had my two boys. I had to make sure they were square too."

If Banks had his boys staying with him, they'd leave for school around 5:30 a.m. If he didn't, they could push the departure to 6:30. Of course, Edwards would stay up playing video games and wouldn't get much sleep. But much like Little, Banks knew he couldn't impose too many restrictions on Edwards. Both of them understood this, and they also understood they couldn't be a parent to him. Yes, they knew what was best for Edwards, but they'd push him away if they tried to be too overbearing.

"I studied him when he was younger, you couldn't talk to Ant like you was his dad," Banks said. "You couldn't say to him, 'Hey turn that game off and go to sleep.' That was probably some mistakes people made. Ant didn't like structure, but he did. I knew how to handle him. So stay as long as you wanna stay up. I know when I come down here in the morning, your ass getting up, we goin' to school."

The only time Banks told him he couldn't do something—when Edwards wanted Banks to get a dog. Because he knew Edwards would play no role in taking care of it. But overall, even with the late-night video game sessions, Banks said Edwards wasn't hard on him.

"The way I talked to my kids, I couldn't talk to Ant like that," Banks said. "But I really didn't have no reason to talk to him like that because we never had no issues. He never disrespected me, never talked back, never looked at me crazy. Nothing."

After eating breakfast, Edwards would sleep the remainder of the ride to school. That lengthy commute had an effect on his disciplinary record.

Quickly in his first year at Holy Spirit, Edwards was piling up the demerits for being late. Multiple demerits equal detention and multiple detentions equal weekend detentions.

Because of the volume of demerits Edwards was getting, Little and Sotomayor came up with a revised rule. They didn't want Edwards to receive special treatment—that wasn't the way at the strict Holy Spirit—but they also wanted to be sympathetic to his circumstances.

"If he's less than fifteen minutes late, we don't write him up," Little said. "That worked so much better. Because if he was late, it was like 8:05, 8:10."

The next issue was the dress code. Edwards had a uniform at every house he might stay at with Holland, Banks, and Little. Everyone had multiple variations of the uniform. Anderson kept those belts and socks in his office.

"If I was the number one player in the country, and I was seventeen years old, and I'm basically living on my own, I don't think I'm gonna be in dress code, right?" Anderson said. "For him to get to school every day was a feat. To not be in dress code, it was hard for me to reprimand him."

Edwards wasn't the only one who had issues with it. His good friend Bidzina "Buka" Peikrishvili, one of the international basketball players who lived with Little, said a lot of students, including himself, hated that dress code.

"That dress code was just not fair," Peikrishvili said. "You would not expect a five-star athlete to follow that dress code. Like, why the black socks had to be black? Why couldn't it be gray? Oh, why the shirt always had to be tucked in? Facial hair, always clean-shaved. Suit and tie on, shirt tucked in, well-groomed everything. No hair past your ears. For a teenager that's fourteen, fifteen, sixteen, we don't really care about stuff like that, and it was hard to keep up because that school was really strict. But we were trying our hardest."

When Edwards did arrive at school, Sotomayor and Little had the person who was overseeing the front desk check him over for dress code violations when he arrived and before he saw any teachers who might've been itching to write him up for a violation. Socks were Edwards's frequent misstep. He'd wear white athletic socks when the dress code called for blue or black.

"It's like, dude, your legs are long. So when you sit down, they're gonna see that you're wearing white socks," Little said. "In some ways, I think, had he gone to, quote, unquote, 'a more powerhouse private school' . . . people are gonna look the other way if he's wearing white socks.

"I think people probably assume when you're as talented and have this amazing trajectory for your life, in some places you might get special treatment, but that was not the experience. If anything, they made it harder."

Edwards spent more time with Little in his two years at Holy Spirit than probably anybody in his life. He would have study hall with her and he went to her office on lunch breaks, which he usually spent taking a nap. His sleep habits were not the best—video games until late into the night and then attempting to wake up for early-morning practices or workouts.

On Monday through Thursday during basketball season, especially in his second year there, Edwards would sometimes stay with Little and Peikrishvili about forty-five minutes to an hour from the school. Little's mother, Kathy, also moved in to help her with all her duties. Little would take them to practice and then she would sleep in the back of her car before school. She'd take them home after school and take them to games. There were usually games on Friday, and so Edwards would leave those and return for the weekend with his family or Banks. Edwards's days were nonstop, Peikrishvili said. First came those 6 a.m. practices, which required a 4:45 a.m. wake-up call. Then school from around 8 until practice again at 4. Practice would last until around 6:30.

"By the time the 6:30 hit, I would be dead," Peikrishvili said. "And he would still get a ride from a trainer, go put another hour and thirty minutes of individual working, and then come home at like 9 p.m."

Of course, Edwards didn't go right to bed; there might be school-work he had to do, but he and Peikrishvili also played a lot of *Fortnite* and *Call of Duty* in their shared bedroom. At this point Edwards had moved away from playing *NBA 2K* so much and into these games.

"Crazy part is he didn't even need eight hours of sleep," Peikrishvili said. "He could just sleep for an hour, and he would be fine to go next morning."

Really? Just one hour of sleep?

"Yeah. He didn't need any sleep at all," Peikrishvili said. "He would sleep on car rides. I never remembered him awake on car rides."

Enter "Slick" Nick

There was somebody who was often a part of these late night *Fortnite* sessions with Peikrishvili and Edwards, someone who would become one of Edwards's closest friends and confidants—Nick Maddox, known affectionately as "Slick." Just before Edwards entered the NBA Draft in 2020, he asked Maddox, who was playing college baseball at Toccoa Falls College, to join him on his path to the NBA and be one of the people who would play a large role in his future. Maddox sits next to Edwards's brother Bubba at Wolves home games, is frequently at road games, and starred alongside Edwards in some of the commercials Edwards filmed for Adidas. He even got his own custom version of the AE1 shoe in December 2024—"Nick's Gift," Adidas called it. Their friendship began at Holy Spirit.

Maddox played basketball and baseball at Holy Spirit, and he grew up not too far from Edwards. By the time they met, Maddox had his own car and was making that laborious hour-long commute. Edwards would sometimes need a ride back to that part of the city, and on those car rides, Maddox and Edwards formed a connection.

On one of their first rides, Maddox said he turned on the classic song from the Temptations "Just My Imagination (Running Away with Me)," and Edwards sat up as if to say, "You know that song too?"

"We both old souls," Maddox said. "It was always like a song we both liked, then we found out we both loved *Sanford and Son*. Everything was just genuine. It wasn't forced. We both loved sports, music, liked to have fun, have a good time. Get our work done and do what we wanna do."

Maddox knew about Edwards's family situation before he met him, and like Little, he was surprised to see just how upbeat and energetic Edwards was every day. There was no hint that Edwards had dealt with such heavy losses in a short amount of time.

"Nobody can deny that boy is always smiling," Maddox said. "Sometimes I think about to this day how I would be if my mom, grandma weren't here. The fact that he lost them at such a young age and to grow up and mature as fast as he did . . . very commendable, man."

Maddox was ahead of Edwards when he got to Holy Spirit and they spent just one year in school together, but that was more than enough time to form a lifelong friendship. They bonded during those shared car rides, and they were some of the only Black students in a predominantly white student body. So Maddox would always check in with Edwards in his early days at Holy Spirit to make sure he was doing okay.

"During classes we'd be looking at each other like, 'You straight? You all right?' Because this is very new to us coming to situation like that, not many people looking like us that can relate to us," Maddox said.

Maddox also interacted a lot with Little, and he and Edwards both had teachers that didn't seem to particularly care for them. Little was always there to help. Maddox had an issue with a chemistry teacher in his senior year, and Little "got on they ass" to fix the situation.

"He put me through hell," Maddox said. "But she came to my side. . . . She understood my perspective. It was like we weren't trying. Some of them teachers have it out for us. Everybody doesn't want to see him go to the league. Everybody don't want to see you succeed. Man, the fact that she stepped in the way she did—I'll do anything for that lady."

There was a time Little had to come to Edwards's help in a similar way just before he graduated, and that help may have saved Edwards from making a life-altering decision. Edwards felt at ease when he was around Little and trusted her because Edwards sensed she was someone who just wanted to help him—and that wasn't out for anything more. Throughout his life following the death of Yvette and Shirley, this characteristic has been a constant of Edwards's. He is hesitant to let people in; he may smile and greet you warmly, but he can sniff out when you are trying to use him for your own personal gain. With Little, he never sensed that.

"I said he sees you like a big sister, as someone that he really trusts," Sotomayor said. "They had a really beautiful relationship."

Added Maddox: "A lot of kids from where we're from, you'd be automatically like, 'You ain't my momma. You ain't got to tell me nothing. I ain't listening to you.'"

That was never an issue between Edwards and Little. There was a time Peikrishvili, who is from the country of Georgia, said he had a distrust of Little. Looking back on that period, he said he was homesick and missing his family. Perhaps he also was being a typical teenager rebelling against the person who had authority over him, which at this time was Little.

"At first I was kind of like an asshole to Rachel and her mom," Peikrishvili said.

For a while, Peikrishvili thought Little was trying to usurp his family's place in his life.

"I don't have any family in America. I'm far away, and I'm still young," he said. "I was thinking that Rachel was taking that role, and I was like, 'Oh, do I allow her?'"

Edwards ended up convincing Peikrishvili that Little was there to help them, that she could be trusted, and he shouldn't be treating her and her mother with disrespect.

"We had long conversations for hours of him proving to me that Rachel was legit, legit there to help us get better at everything and she was helping us survive," Peikrishvili said.

Edwards and Peikrishvili became fast friends from the time they met when Peikrishvili was fifteen. At first Peikrishvili didn't speak much English, but he said Edwards made him feel welcome.

"I had an accent, like broken English, and he would just say, 'I love your accent,'" Peikrishvili said. "'I want to go to that country and meet people, how they speak, hear the language.'"

Edwards hasn't made it over to Georgia, yet, but whenever Peikrishvili would FaceTime with his family, Edwards would hop on the calls so Peikrishvili's dad could teach him some Georgian words, including some curses.

"But he wanted to know the actual conversation holders and not the bad words," Peikrishvili said. "He knew everybody of mine, grandmas, uncles, everybody. They all want to FaceTime him."

Before the Olympics began in 2024, Peikrishvili said Edwards invited him to Abu Dhabi for Peikrishvili's birthday when the team was there playing some showcase games prior to arriving in Paris. Edwards introduced him to all of his teammates.

"He said, just come to Abu Dhabi and just spend time, spend your birthday with me, and we just had a great time," Peikrishvili said.

Peikrishvili added that a few weeks later, after the Olympics, he was FaceTiming with his grandmother and Edwards joined the call. Peikrishvili's grandmother implored Edwards to visit Georgia after the Olympics.

"The dude's been gone from his home for like, two, three months for preparation, he's not coming to Georgia," Peikrishvili said. "But it's hard to tell a seventy-year-old lady that."

Peikrishvili and Edwards helped each other get through the unique experience of being newbies at Holy Spirit. Edwards's first year was filled with late arrivals and dress code issues, but Sotomayor said he stayed out of serious trouble.

The Drama of Reclassification

Edwards was improving by leaps and bounds and jumping up the recruiting rankings. He was slated to be a part of the recruiting class of

2020, after he had entered Holy Spirit as a sophomore in 2017. But entering the next school year, Edwards's people delivered Holy Spirit some surprising news—Edwards was going to reclassify and become a part of the 2019 class after all. He would be graduating at the end of the 2018–19 academic year in part because of something Edwards scribbled on the walls of his grandmother and grandfather's house a few years earlier: becoming a McDonald's All-American. That was within reach, and he wasn't going to let it get away.

Any story that journalists write about athletes who reclassify tends to treat that term as a footnote, like it's merely a business decision for a player to go pro a year earlier or later than anticipated. What they don't write is just what may be involved with that process behind the scenes, and in Edwards's case, reclassification almost derailed his ability to attend Georgia and altered his basketball future.

Becoming a McDonald's All-American had some stipulations that came with it, namely this: nominees have to be on schedule to graduate the year of their nomination. Naturally, it came to Little to figure out how to make this happen. She was less than thrilled.

"I was just like, are you kidding?" she said.

Holy Spirit was about to embark on a national schedule to highlight Edwards and the program, and that meant time away from class for out-of-state games. Edwards was also going to be taking recruiting visits throughout the fall. Not to mention there were the difficult logistics to navigate in just getting to school every day, no matter where he was staying.

That all didn't matter. Little had to figure out how Edwards could get a diploma by the end of May. So she sat down with Sotomayor, and they looked at just how many credits Edwards had accrued toward state requirements for graduation in his five semesters of high school. They concluded that Edwards would have to take four separate online classes in addition to a heavier course load at Holy Spirit in order to graduate on time.

"It was just gonna be an onslaught year for me chasing him down and saying you have to do this, you have to do that, and that's ultimately what it was," Little said.

At least with the online courses, Edwards could do those on his own time. He often stayed with Little and the rest of her crew multiple days per week during basketball season, and she saw him during his study hall and again during his lunch break.

As for the basketball season, Holy Spirit was playing that national schedule, and that included out-of-state road trips, like one they took to play James Wiseman's team in Memphis. That was a necessity for Edwards because their regular league schedule didn't have the stiffest competition. Edwards's days were still filled with frequent demerits and detentions, no matter how hard everyone tried to keep him in dress code. Anderson would even delay the start of practices for Edwards to get out of detention. He also had to delay them for another reason.

"He always had to take a shit before practice," Anderson said. "For some reason, the bowels always started to move like, right before practices started."

So everyone waited for Edwards to clear detention, clear some other things, and get to the floor. Edwards's games were an event around Atlanta, and the small gym at Holy Spirit was at capacity for each of his games. There would be requests for autographs outside the arena and wherever Holy Spirit ended up playing on the road. But inside the school, Edwards could move around as if he was just another student. That was one tangential effect of the school not having placed a premium on athletics in the past and the intense culture that existed there. It wasn't conducive to having a so-called big man on campus. Certainly, Edwards's teachers weren't having any of it.

"Yes, he was popular, but teachers don't care about that," Sotomayor said. "I think they made it difficult as well."

The discipline at Holy Spirit got to the point that Edwards had to serve Saturday detentions, including one prior to a Thanksgiving weekend matchup with Atlanta powerhouse Wheeler. Edwards was adamant he wasn't going to that Saturday detention. Anderson was getting nowhere with him, so he turned to Little for help.

"I'm like, why do I get all the bad jobs?" Little said with a laugh.

Edwards had just finished up a practice in the gym, and Little sat with him on the bottom set of bleachers.

"I put my hand on his arm, and said, 'I need to say some things that you're not going to like, but I need you to hear me completely before you respond,'" Little said.

Little started explaining to him that he had to attend that Saturday detention. Edwards began firing back at her. She told him to let her finish.

"I said, 'Your team is counting on you,'" Little said. "'You do not want to upset your teammates. This is a national tournament. It's going to be really important to everybody. You have to show up. So I'm going to bribe you. I will get you Chick-fil-A for lunch every day for the next two weeks after Thanksgiving break.'"

That got Edwards to agree. Despite the detentions, Sotomayor said Edwards always had a good attitude around the school. Always engaging, making friends with all different kinds of students, not just his teammates on the basketball team. On the court, that uplifting personality was how Edwards led, and it was a harbinger of how he would affect the Timberwolves in his first four seasons of the NBA. Before Edwards's last season at Holy Spirit began, Anderson pulled him aside and said he needed Edwards to be the leader of the team. Edwards demurred.

"Listen, you tell me you don't wanna be a leader. That's because what your idea of a leader is very surface level," Anderson said he told Edwards. "Leadership can come in so many different ways. And so like it or not, you are our leader. And here are the ways that you do it. Let's see if we can just be a little more conscious of the ways that you affect people and you can harness that a little bit in your own way."

Anderson could see that Edwards's emotional intelligence was off the charts for someone his age. The way he interacted with students, teammates, and teachers was unlike many of his peers.

"His self-awareness is extremely high," Anderson said. "He's still got like that teenager whimsy that I think a lot of people wish they could hold on to. He holds on to it partly because he doesn't grip it."

He would also introduce his teammates to the college coaches who visited their practices. At the University of Georgia, he'd do the same thing—try to bolster his teammates by introducing them to pro scouts. Edwards could also sense when someone needed some picking up. He could know when someone needed a little ribbing to get going.

"Like marginalized kids on a team who maybe weren't as funny [as others]. If he takes their side in a *Lord of the Flies* situation all of a sudden now they're one of the cool kids because Ant's the cool kid," Anderson said. "Ant decides who's the cool kid. That type of leadership has a lot of depth to it."

Peikrishvili said Edwards was positive at all times. He would encourage players to do what they were best at, and if they weren't doing those things or were hesitant in a game, that could have a negative impact on the team.

"You need to have those people on your team," Peikrishvili said. "I never seen a sad face on his face. Never even the state championship."

Holy Spirit lost its state title game to Heritage 67–64 in a performance Anderson called one of the most impressive he saw from Edwards, who was playing through knee tendinitis that night. At halftime Anderson told Edwards to sit the rest of the game out. But Edwards checked himself back in during the third quarter anyway.

"There wasn't really anything I could do to keep him off the court, but wanting to play through that was certainly a moment that I won't forget," Anderson said.

Edwards was named a McDonald's All-American, the thing he wanted to accomplish on his checklist. But after the season was over, Edwards still had work to do before he was through at Holy Spirit. All those extra classes were still hovering over his head. The calendar turned to May, with graduation in sight, but that month was about to be the most stressful of Little's time with Edwards at Holy Spirit.

"May was terrible," Little said.

It started when Edwards told Little that he didn't take a required English online course.

"What in the ever-loving you-know-what," Little said. "Every night that month, he had to come home with us. 'Sit down. I am watching you do it.'"

About two days before Edwards had to report to the University of Georgia that spring for his first workouts, Little called the school to tell them he had posted a grade in that course, so he would be academically eligible to come onto campus.

But that wasn't the worst of it. Once exams were over and before graduation, Little would get failure reports for students who had not passed certain classes. The administration would then go over the grades to see if there was a way they could work with the students and teachers to rectify the situation. Little nervously held her breath, because she knew Edwards was on the border of failing history. The thing was, it wasn't like Edwards lacked intelligence or work ethic. Little said Edwards could be an excellent student if he devoted the time he put into basketball into academics. Edwards was calculated in how he delegated his focus and attention.

"He was always able to figure out percentage-wise exactly which homework assignments he had to do to keep his grades where they needed to be," Little said. "He used the same method before a test to figure out what grade he needed. He could learn material pretty quickly and knew when to be 'on' or when he could be a little less focused. It takes a uniquely smart person at that age to know where to put his time and energy that allowed him to manage his insane schedule."

Peikrishvili said Edwards was especially smart in math. Their first year together, Peikrishvili said he knew more than Edwards when they began studying geometry, but by the end of the class, Edwards was tutoring him.

"My man didn't know anything before," Peikrishvili said. "Went to tutorials . . . and I think dude became smarter than the actual teacher."

But the reality of his situation was he had to spend so much time on basketball that academics just naturally took a back seat when millions of dollars were at stake in his future, and none of the classes were cupcakes.

"Because the one word that describes every syllabus at Holy Spirit is 'rigorous,'" Maddox said.

The history teacher and Edwards didn't have the best relationship, Little said, and so she sifted through the failure reports, and her worst fear came to life: Edwards's history grade was a 69.4. A 70 was passing, which meant if Edwards even had a 69.5, it would have rounded up to 70 and he would have passed. That 69.4 was cruel, and Little was livid.

"I was like, abso-freaking-lutely not," Little said. "We are not going to be the roadblock that keeps this kid from the rest of his life and going on this new path that could change his life, change his financial future, change his family's financial future because of one-tenth of a point that we're bitter about. I'm going to die on this hill that we're not going to do this."

When she told Edwards about it, it was one of the few times she said Edwards was visibly upset and fed up with the way Holy Spirit was treating him, and he was ready to throw his whole future into doubt over that grade.

"He was so done. I was so done," Little said. "So when I told him, he said, 'I give up. I'm just gonna go play overseas. Forget college, forget it. I'm just gonna go,' and I was like, 'Calm down. I have a plan. We're gonna figure it out.'"

Little met with Sotomayor and she agreed they had to take action. But Sotomayor was on her way out as principal, and her successor, Dr. Edward Lindekugel, was already on campus. Luckily, Lindekugel also agreed this could not stand, and he happened also to be a history teacher. Together they looked at every quiz, test, and homework assignment Edwards had accrued in the teacher's grade book. There was an 18 for a test in there. It was just an exam that Edwards couldn't prepare properly for in the natural ebb and flow of his chaotic year, and the teacher showed no mercy in grading the exam. This was their out. He would retake this test.

So Edwards came into the school just before graduation and Lindekugel taught him the material on the test that morning. He asked if Edwards wanted a day to review it at home so he could retake the test the next day. Edwards told him he didn't have to; he was ready to take it right there.

He didn't do so well on the essay portion of the test, but he did great on the rest, and the grade was a 75. That was enough to lift his overall average above a passing grade. Edwards was on his way to graduation, finally. After two strenuous years, Edwards got to the finish line of his Holy Spirit experience. At graduation, his family couldn't be prouder. His sister, Antoinette, who had just had a baby, took so many pictures of her brother.

"I remember he was all smiles," Sotomayor said. "They were so proud. It was beautiful. . . . All smiles, and it was a big accomplishment. I'm telling you that boy that came to me in tenth grade that I was like, 'Oh my God, how are we going to do this?' But he did it."

He did it without shortcuts, without anyone fudging his grades or letting him skip class so he could put more shots up in the gym. Edwards earned that diploma, even if it took all of Little's efforts to get him to that stage at graduation.

"When he passed that exam . . . I felt like that meme where the guy comes in from work with his backpack and then he just like plops down," Little said. "It was the most insane year ever."

From that experience, Little became Edwards's favorite white person of all time. Little has been to multiple games since Edwards joined the NBA, and he's always happy to see her. One time, he told her to test-drive his Lamborghini on the frozen streets of downtown Minneapolis and expressed bemused disappointment when she didn't go over 25 miles per hour. On another of the visits, Little was talking to Edwards about all they went through at Holy Spirit—the detentions, the demerits, the close calls with the grades, the online courses. He remembers that dress code. After a playoff game against the Denver Nuggets in 2024, Edwards was swapping stories with Karl-Anthony Towns and Naz Reid, who also attended Catholic schools, over who had the strictest dress code. When Edwards posted a video to Instagram putting on his outfit for the opening ceremonies of the 2024 Paris

Olympics, a fit that included a Polo blazer, dress shirt, and tie, the caption read, "The HSP way."

While the exams, the pressure of making grades and getting enough credits, may have left his mind, there is one exception.

"It's hilarious, because he hardly remembers any of it," Little said. "Well, he remembers that one history teacher."

CHAPTER 5

(LESS THAN A) YEAR AT GEORGIA

The first time Amir Abdur-Rahim saw Edwards work out, it was on a weekday at 6 a.m. during his sophomore year at Therrell. As Abdur-Rahim, an Atlanta native who was an assistant at Texas A&M at the time, watched Edwards, his jaw fell to the floor.

"You just look at the way somebody moves sometimes, and you can tell," Abdur-Rahim said. "Sometimes you can look at just their features, how tall they are, the length of their arms, things like that. But then sometimes, man, you find a dude that has all of it, the length, the athleticism, and when he moves, it's like poetry in motion."

As time went by, and Abdur-Rahim saw how competitive Edwards was, he began calling people he knew in the Atlanta area with one message: "Edwards could be the best player ever to come out of Atlanta and the state of Georgia." More than one person scoffed, because that meant Edwards would be better than Amir's own brother, Shareef Abdur-Rahim, the former NBA All-Star who played twelve seasons in the league, from 1996 to 2008.

"I'd say, 'I know who my brother is,'" Abdur-Rahim said. "But serious, the dude is the real deal. I thought he was the best player in the country, regardless of class, from that moment I saw him. I remember going back to A&M and telling our staff this is the dude we gotta have."

After his sophomore year, Edwards shot up the rankings and was the top recruit in the 2020 class before reclassifying. Then he was still the top recruit in the 2019 class after he officially reclassified.

That accomplishment is almost unheard-of in the world of recruiting. After that first workout, Abdur-Rahim struck up a conversation with Edwards, and the two bonded over their shared Atlanta roots. Under NCAA rules, Abdur-Rahim said he couldn't contact Edwards, but if Edwards wanted, he could call Abdur-Rahim, so the two made a standing appointment for a check-in, every Thursday at 8:30. Edwards never missed a call.

Then Tom Crean became the head coach at Georgia in March 2018. The former Marquette and Indiana coach was coming to Athens in an attempt to revitalize a program that many had tried to jolt back to life previously, but could not. Being on such a football-dominant campus can do that to a basketball program. As of 2024, Georgia men's hoops had been to the NCAA tournament only five times this century and had not advanced to the second weekend of the tournament since 1996.

When Crean took the job, landing Edwards was a chance to inject a shot of adrenaline into the program. So Crean made a logical move to hire Abdur-Rahim to his staff a few months after he took the job.

Abdur-Rahim joined with fellow assistant Chad Dollar, who had also been keeping tabs on Edwards for as long as Abdur-Rahim had, in a tag-team recruitment of Edwards to the Bulldogs. Dollar, also an Atlanta native, said the pair was able to really get close with different members of the tight inner circle Edwards kept, and that helped give them a leg up on every other school.

"With someone of his caliber, I'm a firm believer that you can't do it by yourself," Dollar said. "We did a good job of breaking up his inner circle so we knew exactly what was going on. I had a group of guys, Amir had a group of guys, and obviously you had Coach Crean, and that was very instrumental in helping us recruit him."

With those phone calls, Edwards and Abdur-Rahim began building a relationship, and Abdur-Rahim knew that bond would mean something to him in the recruiting process, even as the crush of blue-blood programs (with Kentucky leading the way) eventually descended on him with their flash and promises.

"They all start coming in and trying to wow him," said Abdur-Rahim, who was the head coach at South Florida when he spoke for this book about two months before his unexpected death following complications from surgery in October 2024. "I was never worried about it, because he's not somebody who can be wowed."

The Georgia staff figured out Edwards keeps a tight inner circle, and he has a good bullshit detector to weed out those who don't have his best interests at heart. They didn't have to worry much about hangers-on or new people entering his life trying to get something out of him. As long as they stayed true with Edwards and that circle, they were good.

"We felt like we had put in the work," Dollar said.

One of Edwards's innate gifts is his ability to command a room, and he would meet with some of these street agents and other businessmen who'd pop up at his games in Athens. He could smile, carry on conversation, and make them feel like they were long-lost friends. This was Edwards "the politician" at work, as Holland said. As Crean put it, "He can smile at you and he can talk to you, but that don't mean he's going to do what you want. He's not an overly trusting guy."

Edwards constantly has people trying to gain access to him or to ask him for a favor. He has changed his phone number dozens of times and tries to limit the number of people who end up receiving it. Dana Watkins said he sometimes receives calls in the middle of the night from Edwards just so Edwards can let him know he changed his number again. One of his longest-tenured Wolves teammates, Naz Reid, joked that he has about five numbers for Edwards and "I never know who to text."

"People might want him to help put businesses together, like a barbershop or car wash," Dana said. "It's like, well, put together a business proposal and get back to me."

Those proposals rarely come. Holland joked that they were paying phone bills for numbers long discarded by Edwards well into his NBA career. But inevitably, people Edwards doesn't want to have his number end up getting it. The process repeats. If Edwards gives someone his number, it's one indication of where you stand with him. A lot of others don't get it.

"As a kid, I can't believe he was able to figure all that stuff out," assistant coach Brian Fish said.

As their relationship grew, Crean said he emphasized to Edwards the importance and power of "being the head of your board meeting." He shouldn't let others speak for him, regardless of the promises they make. Edwards had an innate sense to do this already, but Crean helped instill it.

"It gets really easy for these guys, a lot of times, to let somebody else speak for them, because that's easier," Crean said. "They don't want to deal with it."

Edwards has always been independent in that way, and if he doesn't want to do something, or to invite someone in his life, there's no amount of convincing anyone can do to force him.

All through Edwards's time at Georgia, NCAA compliance people were interested in him, and he had regular meetings every few weeks where they would comb through his phone and make sure everything was on the up-and-up. This was the time just before the NCAA began allowing athletes to earn money based off their name, image, and likeness (or NIL deals) and in 2019 the NCAA was still suspicious that Edwards was receiving even small gifts. One time, Dana attended a Georgia game with Banks, and he said Banks would point out people in the crowd and tell him what they had asked from Edwards's camp.

"'See that guy over there? See that guy over there?'" Dana said. "You see that trajectory. They were the street agents, and I've seen it too many times to count."

Added Fish: "There would always be somebody in Atlanta saying I gave them this or I gave them that. Georgia would research it and put it to bed."

Edwards and Georgia never received any NCAA discipline.

Bullish on Bulldogs

Bit by bit, Crean formed a bond with Edwards through the recruiting process. It wasn't something the coach tried to fake and make happen right away—it helped that Abdur-Rahim and Dollar had already laid the foundation—but Crean let their communication evolve naturally. Crean said there came a moment one night as he was texting Edwards something about late-game offense, and Edwards replied back: Will you let me have the ball at the end of games?

Absolutely, I'll do everything I can do to help, Crean said he texted back. You deserve to earn the ball at the end of games, and I'm betting on myself as well as you. . . . I think that was a moment for him that bonded us. He appreciated the fact that I would tell him what he needed to get better at, and I would have a plan on what it would look like.

People to trust were in short supply. In Crean came with the chops to mold recruits for the NBA, as he did with multiple players over the years like Dwyane Wade, Victor Oladipo, Noah Vonleh, and Wesley Matthews. Georgia needed Edwards to stay home; this was Crean's best chance to jump-start the program, and they did whatever it took to keep Edwards in state. On one unofficial visit, the staff made sure Edwards ran into Crean's former protégé Wade, who was making college visits with his son Zaire.

When Edwards came on an unofficial visit, Abdur-Rahim said Crean sat with Edwards for a lengthy film session—something Crean often does with recruits—and observed how Edwards's attention never wavered.

"Most recruits would get to a point where they would doze off, or their body language will change," Abdur-Rahim said. "Not Ant. He was up the whole time asking questions. This dude was different."

In December of his last year at Holy Spirit, Edwards had his official visit in Athens. He wanted Peikrishvili to join him, but Georgia couldn't make that work under NCAA rules. Edwards was on campus for parts of three days, and the itinerary included a forty-five-minute film session with Crean. At 8 p.m. on Sunday, Georgia scheduled a bowling and team dinner event for Edwards, since bowling is one of his favorite hobbies. Also on the visit was Antoinette, and Georgia sold Edwards on being near his family for one more year. Kentucky, who was among the finalists for Edwards, didn't have this card to play. This was the same teenager who wanted to stay with his family as much as he could, so staying home one more year was valuable to Edwards.

"We sold that," Crean said. "Your life is going to change, no matter what. . . . But the bottom line is, it doesn't have to change yet, and we can help in every possible way, help you get ready for when that change comes."

Not that it wasn't close. Kentucky came in strong. Maddox said Edwards called him a few days before he made his decision and Edwards told him, "I'm thinking about doing the Big Blue, man."

"I said they do have pro training over there," Maddox added, but he said he was hoping Edwards would choose Georgia because he was still only an hour from campus and could make the drive to Athens to visit him often. Maddox walked into one of his classes the day Edwards was about to make his announcement. He had no advanced knowledge of where Edwards would go. He was on Instagram Live watching Edwards make his choice when his professor told the class they had a pop quiz.

"I said I got a family emergency, I need to step outside. I'll be right here if you need me," Maddox said.

After about thirty minutes on that broadcast, Edwards selected Georgia. He was staying close to home.

Before Edwards arrived on campus, Abdur-Rahim got an offer to be a head coach at Kennesaw State, just north of Atlanta. Prior to taking the job, Abdur-Rahim said he called Edwards to tell him about the offer, and that he wouldn't accept it if Edwards wanted him to stay on staff at Georgia.

"Man, that was the goal for you, right [to be a head coach]?" Edwards told him. "Coach, I'm only gonna be there six months. Naw, you gotta take that."

"Y'all have no clue how hard it is to get a head coaching job," Abdur-Rahim added. "I'm forever grateful and thankful that kid was so understanding. He saw the big picture. He got the big picture. He could've easily said no."

It was something Abdur-Rahim never forgot, and he was advancing up the ranks in his coaching career at South Florida before his death on

October 24, 2024. He was forty-three. Edwards flew from Minneapolis to Atlanta on an off day during the Wolves season to attend services and pay his respects.

First-Time Weight Lifter

Edwards was the head of a strong recruiting class for the Bulldogs, who were also bringing in four-star prospects Christian Brown, Jaykwon Walton, and Toumani Camara, and three-star guard Sahvir Wheeler. For the first time in a long time, there was excitement around Georgia basketball, and Edwards brought instant buzz to campus.

"He took over the town," said Bulldogs teammate Tye Fagan. "That's all everybody was talking about—football guys, basketball guys—like it was insane."

Added Crean: "There was an air of confidence, there was an air of competition, but there was never a guy that walked around like everybody was looking at him. He just fit in, like he was from Atlanta. That's part of what makes him great, and he's very, very comfortable wherever he's at."

Behind the athletic department's weight-training facility, which all sports use, there's a sign that reads, "Due to NCAA regulations, solicitation of autographs is prohibited on athletic association property."

Of all the athletes who have come through Georgia, Edwards was the one who caused the school to put the sign up. Such was the demand for his signature.

"That was put up specifically for Anthony," Sean Hayes, strength and conditioning coach, said. "There's no way his life was normal. Whenever we got off a bus, people were waiting in line for autographs."

Fagan said Edwards requested him to be his roommate after Fagan helped show Edwards around on his visits. He was getting more than he bargained for in his new roommate. Like in high school, Edwards wasn't one to sleep a lot, and he'd play video games and loud music well into the night. Sometimes Edwards would come back and wake Fagan up from a dead sleep.

"He's an a-hole," Fagan said with a laugh. "There was sometimes he'd knock on my door, 'Hey man, stop all that old shit. You ain't asleep. Open the door.' I'm like, 'Leave me alone, bro. I got class eight in the morning. You don't.' Talkin' 'bout stop that old shit. Man, we're a year and a half apart."

They even adopted a dog named London while they were roommates. But Fagan said he was the one who ended up taking care of her.

"That was me walking her outside in the forty-degree weather, thirty-degree weather," he said.

Over that summer before classes began, Fagan's and Edwards's early wake-up calls were for conditioning and lifting. The schedule was lifting Monday, Wednesday, and Friday from 9 to 10 a.m. Tuesdays were agility drills in the beach volleyball sandpit. Hayes had to start at the beginning with Edwards, who didn't lift weights much at any point in his life, even in his football days.

"Week one we're doing just basic stuff, like bench press, and we had ninety-five pounds on the bar," Hayes said.

Edwards was like a lot of other athletes Hayes encountered; he had to build their habits from the ground up.

"You're teaching them discipline, culture, and work ethic, and you raise your voice, you yell and you motivate," Hayes said.

But one day, Hayes got on Edwards, who was socializing with one of his teammates, and told him to "cut the shit," since they only had a limited amount of time to work out, per NCAA rules. Hayes said Edwards got quiet and finished the workout. When it was over, Edwards walked over to Hayes and put his arm around him.

"'Coach Hayes, you know you don't have to yell at me. Just tell me what you want me to do and I'll do it,'" Hayes said Edwards told him. "He's seventeen years old at the time, and he just had this mature, grown-up conversation. I said, 'We're on the same page,' and he said, 'Perfect, coach,' then gave me a pat and walked off."

From that moment, Hayes never had any difficulty getting Edwards to do any exercises, except the only one Edwards didn't want to do—and Hayes never forced him: front squats.

This wasn't quite the approach Crean took when he worked with

Edwards. There would be yelling, and a decent amount of it. According to Fish, Crean liked to say he would "pierce you, and then bring you back" by offering some positive reinforcement. During a workout in August, Edwards almost had enough of Crean piercing him.

The Bulldogs were having one of their first team workouts since NCAA rules limited them to individual or small group sessions over the summer. Crean had worked with Edwards to improve the basics, little things about his game he never had to tweak previously, like how to catch the ball more aggressively and having the right footwork.

"When he first got there, it took about three weeks for him to realize like I was going to back up what I said we were going to do," Crean said. "Practice [previously] for him was pretty much on his terms—scrimmage, shoot. Those kind of things. He had to learn a lot about small group workouts. He had to learn a lot about the fundamentals."

During one of these sessions, Crean was not letting up on Edwards as they were going through some dribbling cone drills.

"Tom demands you come full speed, going in and out of cones, right- and left-handed and then stepping through, demanding the ball to be crossed over low, things like that," Fish said.

It's the type of drill that doesn't carry instant gratification like making a shot or getting a stop on defense. The eye of the evaluator determines whether a player does well in the drill or not. Crean wouldn't let up.

"I think it was the first time somebody told Anthony we're not accepting really good, we're going to demand greatness," Fish said. "[Crean was] very loud, very demanding, matter-of-factly."

Fish described what happened next as a "meltdown."

After several minutes of Crean harping, Edwards stopped doing the drill, backed away and retreated to a wall, and put his head against it. To Fish this was a "defining moment" for the season, for the program, and for Edwards. Edwards was not powerless in this dynamic with Crean. Crean and the Bulldogs needed Edwards, and if Edwards walked out, it would be a devastating blow. If he didn't want to accept the coaching, it could set a bad example for the rest of the season. For three or four minutes, Fish said, Edwards remained against that wall.

"I'm going to push you to the highest level. This is what you want. This is what you said," Crean kept telling Edwards, even as he was against the wall.

"There's not a single person not watching this confrontation," Fish recounted. "This is the stare-down. Is Russia gonna shoot the missiles or are we gonna do it? It's the Cuban Missile Crisis in Athens."

Practice continued in an awkward fashion as Edwards remained against the wall.

"In my thirty-five years in college basketball, it's right there as one of the most defining moments I've seen," Fish said. "Because who challenges a player of that stature? Who does that? And as a player of that stature, who accepts that?"

Eventually Edwards turned around and Crean came over to him.

"Tom goes over and hugs him. Anthony hugs Tom, and they have a moment together," Fish said. "And it's on. I feel like those two hitched themselves to each other at that point."

Edwards and Crean still have a strong relationship where Crean texts him advice and checks in on him. Even in the Western Conference Finals in 2024, Edwards made public mention of advice he received during the series from Crean. Edwards recognized that Crean was ultimately out to help him, no matter how much Crean got on Edwards, and he was on Edwards a lot.

"There was no subject that I wasn't going to touch, but I was always coming from a place of help and what was best for him," Crean said. "Knowing that he needed to have more tools in the toolbox as he left."

There was no sugarcoating from Crean. Graduate assistant Reed Ridder said that one time Crean yelled out to Edwards, "One of these days, you're gonna miss hearing my voice."

Even though Abdur-Rahim was coaching in Atlanta at Kennesaw State that season, he still made time to travel for some of Edwards's practices in Athens, and he saw how intensely Crean coached Edwards in these practices. Edwards always accepted it.

"Anthony doesn't want to hear you're great, you're this, you're that," Abdur-Rahim said. "He wants to hear what he needs to get better at. That's why he and Coach Crean, their relationship was always so good. . . . He wasn't just telling them how awesome he was."

Midnight Oil

When Edwards came on campus, Ridder was in his second year as a graduate assistant and Crean handed him an important responsibility—he would lead Edwards through his late-night workouts. NCAA rules said the head coach or assistant couldn't do it, Ridder said, so the job came to him. Ridder and Edwards became fast friends.

Edwards had been a creature of late-night workouts extending back to his days with Holland, so he was used to hitting the gym late at night. This didn't change at Georgia, even as Edwards dealt with the facade of pretending to take his studies seriously for the one and a half semesters he was there. There were times he would tell the assistants, Fish said, that he was skipping class to go to the gym and get in an afternoon workout. It often fell to Ridder to tell him that he needed to get to class.

Maddox would drive to campus and stay overnight with Edwards and Fagan. Inevitably a coach or staffer like Ridder would knock on Edwards's door to tell him he had to get to class. One time, Maddox let him in, much to the chagrin of Edwards. Maddox was also worried what the coaching staff would now think of him.

"They gonna look at me like I'm a bad influence," Maddox said.

But Ridder, who played Division II hoops and professionally in Australia and Spain before entering the coaching world, was able to hold Edwards accountable. Edwards may have skipped some classes, but he made sure he did what he had to do in order to stay eligible.

"I'm a GA, honestly, the bottom end of the totem pole," Ridder said. "I knew my role. I never one time was like, 'Listen to me.' I'm not dumb."

But Ridder asked that Edwards respect his time, and one day when Edwards was late to an afternoon workout, Ridder told him this was not how you handle business.

"'Respect me. I respect you,'" Ridder said.

They had a standing time throughout the season for their workouts—9 p.m. Ridder was also with Edwards throughout most of the day, and he'd take him around campus at times on a golf cart, with Edwards hamming it up in the back seat.

"He loves the golf cart," Ridder said. "He'd sit in the back like this [arms extended], it was funny. He'd just say, 'I got my dawg Reed driving me, man.' If he had class at nine a.m. how do you think he's getting there?"

Ridder had two jobs: make sure Edwards kept working on things the coaching staff wanted him to keep doing, but also allow Edwards the freedom to dictate their workouts, practice the things that he wanted, and keep Edwards in a good frame of mind for games. Ridder became so essential to Edwards's life on campus at Georgia that he was a contact in Edwards's second phone, which few knew the number to.

At various points that year, Edwards would shout out Ridder in a postgame press conference, and he posted to his Instagram story that he had the "best GA in the country," a video Ridder still has saved to his phone. Ridder could be unvarnished with Edwards, and Edwards would listen and accept it.

These late workouts were a way for Edwards to decompress. No classes, no team practice. No other coaches hanging around. Just him, Ridder, and maybe someone else on staff to rebound. As was his custom, Edwards was in the gym as much as possible, or he was back in his room playing video games.

"Every game, whether we were away, he's coming back and going right to the gym," Camara said. "It inspired me to do the same thing, but I couldn't find the energy to do it with him."

Oh, and Edwards went to class too, even if he didn't always feel like it. Some on the staff even secretly respected the fact that he was up front about his unwillingness to attend classes.

"He was the first eighteen-year-old that I encountered that didn't lie," Fish said. "He just told you the truth. 'Coach, now, I'm not gonna go to class today, but I'm gonna go in the gym in here and shoot for two hours.' Then he had to figure out how to make up the class."

Gutting Through the Season

But just like at Holy Spirit, Edwards made sure to stay eligible and out of trouble. Entering the season, the media preseason poll had the Bulldogs finishing ninth out of the fourteen SEC teams, so external expectations still weren't high even with Edwards and a highly touted recruiting class. The Bulldogs started the season 4–0 with a win over Georgia Tech before going to the Maui Invitational, where two significant moments happened for Edwards that season.

The first is well documented: his performance against Michigan State, who were ranked No. 3 at the time. This is the game that was the model for what Edwards could be in the NBA.

"A lot of stuff he did don't surprise me," Fagan said. "Like that Michigan State game, it didn't surprise me."

Following a loss to Dayton, the Bulldogs squared off against the Spartans, and the first half was a dud for both Georgia and Edwards. Ant had just four points and the Bulldogs trailed 52–31 at halftime. But in the second half, Edwards erupted for 33 points to finish with 37.

"Once he hit the second shot in that run, it just went to another place," Crean said. "What was so crazy was it wasn't just his scoring, it was his defense, his rebounding and his passing."

He was hitting everything, including contested three-pointers. He was pulling up in transition from well beyond the arc and draining them. At one point he had his back to a defender in the left corner, turned, leapt and shot in one motion, and hit the long two, an otherwise terrible shot that wasn't on this day, because Edwards couldn't miss.

"There was nothing they could do with him in that run," Crean said.

He had three blocks. He had a bounce pass from half-court that hit Rayshaun Hammonds in stride for a layup. Edwards then circled his hands around his eyes like they were glasses, to emphasize his vision on that play for the Spartans bench. He led the Bulldogs back from a 28-point deficit to as close as two, 75–73, but Michigan State, behind 28 points from Cassius Winston, held them off.

Watching that game in the arena was future Timberwolves general manager Matt Lloyd, who was working for the Orlando Magic at the time. Lloyd said Edwards's performance was one of the most memorable he had ever seen in person in twenty-seven years of scouting.

"You go through your time as a scout searching for things like that, and ninety-nine percent of the time you don't see that immediately," Lloyd said. "He just individually carried the team back into the game throughout just this cascading, spectacular moment after spectacular moment."

The blueprint of who Edwards could be in the pros was now on tape for all to see. That's what the basketball world remembers from Georgia's trip to Maui, but Crean and others also remember a moment that showed another side of Edwards in the following game against Chaminade. Maui wasn't a great trip for Georgia, and by the time they faced Chaminade on day three, frustration began to mount as Crean tried to adjust rotations and playing time. Chaminade is the host school for the Maui Invitational and is a Division II school. A loss to Chaminade is not a great look for any school that comes to Maui. But the Bulldogs found themselves in a tight game late, and they needed a late three from Edwards with 0.6 seconds remaining to pull out an 80–77 victory. The team won, but few were happy as they retreated to what Crean said was a "tiny" locker room with the team cramped in there sitting on small benches.

"One of the players was really being disrespectful at the end of a game, and was upset that he didn't play as much and was mad," Crean said.

Edwards hadn't established himself as a leader on the team; he was always reluctant to call out teammates, dating back to his time at Holy Spirit. He never wanted to embrace the label of leader, even if he was by default. But as the best player on the team, Edwards's voice carried weight, whether he wanted it to or not. He used it here.

"I can't remember what he said word for word," Fagan said. "But it was along the lines of, 'Bro, we won. At the end of the day, I don't care if I get eighteen or twenty. We win, I'm happy. Like, I get you want to play more. Everybody wanna play more. But we won, brother. You can't be selfish like that.'"

"He had my back," Crean said. "He also knew that it was ridiculous what the player was doing. He spoke up in the sense to say, 'No, we're not talking to coach like that, and we're not acting like that in here.' It was really strong, man. He's got a lot of natural leadership in him. It just needed to be manifested, to be brought out."

To Ridder, Edwards earned that moment to check his teammate, because he would so often encourage and talk up his teammates. Edwards would be the one calling attention to his teammates for the NBA scouts who showed up to Georgia practices, which Fish joked "kind of hurt us" because teammates started thinking they were as good as Edwards. Fagan said there were times Edwards would show he was eighteen years old, and there were times he showed how elite he could be on the court. This was different.

"It was a surprise in that moment," Fagan said. "In that moment, he stepped up and was being the alpha that maybe Coach Crean had been trying to make."

Said Camara: "We were just struggling, trying to figure out our identity. A lot of people start putting their personal agenda into it, and we didn't really have a leader at the time and Ant was the guy everybody was already looking up to, even as a freshman."

If Edwards's season at Georgia was a movie, this would've been the scene halfway that turned the fortunes of their season around, and they'd go on a magical run into the NCAA tournament and possibly a national championship. Unfortunately, that didn't happen.

"We didn't have a year nowhere near what we expected," Fagan said.

The Bulldogs' youth caught up to them once SEC play began. The team had nine freshmen overall on the roster. It didn't help that the previous spring, the program was a bit taken by surprise that center Nic Claxton declared for the draft. Claxton would have been a perfect piece to complement this year's team, Ridder said.

"With a young team, it's hard to be as consistent, especially down the stretch," Ridder said.

Georgia began with a tough portion of its SEC schedule with its first five games, including two matchups against a top-15 Kentucky team and a road game at No. 5 Auburn. Georgia lost four of those first five, then followed with a pair of losses to Ole Miss and at Missouri. The Missouri loss, 72–69, typified one of the issues Georgia faced that season—it couldn't close out games even after building double-digit leads.

"We were talented enough to be close. We weren't experienced enough to close it," Ridder said. "It's one thing to compete. It's another thing to beat."

The Bulldogs led in Missouri by as much as 20, and they led through most of the second half before Missouri pulled out the game in the final minutes. Edwards had 23 points but on 9-for-24 shooting. Fagan said at times he and the players felt the coaching staff was trying to put too much on Edwards's plate, that they were trying to get him to be this alpha scorer down the stretch when his natural inclination was to make the right play, whether it was a shot or a pass.

"He is a microwave and can get it going at any moment," Fagan said. "However, he's always been a team player, to his core."

Crean had told Edwards when he was recruiting him that Edwards would have the ball in his hands late in games. For all his talent, he was still a freshman, and Georgia was going to live with how Edwards played in these clutch moments and the decisions he would make, right or wrong. The same went for the rest of the young roster.

"There's so many learning processes that you go through, and we went through them with Ant," Crean said. "Because the bottom line is he had to learn about the value of winning and what it took to win, and how you've got to continue to stay in the moment and not do your own thing at times."

After a win over Texas A&M, the Bulldogs lost four more consecutive games, which included close losses at Florida, home in overtime to Alabama, and at Texas A&M. It didn't help Georgia that Edwards was battling an illness during that stretch of games.

"That was a bad week," Crean said.

Their conference record was at a miserable 2–10 and by mid-February any hope of reaching the NCAA tournament was gone. Rumors began to circle that Edwards might just bag the rest of the season and prepare for the draft. Crean and the coaching staff weren't too worried about this, given Edwards's competitive drive.

"I think people underestimated a couple of things," Crean said. "How much he loved to play. I think they underestimated that he really enjoyed being a teammate and he loved the competition. He also knew he was getting better."

Crean kept challenging him, even through this difficult patch of the season. If Crean sensed Edwards wasn't in the right frame of mind at the beginning of a practice, he would take him to an end of the gym and just shoot with him for a few minutes to regroup, something he did with other players as well. With this Crean was trying to drive home the value of setting a positive tone, because even if Edwards wasn't a vocal leader of the team, how he carried himself still made an impact on the team at large.

"It became clear early on with the maturity of our team that they were going to be driven a lot by how he went," Crean said. "I think he started to figure that out."

Camara said Edwards kept the team going, even amid the losing, because he was "cool with everybody."

"Making everybody feel like there's no hierarchy on the team," Camara said. "No matter if you're going to the NBA or not, he's treating everybody the same. That was humbling to see."

During this stretch of losing, Crean called a practice the day after one of their losses.

"Everybody beat up," Fagan said, "and he made practice hell."

Edwards's legs were killing him. "I ain't got it right now," Fagan said Edwards told him. That didn't matter to Crean, who went through a hard practice to push his star. He would invoke Oladipo or Wade as motivation, and told Edwards his effort wasn't living up to theirs.

"When it comes to competing, I don't care how his body feels, he turns something on that most guys can't get to," Fagan said. "He got some kind of gift that God done gave him that when competition comes out . . . it's a gear that most guys just can't get to that level. . . . I think Crean knew that and was doing everything to bring it out."

As the team scrimmaged, Crean kept "talking crazy" at Edwards, Fagan said, and Edwards started scoring every time down the floor. He was calling his shots before they went through the net. Those legs were feeling a lot better. Then he posterized a teammate on a dunk, "postered him bad," Fagan said, and Crean finally got the response he was seeking out of Edwards.

"After he did that, Crean was like, 'Practice over,'" Fagan said. "Ant responded in a major way."

The Bulldogs had their second date with Auburn, this time at home, as they began their final six-game stretch of the regular season. The night before, Fagan and Edwards were up late talking about the matchup, with Edwards wondering how he was going to solve the Tigers' defense. They had limited him to 18 points on 6-for-15 in their first matchup, and Fagan saw it as his job to keep Edwards in the right frame of mind after weeks of losing.

"He was frustrated with how certain stuff was going," Fagan said. "So I'm trying to keep his head in the game. I tell him: 'They can't guard you. You can't mentally give in to how good they is and allow their schemes to work. Make them work to guard you.'"

It wasn't a pretty game for Edwards—18 points on 16 shot attempts to go with 7 turnovers. But Fagan remembered Edwards making the right play more often than not, and Georgia limited the Tigers to 31 percent shooting to come away with a 65–55 win.

"It wasn't about the points, it was competitive, it was timely, and he played the right way," Fagan said. "He hit guys when they were open. He was fully himself."

Georgia finished the regular season 3–3 before heading into the SEC tournament. Their first game came on March 11 against Ole Miss, and Georgia played one of its most complete games of the season in an 81–63 win. Watching Edwards that day for the first time in person was then–Timberwolves president Gersson Rosas. That game also happened the same night that Jazz center Rudy Gobert tested positive for the coronavirus, which prompted the NBA to shut down its season. The SEC announced the next day it was canceling the rest of its conference tournament as sports everywhere shut down. This ended Georgia's season at 16–16. When the team got the news the season was over, there was no pretense from Edwards regarding what he was going to do next. That Ole Miss game was his last in a Georgia uniform. The staff and he said their goodbyes to each other, and they thanked him for what he did for the program and for them individually.

"You don't have to give him energy. He brings energy to you," Fish said.

Ridder had been with Edwards more than almost anyone on staff, and even though he was young and just getting his coaching career going, he knew he may never work with someone as dynamic as Edwards. He keeps a lot of the videos he and Edwards made of those late-night workouts as reminders of that time.

"We looked at each other in the hotel room and it's like 'Dang, bro, I guess this is it,'" Ridder said. "I said, 'You know you just screwed me for life, right?' He goes, 'What do you mean?' I said, 'Another player that I coach for the rest of my life will never be like how you are. Skill-wise, but how you are as a person. You just held my standards as a college coach for the rest of my life so high. I'm getting chills talking about it. Because, man, it was such a surreal moment.'"

Edwards maintains relationships with a lot of people from his year at Georgia. Fagan said Edwards helped him when he was in need financially in the spring of 2024. After Fagan was done playing basketball at Ole Miss, he was off the school's insurance when he tore his patellar tendon.

"My mom don't even know this. When I had an injury last April . . . I had to pay for surgery out of pocket. And for anybody that know, when you have a major surgery, how much that really cost."

Fagan was telling Edwards about the costs, and Edwards simply asked Fagan how much he needed.

"I said, 'Bro, I don't ever need one dollar from you.' But this particular moment, knowing how much surgery was, knowing how long I recovered and I paid a lot of stuff out of pocket, I kind of needed the help," Fagan said.

Fagan didn't want to ask for the full cost of the surgery, so he just said $4,000. Edwards sent him the money via Apple Pay seconds later.

"When nobody gave you nothing, a guy who's not even my sibling, no blood relation or nothing. We just built a bond—that meant more to me than anything," Fagan said. "Like me and him don't even speak on a daily. Can't nobody tell me nothing about him as far as our friendship."

Georgia is always on Edwards's mind, or at least never far from it. Even in the most important games Edwards played in his young career, the people he met and things he learned in Athens affected him.

All the Crean drills made an impression. Crean taught Edwards to use the backboard when he would lay the ball up. Ant wanted to finger-roll it in instead.

"I said cute is going to get your shot knocked into the third row and sitting at the end of the bench," Crean said. "I always talked to him like that."

The same went for jump shots. But during Edwards's third NBA season, he began using the glass more and more off midrange jumpers, causing Dollar to laugh anytime he sees it.

"He said, 'Why would you take a bank shot? It's for old-school people,'" Dollar said. "Now it amazes me. That's because Coach Crean said, 'Well, Dwyane Wade shot bank shots.'"

After the Wolves lost the Western Conference Finals to the Mavericks in 2024, Edwards said he had to get in better shape to play the volume of games required for deep postseason runs.

"The year that I was going to college, I think I was in the best shape of my life," Edwards said then. "A lot of stuff that makes me uncomfortable."

Those weren't empty words from Edwards. Shortly after he said that, he began texting with Hayes to ask what the specific exercises were that Hayes ran him through during their sessions.

"What do you do when no one's looking? He does it when no one's looking," Hayes said. "And he does it with a smile."

Edwards and Crean still stay in touch, and he often texts Edwards pieces of advice when he sees Edwards hitting a lull during a season. He was in Edwards's ear during the 2024 Western Conference Finals to remember to "play with joy" after the Wolves fell behind the series 3–0. Edwards took that to heart and credited Crean after the Wolves won Game 4. That's because when Edwards plays with joy, it's infectious.

"All eyes are riveted to him. It's an aura that he has," Crean said. "He was aware of what was out there and how many people were watching him, but there was never any air to him. . . . He doesn't use it in a way that makes people feel uncomfortable. He's himself. I think you see that. He's naturally funny, he's naturally happy. He's got joy."

CHAPTER 6

HEY, MAN, WE FROM ATLANTA

On November 9, 2018, the Minnesota Timberwolves lost to the Sacramento Kings 121–110 and completed an early-season West Coast trip 0–5. That dropped their record on the season to 4–9. After the game, forward Jimmy Butler held court in a somber Wolves locker room and discussed all the things the team was doing wrong.

There was irony in Butler's words, considering he had no interest in being around to fix the problems. The Wolves were in a weird place as a franchise. Butler had made a trade demand of the organization before the season began but was still playing in some games while the Wolves figured out where he might go next. Head coach and president of basketball operations Tom Thibodeau had traded for Butler about sixteen months earlier, with the idea being that Butler, who thrived under Thibodeau when both were with the Chicago Bulls, could form a contender with Minnesota's young stars, Karl-Anthony Towns and Andrew Wiggins.

At the time, the Butler trade filled the Wolves fan base with a hope it had not had in a long time. The franchise's last playoff appearance was in 2004, the team's lone trip to the conference finals with Kevin Garnett leading the way. Garnett had gone to Boston, won a championship, spent some time in Brooklyn, and then returned to Minnesota to cap off his career, and the Wolves still had not reappeared in the post-season. In the interim, Wolves fans went through miserable regime after regime, including the David Khan GM years, which included the Wolves passing over Curry twice in the 2009 draft.

The Butler trade made Timberwolves basketball exciting again—for a few months. On March 1, 2018, the team was the No. 3 seed in the

Western Conference, but a late-season knee injury to Butler caused them to slide to No. 8, and the Houston Rockets made quick work of them in the first round in five games after Butler returned late in the regular season.

To Butler, that season was proof he could not coexist with Towns and Wiggins. He especially took aim at Towns. In otherwise colorful language, Butler would accuse Towns of not being tough enough and not working hard enough. Through anonymously leaked reports to national media (which is how this kind of business is usually conducted in the NBA), he and his representation demanded a trade, and Butler initially stayed away from training camp. Then when he did show up, he took the third-stringers on the roster and beat the starters in a scrimmage that has become the stuff of legend around Minnesota and the NBA podcasting world. The whole thing appeared to be an orchestrated publicity stunt, since after that practice, he sat down for a prearranged interview with ESPN.

Thibodeau didn't want Butler to leave, and he attempted to get Butler to stay multiple times, but despite Thibodeau's best efforts, Butler wanted out, and he never wavered from that position even as the season began. The next day, the Wolves brass agreed to a deal to send Butler and center Justin Patton to the Philadelphia 76ers for Robert Covington, Jerryd Bayless, Dario Saric, and a 2022 second-round pick.

On January 6, 2019, Wolves owner Glen Taylor fired Thibodeau after less than three seasons in charge. Taylor said he was disappointed with how the reassembled Wolves were performing, and he made the move in hopes of a playoff push with interim coach Ryan Saunders in charge. Saunders, who was thirty-two at the time, is the son of the late Flip Saunders, who was the winningest coach in Wolves history and died in 2015 of Hodgkin's lymphoma a few months after he made the decision to draft Towns first overall. But making the playoffs that season was more dream than reality, as the Wolves finished at 36–46 and were back in a familiar place, the NBA Draft lottery.

After the season, Taylor announced he would hire a new president of basketball operations, and in May 2019 he hired Gersson Rosas, who had spent sixteen years with the Rockets working primarily under Daryl Morey. Rosas's first order of business was to hire a head coach, and his finalists for the job included Saunders, Portland assistant David Vanterpool, and a then-assistant with the New Orleans Pelicans, Chris Finch. Finch had worked closely with Rosas in Houston when Rosas ran the team's D-League (now known as the G League) franchise, the Rio Grande Valley Vipers.

Finch and Rosas were close, but Rosas stuck with Saunders as his coach. From his first day, Rosas set his sights on acquiring free agent point guard D'Angelo Russell, aka D-Lo, who Rosas thought was going to be the Minnesota version of James Harden in Houston—someone who would thrive when given the keys to a franchise the way Harden turned into an MVP after Houston acquired him from the Oklahoma City Thunder. The Wolves attempted to woo Russell in free agency but Russell signed a maximum contract with the Golden State Warriors, who had just lost Kevin Durant in free agency to Russell's former team, the Brooklyn Nets.

Despite the initial whiff on acquiring Russell, Rosas never gave up on getting him. Russell was an important part of Rosas's vision for the Wolves' future, and he was determined to pair him with Towns to form a partnership for years to come. The Wolves floundered through the next season with a 19–45 record in a COVID-19-shortened regular season. They had the second-worst record in the league and didn't even receive an invitation to the NBA bubble in Orlando when the league resumed its season later that summer. But during that year, Rosas was biding his time and waiting for his moment to remake the roster.

That opportunity came, again, after a Wolves loss to the Kings on February 3, 2020, just before that season's trade deadline (and about a month before COVID shut down the NBA season). Another Wolves loss in Sacramento, another dejected locker room just before seismic change to the franchise. The next two days were among the most transitory in recent Wolves history. Rosas swung multiple deals, including two that had reverberations for years to come. First he dealt Covington in a four-team trade that netted the Wolves Denver's Malik Beasley, Juancho Hernangomez, and Jarred Vanderbilt, among others, and a first-round pick from the Atlanta Hawks via the Nets, a pick that became No. 17 overall.

He also got his prize, when he agreed to trade Wiggins and a 2021 top-three protected first-round pick (which became Jonathan Kuminga) to the Warriors for Russell. At season's end, the only Wolves who were also on the team when Rosas took the job the previous May were Towns and guard Josh Okogie. Everyone else was new. At a press conference to announce the (many) new acquisitions in downtown Minneapolis, Rosas did a little chest-pounding.

"Why didn't they sign a point guard on July first?" Rosas said. "Because we wanted *that* point guard."

Rosas pointed to Russell. This was supposed to be the start of a new Wolves era. Except it was initially a false start. That new era actually began that August, when the Wolves, represented by Russell on the ESPN broadcast, won the draft lottery for the No. 1 pick.

"Finally catching a break," Rosas said.

The season featured plenty of losing and Rosas had made his moves to turn over the roster, which is never easy on an organization. Then after the NBA suspended the season, Towns lost his mother, Jacqueline, and multiple family members to COVID that spring. Those were losses that reverberated through the entire organization. That lottery felt like the first time something had gone right for the Wolves in years.

"It was pretty apparent to all of us that we needed to add talent to the group," Rosas said. "We needed more upside, and we needed a special talent with some volatility. For us to win that lottery was, I think, one of the most pivotal points for the Minnesota Timberwolves organization."

But Rosas still didn't know who was going to be his pick that night, he said. At this point Edwards was just one of several names the Wolves were going to focus on in the COVID-delayed draft process, and those delays nearly derailed Edwards's chances of being the top pick.

Can It Just Happen Already?

Time tends to rewrite history in the minds of those who don't bother to commit it to memory, and so looking back on the 2020 draft class, it seems like a given that Edwards, a multiple NBA All-Star and All-NBA player by twenty-two, should have been a no-brainer No. 1 pick. That was not the thinking at the time.

Every year, NBA analysts and observers on social media tend to form a consensus around that year's draft class: Is it a "deep" draft? Are there a lot of potential All-Stars? Or is it a draft filled primarily with lower upside, role players? These opinions can sometimes look regrettable years later. The 2020 draft, according to draftniks, wasn't a particularly deep draft, and there were danger signs at the top. Whoever went No. 1, especially if it was Edwards or Memphis center James Wiseman, could turn out to be a monumental bust. As the draft neared, the common view was that either Edwards, Wiseman, or point guard LaMelo Ball would be the No. 1 pick of the Wolves, but the Wolves were also entertaining potential trades for the pick, to find a more established player to play alongside Towns and Russell, whom Rosas viewed as his two tent poles for the future.

Since this was the COVID year, everything on the NBA calendar was pushed back. The draft, normally in late June, ended up happening in November, and that gave the Wolves plenty of time to think about what they were going to do with the pick, and who it would be if they kept it. In interviews with media at the time, Rosas emphasized his draft philosophy was always to take the best player, regardless of roster fit.

But taking Ball, a point guard, seemed out of the question after they had just made a big deal of acquiring Russell. With Towns there they didn't need another center, so taking Wiseman also would not have made much sense. Edwards was a two-guard or shooting guard, and could play alongside Towns and Russell. If Rosas thought Edwards was the best player among him, Ball, and Wiseman, it was also convenient that Edwards made the most long-term roster sense for the Wolves of those three.

This was where the Wolves stood entering this prolonged draft process, a process that was torturous for Edwards and his camp. The eight-month lag between the end of his season at Georgia in March and the COVID-delayed November 18 draft may have contributed to some of the whispers that tried to bring down his draft stock.

Edwards had two concerns that dogged him. First was his shooting—he shot just 29 percent from three-point range at Georgia. Was he destined to be a high-volume chucker from outside at the NBA level? Would he ever develop a consistent outside shot? This was a valid concern, but from the time Edwards was a teenager working out with Holland, his mantra was, "If I ever learn how to shoot, I'm unguardable." Edwards would work and work through his NBA career to develop a more reliable outside shot. As he has reiterated throughout his career, if there was a critique of his game that Edwards has taken to heart, it is this one.

"I don't pride my game on just getting to the rim. I hate when people say that," Edwards said in a 2023 interview with the *Star Tribune*. "I work too hard to be somebody who finishes at the rim. I can score the ball with the best of them."

The second concern was that he didn't care that much about basketball. This theory was more baffling since Edwards lived in the gym since his high school days and had nightly 9 p.m. workouts with Ridder at Georgia.

"That was a joke," Holland said.

"Whoever came up with that idea, I said, you do not know him. What are we talking about?" Ridder said. "I was with this guy every day in the gym and all we would talk is hoop. He loves hoop. Yeah, he jokes around. . . . But he loves hoop more than anything. He loves his family, and he loves hoop and his people. I thought that was obscene."

An ESPN profile that came out a few days before the draft didn't help that perception. In the profile, written by Alex Scarborough, Edwards was quoted as saying, "To be honest, I can't watch basketball," and "I'm still not really into it [basketball]. I love basketball, yeah, it's what I do." For every sound bite from Edwards that goes viral, those who interview Edwards on a regular basis know there are times he can sometimes be short in his answers, and he can be prone to exaggeration and sarcasm (which may not be interpreted as such when the clips go viral). This was one of those moments, Holland said. That interview was also an example of the long COVID pause taking a mental toll on Edwards.

In May the league announced it was postponing the draft from its original late June date. That postponement hit Edwards and his camp hard.

"We get the first push back and it's like, we got to figure out something," Holland said. "Gyms aren't supposed to be open, so we're sneaking in gyms. They had all these rules and everybody is in quarantine. So with that first push back, we took a break from each other. Everybody's kind of getting irritable . . . getting annoyed with each other, and it was just like, let's take a break."

The league originally rescheduled the draft for October 16, but then that got pushed back an additional month to November 18 to allow teams to complete the season in the league's bubble in Orlando, and then have some more time to complete the draft process. This second delay frustrated Edwards even more than the first.

"We were getting drained from doing the same thing over and over," Holland said.

To help with his peace of mind during the process, Edwards had asked Maddox right around the time COVID shut down his season at Georgia if Maddox wanted to come on this journey with him.

"I need somebody I can trust, bro. I need you to come with me," Maddox said Edwards told him.

After Maddox hung up the phone, he thought of all the possibilities for where Edwards could take his life, and how he could help him along the way.

"It was just like, well, he has a chance, with him being rated so high, to impact the world, globally," Maddox said.

He also thought of his favorite basketball player, LeBron James, and one of James's closest confidants, Randy Mims. Maddox could be that for Edwards.

"Hell yeah. Why not?" Maddox thought. "I get a chance to see the world, watch him grow up and become the player he wants to be and see him accomplish his dreams. But for me, I definitely was thinking about, Okay, how can I turn this into a career?"

Maddox wears many hats: he's a confidant to Edwards, friend, truth teller, logistics handler, on-court workout helper and rebounder, actor in Edwards's Adidas commercials, Spades partner, competitor in pool (even if he says Edwards tries to cheat and claims more wins than he actually has). Maddox gave up his collegiate baseball career to join Edwards, and in the summer of 2024, he ended up meeting his hero, Mims, at the same time Edwards was sharing the court with his childhood idol Durant in the Paris Olympics.

"Everything, man, like every aspect of [Edwards's] life, I play a part in it," Maddox said. "It's been an absolute journey, a privilege. When he put it in plain words, like 'Listen, bro, I need somebody who I can trust, who will be there for me. Tell me the truth.' It'll be my honor. Can't wait. Let's do it."

Their first months together came during that prolonged draft prep, with Maddox and Edwards rooming together in Atlanta. They'd try as much as they could to get into gyms, and Maddox would work out with Edwards around their apartment building, where Maddox said he and Edwards would "run the garages." That meant they'd run up and down the several floors of the parking ramps at their building.

But it wasn't the kind of schedule and routine Edwards would normally adhere to. As the process ramped back up in October, Edwards wasn't in his best frame of mind or shape, Holland said. The seven-month limbo had taken its toll, and when Edwards gave that ESPN interview, it came after a long day of doing Zoom calls, Holland said, and it quickly became apparent Edwards did not want to do the sit-down with ESPN.

"One day he had a million Zoom calls, and I'm putting this on the record because I want people to know where this came from," Holland said. "He had an in-person interview. . . . He was being sarcastic in his answers because he was tired. The guy was asking him questions and he was giving sarcastic answers, to the point where the guy started asking crazy questions. We knew the interview was terrible."

So Holland and Edwards's camp apologized for the interview, and would ESPN do it again another day? They agreed, and Edwards had another sit-down that went much better. Scarborough even noted in the piece that Edwards had much more energy in the second interview. But the money quote about not watching basketball came from that first interview session, and Edwards's camp didn't think ESPN would use it. Holland said he thought it was "unfair and unjust" of ESPN to keep that quote from the first interview in the piece after they agreed to the second interview and agreed the first interview was a product of Edwards having a long day. Scarborough didn't respond to multiple email requests for comment.

"It negates everything about the second interview," Holland said. "People misinterpreted that when he said he doesn't watch basketball. These kids now, they don't consume content in a traditional way. Ant's a basketball mind because all he does is consume the sport, but it's through YouTube."

It was a quote and a perception that took Edwards a long time to shake, and it stuck with him for years at the beginning of his NBA career. The mental and physical fatigue of the prolonged process also carried over to Edwards's workouts with teams at the top of the draft— but it also led to a couple of seminal moments in his career.

"It kept knocking the wind out of us every time [the draft] got pushed back. I don't even know what else to say about that. It was a struggle," Holland said. "It got to a point where it was why he wasn't prepared for the Golden State workout."

"He Looked Lazy"

In the weeks before the draft, teams finally began holding workouts and Edwards auditioned not just for the Wolves, but also for the Warriors, who had the No. 2 pick, and the Hornets at No. 3.

Golden State had the first workout. A contingent of Warriors owner Joe Lacob, general manager Bob Myers, coach Steve Kerr, and a few others made the trip to Atlanta, and Warriors brass was able to get an up-close look at Edwards for the first time. Normally, teams would have

draft prospects work out in their facilities and spend the day getting to know them, but under COVID protocols the process was different, and this workout represented one of the few times Edwards came face-to-face (socially distanced or not) with one of the teams that might draft him.

The Warriors representatives watched as Edwards began his workout with Holland. He began by shooting jumpers, and he just kept shooting them as the clock ticked. Kerr said after about twenty minutes Myers turned to him and said, "Do you think he's gonna go any harder?"

"We were thinking at first that was a warm-up, but it turned out that *was* the workout," Kerr said. "So I went down and said, 'Hey, we'd love to see you guys go harder. Can you add some more to the workout? Something with more force, more pace, more energy.' They were a little taken aback."

Edwards thought he had been going hard enough.

"I was going through the drills, and he kept stopping 'em, like, 'That's all you got? That's all you got?'" Edwards said in 2023. "And I'm like, 'Bruh, I'm going as hard as you want me to go. Like what do you want me to do?' I'm sweating crazy."

Edwards picked up the intensity a little bit, but he didn't convince Golden State he was worthy of the No. 2 pick. The whispers about him not being dedicated to the craft seemed to be true.

"We were nervous about him just because, frankly, he looked lazy," Kerr said.

At dinner afterward, Kerr explained to Edwards why he had to work harder. That if he showed up to a Warriors practice to watch Curry, Klay Thompson, or Durant work out, he would realize what he needed to do.

"If you want to be great, you have to learn to work like those guys," Kerr told Edwards.

Edwards didn't get mad, but instead soaked in all Kerr was saying. This was a moment and a meeting that had a profound effect on Edwards's early career.

"Me and my trainer [Holland] went home after dinner, just talking like, 'We've got to pick it up. I don't know how. I don't know what we've got to do, but we've got to pick it up.' I think after that, man, I became a madman in the gym."

The Warriors wanted to give Edwards a second look and scheduled another workout two weeks later.

"That was the reality check," Holland said. "After that we were on it."

Kerr said the difference was dramatic. Edwards "showed way more energy, way more activity.

"He was just so young, so he didn't know a whole lot, but I think in the first workout, we mistook his lack of aggressiveness as he didn't care, or he was apathetic," Kerr said. "Then after the second one, we realized, 'Oh no, he's just young.' He'll learn, and he did."

At one of Edwards's games against the Warriors in his rookie season, he went up to Kerr and told him what a big impact that series of workouts had on his mentality.

"They all played a huge role in where I'm at today," Edwards said. "Because they pitched that to me early."

It wasn't as if the Warriors left those workouts thinking Edwards was suddenly on the trajectory to being an All-NBA player. They still had concerns, especially with Edwards's shooting.

"Questionable shot selection, shaky defense. I think there were a lot of question marks," Kerr said. "But he definitely had all the physical tools. What we know now is what an incredible competitor he is. How willing he is to take the responsibility for his team."

After the Warriors initial workout came the Hornets, and that offered Edwards a chance to meet the man whom he'd get compared to often—Michael Jordan. Jordan was owner of the Hornets at the time, and he made the trip to see Edwards work out, something he made sure to let Edwards know he didn't always do.

"He said, 'I don't come down to see a lot of people. They told me I had to see you, though,'" Maddox said Jordan told Edwards. "It was funny because Justin started doing the Michael Jordan comparisons long before they ever came out."

Maddox said Edwards told him to keep his cool around Jordan, that meeting him was just like meeting anyone else, but even Edwards couldn't help but be in awe when the day was over. Their lunch that day offered a bit of foreshadowing for a conversation Edwards would later have with future Timberwolves president Tim Connelly, who had worked for the Wizards when Jordan was finishing his career. Connelly would sit down with Edwards to discuss habits of the greats of the game, like Jordan, and how Edwards would need to take after them if he wanted to keep ascending as a player.

Jordan ordered a lunch of salmon and salad. Edwards, to the best recollection of his then-agent Omar Wilkes, ordered something more like chicken tenders, fries, and a burger.

"[Jordan] was just talking about his diet, habits, and how things change as you get older," Wilkes said. "Just thinking like a pro, building pro habits off the court, sleep and all that stuff."

Jordan had been an "open book" for Edwards for about two hours where Edwards could ask him anything he wanted.

"You don't always get to see his emotion," Wilkes said. "But he had a 'wow' moment over what had actually just transpired."

They were also happy that the Hornets workout came after the initial Golden State flop, because it got Edwards to refocus before auditioning for Jordan.

"In a way, it was a blessing that he got the tongue-lashing that he did," Wilkes said.

But the Wolves had heard what went wrong with Golden State, and they were determined to make Edwards earn their pick at No. 1.

A Defining Forty-Eight Hours

While Edwards tried not to wear down during the extended draft process, the Wolves were trying to use that time to their advantage. They had two first-round picks and were devoting a lot of organizational resources into this draft, which was looking like a turning point for the franchise. Rosas credited owner Glen Taylor with essentially giving him a "blank check" to spend whatever the front office felt it needed to dig into as many of the top prospects as possible.

"Nobody knew the top prospects as well as we did, not just on the court, but off the court, and that's not a shot to any other team," Rosas said. "We just invested so much time, money, effort, and resources into it that when we made that selection, when we finished our process, we felt so confident about what we had gone through."

From an on-court perspective, Rosas described Edwards as "so raw." It wasn't for a lack of effort on Edwards's part, and it wasn't as if all that time Edwards spent in the gym was a waste. But the Wolves and every other NBA team were looking at Edwards through their lens and comparing him to other players who had played high-level basketball from a younger age than he did. Players who hadn't played football and been late bloomers when it came to hoops, and even international players who spent some of their formative years playing professionally.

All of this added up to Edwards being a diamond in that rough who held incredible promise, but would need a significant amount of polishing. Even though Edwards hadn't played football since he was fourteen, in Rosas's eyes as a scout and longtime evaluator, Edwards still gave him the impression of being "a football player converting to basketball." This wasn't necessarily all bad, though.

"At that point of our organization, we needed grit. We needed toughness. We needed physicality," Rosas said. "We had skilled players. We wanted two-way guys and his physical tools stood out, and we really felt like this is going to translate."

As for Edwards's life off the court, Rosas described what they found as "dicey," that the number of people who had influence, or were trying to get influence in Edwards's life, made it difficult to discern who Edwards was as a person.

"Trying to understand who Ant was as an individual through all that noise was very important for us," Rosas said.

They had a few "serendipities," as Rosas termed them, that helped them in this process. Rosas and the front office had a relationship with Dice Yoshimoto, a former Wolves staffer under Thibodeau who had served as the director of basketball strategy while Edwards was at Georgia. At Klutch, Edwards worked out with Chris Johnson, who crossed paths with Rosas in Houston. It also helped that one of the comparisons that came up for the Wolves in their analysis of Edwards was Wade, and so Crean was the perfect person to help them dissect that. Through their digging, the Wolves learned how great of a teammate Edwards was at all ages.

"He was loved by his teammates," Rosas said. "He was loved by his coaches at every level, high school, AAU, college. . . . He wasn't this selfish guy who only cared about himself, which is very standard at that level. That really intrigued us, because that spoke to 'Hey, the guy cares about more than himself.'"

Despite that, the team still didn't have a real handle on who Edwards was and had not been able to interact with him one-on-one.

"There's always going to be some risk, and that's why there wasn't a knockdown number one pick for that draft. There was risk involved with all the picks," Rosas said.

Rosas and Saunders were set to meet with Edwards in Los Angeles and work him out there with a small contingent from the team. But before that happened, Edwards had a number of Zoom interviews with several different members of the organization. There were breaks in between some of the calls and during one of those, Edwards went to get a workout in. Then he took another Zoom call. After this particular interview, Rosas got a voicemail from assistant GM Joe Branch.

"Hey, interview went great, but slight curveball. Call me so we can discuss," Rosas said Branch told him.

The "curveball"? Edwards showed up to the Zoom call lying in bed while shirtless. For a moment, Rosas was mortified.

"That freaked me out," Rosas said. "It's funny how history affects you. . . . When I was in Houston, we had a player that did that on a Zoom, and we ended up drafting him, and he was a disaster. It was basically foreshadowing."

Rosas couldn't help but think about that experience, and when Rosas eventually sat down with Edwards, "Believe me, it came up," he said. What potential employee, no matter the job, shows up shirtless for a job interview?

"Like, what are you doing? Why did you want to represent yourself like that?" Rosas said he asked him. "It was part of us getting to know him."

Four years after it happened, Wilkes sounded both amused and puzzled at how Edwards thought this would be a good look. But if the Wolves wanted a glimpse at the real Edwards, they got it.

"The concept of reminding him to have clothes on was not even like anywhere in the stratosphere for me," Wilkes said. "Because some things go without saying, you would assume."

Edwards was apologetic and said he thought since it was a supplementary interview to the several he already did, he "didn't think twice about" the fact that he was shirtless, Rosas said. It was the Wolves' first experience of Ant being Ant. He didn't mean anything by it, he just . . . figured it was okay to show up shirtless.

The table was set, literally and figuratively, for what came next in the process—outdoor dinner with Edwards, Rosas, and Saunders at the picturesque Nobu restaurant in Malibu. The dinner lasted about four hours, with Rosas asking him almost everything he could from the Wolves' extensive background check of him, while Saunders broke out his iPad to go over plays and schemes with him. That was the easy part.

"We're putting everything on the table with him. The interview was impactful, because these type of things are not feel-good sessions," Rosas said. "We said, 'We're going to ask you a ton of questions. We're going to get very personal with you. We're going to put you in some uncomfortable situations, and we just want to see how you respond to it.'"

Four years after the interview took place, both Rosas and Saunders, independent of one another, pointed to the same moment that stood out to them, something Edwards said that helped moved him close to being the top pick in their minds.

"I still feel goose bumps thinking about it," Rosas said.

Added Saunders: "If you were there, you felt emotional hearing this."

Rosas was blunt with Edwards. He told him there are different degrees of players in the league: some who want the paycheck and the lifestyle, and some who want to work hard, win, and be great. How could he depend on Edwards to be the latter?

"He said, 'I've been through the worst in life. My mom's died, my grandmother died. I can't go anywhere but up from here,'" Rosas said Edwards told them. "'I'm going to enjoy every day. You're always going to see a smile on my face. I'm going to make the most of every day. I don't know everything. I'm going to make some mistakes, but you can always count on me to know that what I say, my word, is what I mean.

"'I take the responsibility of being the number one pick. I take the responsibility of being a Minnesota Timberwolf as the biggest priority and the biggest responsibility in my life, and I know with your organization's help, I can be successful. I'm giving you my word, I'm committed to this, and I understand the severity of what this situation is.'"

That moment, Saunders said, "hooked all of us."

"This was a young man who was going to make them really proud," Saunders said.

Edwards's response inched him closer to becoming the No. 1 pick, but the next day proved it for sure. The Wolves let Edwards know they heard what happened when he worked out for Golden State.

"We talked about it in that interview," Rosas said. "How am I going to take you number one if you can't even complete a workout with Golden State? How can I feel like you're going to maximize and fulfill your talent when you've never been at a high level of basketball, you've never worked, you've never done these things?

"Some guys will get defensive; he took it as a challenge. 'I'll show you. I'll prove it to you.' I said we're going to see it tomorrow."

From his vantage point, Holland said the Wolves played the whole process "close to their chest." They were the last team Edwards talked to and the last team who held a workout for him. It took place at Kobe Bryant's gym, formerly known as Mamba Sports Academy. Holland felt good about the changes they had made after the Golden State debacle, but he was still worried about what would happen when the Wolves took over the workout.

Holland put Edwards through a revamped, hard thirty-minute workout, with Holland accommodating some of the things the Wolves wanted to see. Then the Wolves asked Holland if they could keep running Edwards through some drills. With just a bit of trepidation, Holland handed over control as Saunders and Rosas ran a good portion of the next part. Holland said he knew the Wolves would be "trying to make [Edwards] break." But there was nothing he could do now. Rosas said Johnson was on one side of the gym "cringing" while Holland was "praying away." This was all up to Edwards. The next part tested his endurance and mental fortitude.

"Sometimes it sounds easier to do, 'Hey, I'm just going to do a one vs. zero workout.' But those workouts, they're tough, they're killers," Saunders said. "Until you get in it, you don't realize what you're up against."

They did full-court drills, dunking drills, sprint drills, suicides. The Wolves weren't just putting Edwards through a gauntlet, they were trying to mess with his head too. Rosas said they were making sure they repeated a lot of the knocks that were out there against Edwards as he was struggling his way through.

"People say you don't work. People say you don't compete," Rosas said they told him. "People say you failed that workout. People say you're a football player. We were going at him."

Holland could see all this was having an effect on Edwards. He was slumping with his head down, and Holland walked over to encourage him. It wasn't going well. They certainly didn't need another team thinking he was lazy and couldn't handle a tough workload. In normal times, this likely would not have been a problem for Edwards, but this was around month seven of the draft process. He was exhausted in more ways than one. Anything could happen in this moment, and Holland knew it.

"I saw it in his face," Holland said. "He had reached that limit where he's about to say, 'I'm done. Fuck it.' I go over to him. 'Young fella, we are not gonna quit.' We're leaning over, I'm whispering in his ear . . . and then I hear another voice."

Someone yelled out: "Hey, man, we from Atlanta, this ain't what we do."

The voice belonged to A. J. Moye, the former 2000 Georgia Mr. Basketball who made it out of his own rough situation growing up in Atlanta to reach the national championship game with Indiana in

2002. A stroke had ended Moye's professional career, and he became a college coach and skills coach affiliated with Sports Academy. He was in the gym watching Edwards work out that day. Before the workout began, Holland was surprised to see Moye at the facility. The two were acquaintances—Holland used to attend a bunch of Moye's high school games at Atlanta's Westlake High School—but they hadn't seen each other in a long time.

"I turned around that day and saw Justin, and it was like, 'What are you doing here?'" Moye said. "He said, 'Ant's about to have his workout. . . . If you have the urge to share some advice with him, share it with him.'"

Moye had watched Edwards play when he was a freshman at Therrell, but the two didn't have a relationship, and Edwards didn't know who he was that day. Holland gave Edwards a quick history lesson.

"I said that's A. J. Moye, former Georgia Mr. Basketball, a legend," Holland said.

Moye then came over to share a few quick words with Edwards.

"Hey, man, we from Atlanta. You know how we came up," Moye said he told Edwards. "You know how we were raised. You know we been through much harder stuff than anything that can happen to us on a basketball court. . . . Ant just looked at me and shook his head. He didn't say anything. He looked me dead in my eyes and shook his head like, 'I got you.'"

This ATL moment provided the final push needed to send one of its sons on his path to a bright future elsewhere. The determination returned to Edwards's eyes, his body perked up, and Holland said Edwards told him, "Nah, bro, we finna do this. We can't let them see us sweat. We from Atlanta."

All those suicides in football practice with the Vikings when he would have to stay after practice. All those suicides with Dana Watkins when he would lag behind, only to have Watkins blow the whistle and say they had to do it again until Edwards finished first. Those demanding years were leading to this moment.

The promise to make it out of Oakland City, to secure his family's future. Honoring Yvette and Shirley, and all they had done for him.

Did he want it badly enough to be that top pick? Was he going to let another player get by him at No. 1? Did he want to be the best in his class, and keep striving to be?

"I told him afterwards, 'You represent all of us,'" Moye said. "'You're not making it just for you. You're making it for all of us. There's a lot of cats before you that had all the ability in the world, but we just didn't have the platform that you have now. Take this platform and take it all the way.' I'm so proud of him, man."

Moye's words were just the reminder Edwards needed.

"That was an Atlanta thing right there, in the moment," Holland said. "He got up, stood up, 'Let's finish this,' and he knocked it out."

From his vantage point, Saunders didn't see much of Edwards's struggling—he was just experiencing a tough moment in a demanding workout. But he had a gut feeling from how Edwards talked at dinner that no matter what they threw at him, Edwards wasn't going to back down.

"After hearing him say that, it was something I felt connected to having lost my father, and understanding the depths of grief and how you can generate strength out of that," Saunders said. "That made me feel like he wasn't going to quit."

The execution of the drills didn't even matter to the Wolves. They weren't concerned with how many makes or misses he had, how well he went through the drills; they already knew they had their work cut out for them honing Edwards's skills. It was all about the effort. Edwards gave it his all. Rosas and Saunders could see it.

"He did everything we asked," Rosas said. "He didn't quit. He competed, and he got our respect."

Added Saunders: "Whenever we asked for something else or something more, he obliged. It was really impressive."

Of course, the Wolves didn't let Edwards know how they felt in the moment.

"It was poker faces," Holland said. "Good job, great workout, but not a lot of enthusiasm or emotion. We had dinner plans, but not like anything that showed us it's a done deal."

But Holland knew Edwards had killed it, and they left that day feeling good about Edwards's chances of being the top pick. What they didn't know was before Rosas left the gym, he called Taylor.

"Glen, I got our number one pick," Rosas said. "This is the guy."

The Moment Finally Arrives

The ESPN story dropped on November 15, three days before the draft, and despite Edwards's strong workout, the story set off alarm bells for both Edwards's camp and the Wolves. When he saw it, Rosas rang up Wilkes. Rosas said Wilkes was a big help throughout the process but that on this phone call, he gave Wilkes "an earful."

"Omar, do you not want him here in Minnesota? . . . How does this get put out? Unless you ran it, and gave the green light?" Rosas said. "He basically said, 'Gerss, we were surprised by this. This wasn't something that we expected, and it's disappointing that we're having to go through this.'

"You want to make people nervous? You guys have made people nervous."

Wilkes estimated that among Rosas, Myers, and Charlotte president of basketball operations Mitch Kupchak, he made over twenty calls to put out the fires Edwards's quotes created.

"People didn't understand his personality and how he talked at that time," Wilkes said. "If you don't know him and how he communicates, you can misconstrue things. Obviously he loves basketball."

Rosas told Wilkes the timing of the article "couldn't be worse."

"I did want them to be nervous," Rosas said. "And I did want them to understand the ramifications of that, because for us, it was going to be another hurdle. . . . It didn't shake us, but it did give us an opportunity to put Ant in a position to hold him accountable and to tell him this isn't acceptable. . . . You're going to be in a different light . . . and it humbled him, and we needed him to come in as a humble number one pick."

Rosas's lasting positive legacies of his time running the Wolves were his eventual hiring of Finch as head coach, signing center Naz Reid as an undrafted free agent in 2019, and November 18, 2020, draft night. Going into the day, it was still not publicly known what the Wolves were going to do. But the tea leaves were there for those paying attention to how Rosas was constructing the Wolves.

This being COVID times, Commissioner Adam Silver announced the first-round picks from an empty studio without a crowd or audience, and the draftees were not present. Edwards's camp rented an Airbnb and didn't give out the location until a few hours before the draft. This was still pre-vaccines, but on this night protocols were out the window.

Holland told Edwards to invite anyone he wanted. It was a night when a lot of people who were instrumental in Edwards's upbringing met each other for the first time. Dana Watkins said he met Holland that night. Winfred Jordan was there, and so was Banks, among other friends and family packed into the house.

Of course, the day was anything but normal. Holland was still trying to ease concerns the ESPN piece had created for their camp. They had no assurances where Edwards was going to go in the draft. Holland and Wilkes had not heard from the Wolves prior to draft day on their decision. Edwards had a morning workout, and the day went on as normally as it could before they all gathered at the house. Even with the ESPN piece, Edwards knew he was likely going in the top three, but No. 1? There was doubt.

"I'm gathering the family, everybody is calm, but it's like a zoo getting everything set up," Holland said. "We rented a place, had a chef there, we had music."

But there was still plenty of anxious energy. Sometimes draft picks know they will be going No. 1 and the drama on TV is just for show. But in Edwards's case, nobody knew until the time the draft began. Holland was clued in when Wilkes got a phone call just a few moments before Silver went to the microphone. He saw Wilkes leave the room and come back, but Edwards's back was to Wilkes, who was behind the couch where Edwards was sitting.

"We were nervous up until maybe fifteen seconds before," Holland said. "Nobody knew."

But before they could tell Edwards anything, Silver announced the pick. This was how Edwards actually found out he was the No. 1 pick, the same time as everyone else. As Silver read the selection, the camera cut to Edwards on the couch. Seated near him were Bubba and Holland, but flanking him on each side on the couch were paintings of Yvette and Shirley done by an artist, Erica I., who goes by @heypaintella on Instagram. Antoinette had the paintings commissioned for this moment. Edwards put on a Timberwolves hat that Bubba handed him.

"It's an undescribable feeling," Edwards told ESPN's Malika Andrews on the telecast. "I feel like when I get off here, I'mma get emotional and I'm just blessed beyond measures to be in this situation."

That was the feeling in the room. Tears, smiles, joy. All those years of struggle, of perseverance culminated in this moment.

"Even though you didn't know half the people there, everybody was just high-fiving," Dana said. "If only Yvette could've experienced this. Drew was sitting there, crying like a damn baby. I'm happy, just overly excited, overly proud."

Added Rosas: "It was very cool to get back on the phone with him and feel his emotions, his sincerity, his genuineness—it was very special."

That moment was something Holland will never forget, given how tough the previous eight months were to get through.

"People always say, 'Do things the right way,' and while you're doing that, everybody's questioning everything," Holland said. "To quiet the naysayers that night was something real big."

CHAPTER 7

A1 FROM DAY ONE (SORT OF)

Edwards's pick was the start of a busy night for the Wolves, who were not done making moves. Rosas still had work to do. He had more ammunition in the No. 17 pick he acquired in the Covington trade, and he used it to maneuver around the board—while bringing back a fan favorite in Minnesota.

This might be hard for casual fans outside of Minnesota to believe, but the pick of Edwards at No. 1 had competition for the main headline in the local press that night. Rosas traded that No. 17 pick and made multiple trades to move back in the draft, eventually ending up with picks Nos. 23 and 28. One of those deals Rosas made was with the Thunder (after they had just sent Chris Paul to the Suns) to bring back Ricky Rubio, who was one of the best parts of rooting for the franchise in the lean, post-Garnett years. Rubio's positive attitude and flair on the court for six seasons had captivated a fan base that was sad to see him go when Thibodeau opted to replace him with Jeff Teague.

"We needed a mentor," Rosas said. "It didn't hurt that Ricky had good history in Minnesota and he could help us from a point guard perspective, which we really needed."

Rubio was set to be that veteran mentor for Edwards the way he was for Donovan Mitchell in Utah and Devin Booker in Phoenix. It was not an accident that when Rosas decided to draft Edwards, he also set his sights on acquiring Rubio. Rosas said he learned from former Jazz general manager Dennis Lindsey how important Rubio was to Mitchell's development, and in the predraft process, Mitchell was one of the comps the Wolves used for Edwards.

"I said, 'Ant, I'm bringing in a guide for you, to mentor you and to make your life easier, but you have to be committed to it, and I'm not wasting my time. Ricky's not wasting his time,'" Rosas said.

The two got along just fine, with Rubio never afraid to pull Edwards aside and offer advice and constructive criticism. He also was Edwards's first example of what it meant to be a professional in the NBA, like in how Rubio took care of his body or was on time for treatment and workouts. Even if these lessons took a few seasons to sink in with Edwards, Rubio helped plant the seed for why they were important.

Rosas had one more significant move for the franchise's future left that night. After drafting Argentinian guard Leandro Bolmaro at No. 23, whom the team would move to Utah in the Rudy Gobert trade in the summer of 2022, Rosas took a lanky forward with an occasional temper out of Washington at No. 28—Jaden McDaniels. He had gone to Washington as a highly regarded five-star recruit, but he had an underwhelming season that included many technical fouls. Rosas said the team still liked McDaniels's size, ability to guard, and potential to develop offensively. Rosas also wasn't scared away by McDaniels's fiery demeanor. The Wolves needed toughness and McDaniels would fit right in with the kind of team Rosas was trying to build.

"People criticized him about the technical fouls. I loved that about him," Rosas said. "He was competitive. I still love that about him. Give me a guy who's willing to compete instead of a guy that I got to turn up."

McDaniels would develop alongside Edwards and Naz Reid into an integral part of the team's future, thanks in large part to his defensive prowess. McDaniels's fiery nature is both a blessing and a curse. It fuels his motivation to shut down an opponent's best perimeter threat on a nightly basis, and he earned All-Defensive Team honors in the 2023–24 season. But from time to time it can go overboard. McDaniels and Edwards had to bide their time to make an impact off the bench at first in their rookie seasons.

Nonstarter

Edwards came into an abbreviated training camp oozing with confidence. There was one practice, he said, when he was scrimmaging on the same team as Towns and Russell and they were trailing late (it turns out, contrary to what the Butler practice story would have people believe, the starters sometimes lose scrimmages to the bench players). Towns and Russell were higher on the organizational pecking order at this time of Edwards's career, but it didn't matter to him. With the scrimmage on the line, Edwards was taking the clutch shots.

"I came down and took the game-winning shot," Edwards said. "And I missed."

Rubio pulled Edwards aside to offer some advice.

"Young fella, this is not the shot that you take. You let them take the shot," Edwards said Rubio told him. "In a minute, you'll be able to take this shot. But not right now."

As Edwards recalled that story after a shootaround in Houston during January 2024, Towns walked by and interjected, "Man, he ain't listen to that shit one time." Edwards laughed.

"I didn't listen to it," Edwards said. "Then I think like three months later he was like, all right, now you can take that shot. That's one of the memories I have. Him just making the game easier for me, telling me little things every game, like coverages I'll see."

Said Saunders: "It always means more coming from your teammate. Ricky had everybody's respect, especially Ant's. For him to say that, I think it helped Ant understand that we had a plan for Ant."

Edwards had to get to that point in his career where he could take those kinds of shots. In practice, he had an immediate impact on the dynamics of the team thanks to his personality. Even though he would struggle to start the season, glimpses of who he could become in the league began to emerge. Saunders said Edwards gradually got accustomed to the speed of the NBA during that season, while teammates like Jordan McLaughlin could see how "special" Edwards was immediately.

"He just had so much charisma and a positive attitude and an energy about him that just lifts everybody that's around him," said McLaughlin, who was teammates with Edwards for four seasons.

Instead of having about four months between the draft and the start of the season, the 2020–21 NBA season started on December 23, just over a month after the draft. There was no offseason plan the Wolves could get Edwards started on the way they could in a normal year, and training camp was shorter than usual. Saunders had Edwards come off the bench initially because Russell was starting and he could play Rubio and Edwards together in the second unit.

Edwards struggled with this weird offseason and it led to a slow start. That perpetuated the chatter that Edwards was maybe a bust. There was an 0-for-8 night against the Spurs, 1-for-6 against Memphis, 2-for-12 against Atlanta. Through his first 16 games, Edwards averaged 12.3 points per game on just 34 percent shooting, and he wasn't happy with his bench role.

"He hated. Oh my God, he hated it," said his player development coach, Chris Hines (no relation to the author of this book). "But he took it so well. 'Whatever coach says is cool.' But he also was like, 'Ain't nobody better than me.' That's his thing, and that's a real thing about him, that confidence."

Even if Edwards was quietly seething, he never let that show in practice or around Saunders.

"He was great about it," Saunders said. "He did not let it affect him in terms of his personality. When he might have had a question or wondered why something is like it is, I really respected him, he came to my office and asked me. It was never combative."

The Wolves played consecutive games in San Francisco against Kerr and the Warriors in late January, and entering the second of those two games, both Towns and Russell were out. Edwards still didn't start. This was the last time he would come off the bench. He scored 25 points on 9-for-19 shooting, which included 5-for-8 from three-point range in a Wolves loss. The next game at home against Philadelphia, Saunders put Edwards in the starting lineup, where he hasn't left since.

To Hines, this was the game that made a believer out of him and some others.

"That's when I think I saw it. At the time Curry is the face of the league. He's probably the biggest name Ant's played against. I wanted to see how he responded to that. He met him at the level of competing, and that's where I was like, 'Oh he's not scared of the light, the moments and stars.' Some players are in awe a little bit of who they're hooping against. There was no awe leading up to that game."

That promotion to the starting lineup didn't mean things suddenly went smoothly for Edwards. The shooting struggles were still there; natural for a rookie, but when one of your draft red flags was your shooting acumen, that gets magnified. Not to mention, the team was losing. Towns had a difficult start to the season. In the second game, he hurt his wrist in a win over the Jazz and missed the next six games. Then, shortly after he returned, he went right back out of the lineup because of COVID and missed another thirteen games. When he made it back on February 10, the Wolves were 6–18. It had now been more than a calendar year since the Wolves made the trade to get Russell in the hopes of creating a lasting partnership with Towns (and subsequently Edwards), but Russell and Towns had played together in just five games since the trade happened. Towns had also injured his wrist late in the 2019–20 season before COVID suspended it. This was one reason why Rosas was ticked the Wolves didn't get a chance to participate in the NBA bubble—they didn't get that time for Towns and Russell to play together. It was hard for the Wolves to determine what they had with players coming in and out of the lineup.

Holland said he tried to stay as positive as possible with Edwards during this season. He was living in downtown Minneapolis near Target Center and the Wolves' practice facility. At the time, COVID restrictions were still in place. Office buildings were empty and the trial of former police officer Derek Chauvin, who would be convicted of murdering George Floyd on April 21, 2021, was taking place at Hennepin County Courthouse, just blocks from the arena and practice facility. The mood in Minneapolis was tense, and that was only heightened by all the security precautions put in place, like barricades, for the trial.

"That year, I did a lot of just encouraging and coaching him through it," Holland said. "It was a day-to-day thing. Him feeling like he, at some point, 'Am I good enough? I'm rarely playing. They're telling me to stand in the corner. I'm not getting the touches.' His mind was all over the place for a while until he found his niche. . . . It was the first time in his life that he had that kind of adversity, finding his place on this franchise and on that team."

But Edwards remained a presence in the lineup, and as the season progressed, there were flashes of just how fun of a player Ant was going to be. One of Edwards's all-time highlights came in his rookie year, on February 19, 2021, in a game against the Raptors. As time was running down in the third quarter, McLaughlin passed it to Edwards in the left corner. His defender went for the steal and missed, offering Edwards a clear driving lane to the rim.

Waiting for him at the rim was Toronto's Yuta Watanabe, who leapt at the edge of the restricted area as Edwards took flight. Edwards rose with almost perfectly straight posture to the rim over Watanabe. He used Watanabe to hang in the air for longer than seemed normal. He dunked it over Watanabe and fell on top of him as an added insult.

"We had seen him do it a couple times in practice, like doing windmills and stuff, saying he could be in the dunk contest," McLaughlin said. "We knew how much bounce and authority he had. So when he did that, we weren't surprised."

The ascension spread like wildfire over social media, with several posts saying it was the dunk of the year. Each electrifying moment at the rim Edwards had the next few years was measured against it. While Edwards's dunk received widespread reaction on social media, one reaction in particular also went viral, that of NBA analyst Nate Duncan, who noted in a tweet that while Edwards's dunk was fun and all that, he still went 3-for-14 in the game, 0-for-7 on threes. Duncan's tweet spoke to the microscope Edwards was under when it came to his efficiency. Edwards, to his credit, wasn't jubilant in his postgame reaction after a 5-point Wolves loss that dropped them to 7–23.

"I'd be talking about it highly right now if we would've won," Edwards said. "Due to the fact that we lost, it's nothing to be excited about. It was a great dunk, but we lost, so it don't mean nothin' right now."

The Wolves weren't expected to be great in Edwards's rookie season, but they were struggling more than Rosas thought they should have been. They had issues closing games, even as Towns and Russell took turns sitting out because of illness or injury. That Toronto loss marked their ninth loss in eleven games, with none of them coming by more than eight points.

In one game against Indiana, the Wolves lost a late lead but had a chance to win with the game tied at the end of regulation (Russell did not play this night). Edwards, who finished the night 3-for-15, called an audible on the final shot with the score tied. Saunders drew up a play to get mismatches with Towns and Edwards, with the idea being that Edwards would go toward the basket once Pacers center Myles Turner switched on him. Instead, Edwards took a stepback three from the top of the key over Turner that missed, and the Pacers won in overtime. After the game, Rubio told the media he liked that Edwards had the confidence to shoot that shot despite having an off night.

"I told him that's what a special player does," Rubio said then. "It went in and out. He had confidence. When he missed, you could see in his face he was surprised to miss, and when you're not having your night and having that attitude, that means a lot. Give him credit."

Towns also backed up Edwards, saying he was "proud" Edwards shot it. It didn't seem to bother Edwards much after the game, because later that night when he got home, Edwards went live on Instagram and was dancing with his dogs.

The dunk over Watanabe came a few games later, and on the Toronto bench with a front-row seat was Finch, the runner-up to Saunders in the coaching search of 2019. Finch was the lead assistant with the Raptors under his friend and former rival Nick Nurse, both of whom came up through the ranks coaching in Great Britain. It was around this time that Rosas made up his mind to dismiss Saunders and hire Finch as his replacement. Two nights after the Toronto loss, the Wolves lost another close game against the Knicks in New York, and Rosas fired Saunders that night. When news of the firing began to leak via NBA media, Rosas's decision to hire Finch came right after. This was unusual for the NBA, for one team to fire a coach midseason and hire someone from another team as his permanent replacement. There was no interim tag for Finch. He was Rosas's guy, and he would coach the Wolves' next game in Milwaukee on February 23.

Finch's hiring came with some baggage. Rosas received flack for not having an inclusive hiring process, with some players, like Portland's Damian Lillard, criticizing the Wolves for not giving the interim job to Vanterpool, who was also a finalist for the head job in 2019 and was lead assistant under Saunders. National Association of Basketball Coaches president Rick Carlisle even issued a statement that said the organization had a "deeper concern" and "level of disappointment" at the lack of Black and minority candidates in the Wolves coaching search. Carlisle later apologized to Finch for the statement during one of the association's meetings that summer. Rosas blamed the pandemic for making a search difficult, plus he had all the information he needed on Finch to know that's who he wanted to hire. Edwards was at the top of Rosas's mind when he made the switch, he said.

"In full transparency, it was probably the number one reason why we made the coaching change when we did," Rosas said. "Ryan was a strong player development coach. Ryan was good for Ant in a lot of ways, and he connected with Ant, but we needed high-level coaching and high-level accountability for Ant, and it's one of the reasons why we brought in Chris so soon as we did."

Towns spoke to the media after shootaround in Milwaukee and was asked about his commitment to the franchise amid so much losing during his tenure. This is the era of NBA player empowerment and any unhappy star player could ask out of a team and likely get traded within a few months. Towns was on his sixth season with the Wolves and was now on his fourth head coach. But he always maintained he wanted to be part of a contender in Minnesota. He never wavered from that position.

"I'm a loyal guy, to a fault," Towns said. "I've said it before, I would love to finish my career here in Minnesota. . . . I want to build something great here. I want to build a legacy in Minnesota."

That seemed a distant dream during that season, especially after Finch took over. Sometimes teams receive a bit of a temporary surge when a new coach takes over, but the Wolves' problems only got worse. They lost the first five games of Finch's tenure by an average of 21.4 points, and that extended their losing streak to nine. The worst of those losses came at home against LaMelo Ball and the Hornets on March 3. Ball, who had become the favorite for Rookie of the Year by this point, had 19 points on 7-for-13 shooting to go with 7 rebounds and 5 assists. Edwards had 19 points on an inefficient 8-for-24, 1-for-10 from three-point range. This was the final game before the All-Star break, and afterward Finch challenged his team to come out of the break ready to compete.

"Those first five, six games, I was thinking, Will we ever win?" Finch said.

"Finchy"

Finch's path to the Wolves' head-coaching job was a circuitous one. He played college basketball at Division III Franklin & Marshall College, located in Lancaster, Pennsylvania, near where Finch grew up as a Philadelphia sports fan. Finch, or "Finchy," as most call him around the Wolves, despised the Celtics, then later in life became friends with and worked as an assistant with the Rockets under Boston legend Kevin McHale. He played in Europe for a short time after graduating from Franklin & Marshall in 1991. But at twenty-seven he was playing for Sheffield in England when he got an offer to become the team's coach. He accepted, and so began a twenty-three-year coaching odyssey before he got his shot as an NBA head coach.

He coached in multiple places in Europe, including a stop in the early 2000s in Belgium, where he also was the team's de facto general manager. Finch didn't have the money to sign a big man, so he made a decision that would change his life—he played small. The small-ball strategy was a big success, and at the time, the Rockets, with Yao Ming's playing days almost over, were noticing through analytics that small ball and spacing the floor was where they wanted to take their franchise in the 2010s. They took note of what Finch was doing in Belgium and during Summer League in Las Vegas in 2009, then–Rockets front office member Sam Hinkie reached out to Finch to set up a meeting with Rosas. Houston was starting its D-League (now G League) franchise, the Rio Grande Valley Vipers, under the direction of Rosas, and Finch agreed to become its head coach. There Finch conducted a lot of the experiments that the Rockets analytics department was curious could work at the NBA level. Soon he was an assistant on the NBA roster as the Rockets entered an era of sustained success following the James Harden trade with Oklahoma City.

Then came stints in Denver, where Finch worked under his future boss in Minnesota, Tim Connelly. Then he moved to New Orleans, where he was handed a problem that was the opposite of what he faced in Belgium: How do you make a lineup with two bigs (DeMarcus Cousins and Anthony Davis) work? On a podcast, Davis later credited Finch for unlocking the potential in those Pelicans teams before injuries hampered Cousins's career. He had a reputation as a bright offensive mind when Rosas made him the fourteenth head coach in Wolves history.

When Finch came aboard, the Wolves were facing a pivot point in their season and the franchise's future. Nothing was working, and Edwards's development was coming along slowly. Some of that wasn't his fault, given the constraints COVID placed on training camp and practice times. But the Wolves were a mess. They were 7–29, and to make matters worse, they owed their first-round draft pick to Golden State as part of the Wiggins trade, unless it was a top-three pick. So if the Wolves wanted to keep that pick, they had to tank—and tank hard.

But given where the Wolves were as an organization, they couldn't afford to tank. They had to see what they had, so Rosas and Finch came out of the break trying to win as many games as possible. The Wolves gave Finch his first head-coaching win in New Orleans out of the break. In a video that went viral on social media after, the team drenched Finch in water after the game, but Edwards had his head down at his locker, not realizing this was a tradition. After everyone was done, Edwards realized his mistake, got up, and soaked an already wet Finch in one last bottle of water. It's a memory that still elicits laughs from Finch years later.

"The thing I've always loved and admired about Anthony is how much he enjoys his teammates' and his coaches' success. He really does," Finch said.

The connection between Finch and Edwards would set Edwards's career on a gradual upward trajectory from year to year. In each of his first four seasons, Edwards got better, and with that came team and individual accolades—three playoff appearances in his first four seasons, multiple All-Star appearances, an All-NBA team appearance, and a spot on the 2024 US Olympic team. But when Finch first took the job, he also saw a raw "football player" trying to learn basketball at a high level.

"If you ever watch a football player play pickup, sometimes they have the athleticism and maybe the skill but not quite the connectivity," Finch said.

As Finch coached Edwards within his first ten games of arriving in Minnesota, he experienced some moments of frustration. Finch knew Edwards was young; he didn't realize just how green he was. There was one night a few weeks into taking the job that Finch vented some frustration to Rosas in a late-night postgame phone call.

"At that point in time we'd probably seen enough in Anthony to know that he could be a good player," Finch said. "But there was still massive lapses in effort and concentration. I made one of these emotional overreactions, and I was just super frustrated: 'This kid's never gonna get it. He has no idea what he's doing.' I'll never forget, Gersson said to me, 'That's why you're here. You got to teach him.' It was an aha moment for me, because I realized he's right. This is about Anthony's development more than it is anything else right now."

There was another aha moment, perhaps the most important moment for Edwards in his rookie season, for Finch and the team coming shortly after his outburst on the phone with Rosas. The Wolves were 2–2 out of the All-Star break when they took a trip to Phoenix for a pair of games against the team that would eventually represent the Western Conference in the NBA finals that season. Here was one of the first truly great performances of Edwards's career, and a moment that vaulted him to a different plane the rest of the season.

Edwards had been building to this moment in Phoenix out of the break with a 34-point performance at home against Portland in which it seemed everything he tried was working. He hit six threes, the most in any game to that point. As they went to Phoenix, Russell was out and the Wolves rolled out a starting lineup of Rubio, Edwards, Towns, Jake Layman, and Jarred Vanderbilt.

The on-court chemistry between Towns and Edwards popped. Finch had placed an emphasis on the two figuring out how best to play off the attention each would get from opposing defenses, and Towns especially was locked in that evening. Anytime Phoenix would double Towns on an action with Edwards, he found Edwards going downhill, and he ended the game with eight assists. Five of those assists set up Edwards's layups. Edwards had a big second quarter, when he had 15 points to boost his total to 22 by halftime. Towns had 19, and they combined for 41 of the Wolves' 53 points at the half.

That combustible combination from Towns and Edwards would serve as the blueprint for what the Wolves would strive for on the offensive end the following season, when they had the No. 1 offense in the league from January onward. Edwards finished with 42 and Towns had 41 as the Wolves beat the Suns 123–119. The celebration afterward on Phoenix's home court was cathartic for Edwards and Towns.

"It's always happiness when we're winning," Edwards said afterward. "Me and KAT were just expressing our feelings of winning after the game."

"I just want to celebrate with him as much as possible," Towns said. "It's a special moment."

The impact of that one game wasn't lost on those within the team. Rosas appreciated that Edwards's big night came with smart decision-making and few mistakes. When asked if it was the first moment he sensed Edwards could become a player who lived up to the billing of the No. 1 pick, Finch said, "It was for all of us."

"He just took over in the way we wanted him to take over," Rosas said. "I really felt like he turned a corner."

"Of Course He Cares"

One of Finch's primary jobs that first season, he said, was to get Edwards to take more efficient shots. The analogy Finch says he often uses with high-level players is that they are already wearing the Armani suit, and "I just want to tailor it." Meaning they could become really special players in the league if they allowed him to tailor their games toward efficiency. Working with Edwards early on reminded Finch of working with Brandon Ingram in New Orleans, when they tried to limit the inefficiencies in Ingram's game. Finch was on staff with the Pelicans when Ingram won the league's Most Improved Player in 2019–20.

Edwards was a better shooter than Finch thought when he arrived, and the Wolves quickly discovered Edwards could be very good at catch-and-shoot threes. They also tried to get him to drive the ball more instead of settling for stepback threes off the dribble (which he was worse at than catch-and-shoot threes) or midrange jumpers. Edwards is a player who is always engaged and focused when he has the ball in his hands or is guarding the player with the ball one-on-one. Where he sometimes struggles or loses concentration is when he plays off-ball or has to guard off-ball. Those moments can sometimes lead to him looking apathetic or seemingly asleep on defense. Finch learned, though, that Edwards made these errors not for a lack of caring.

"Of course he cares," Finch said. "He just doesn't know [those situations]. He hasn't been in it before, hasn't seen it enough times."

Finch didn't come into the job demanding these things out of Edwards. He realized that it took time to build Edwards's trust, and his preferred way of building relationships with players was to do so organically over time. He did discover early on that Edwards responded and appreciated hard coaching and someone holding him accountable, which merged perfectly with how Finch preferred to operate.

"He identifies that as 'If this guy cares this much, then this must be a good thing,'" Finch said.

Finch said he was also sensitive to how turbulent Edwards's first year was, complete with the restrictions from COVID, not having a training camp, and now facing a coaching change in the middle of the season. But he also hoped Edwards would identify with him in another way—that people were doubting both of them, that this was Finch's shot to be an NBA head coach after decades of working to get here. Similarly, people were doubting Edwards would make it long term, or live up to the hype of being the No. 1 pick.

"We do have a commonality. We were both trying to prove ourselves," Finch said. "I don't know if he recognized in me that quality, but it was my big chance as well as his big chance. So we walked that path together."

Edwards began making strides that year while Russell was out, but the looming question was, How would it all look when Russell was back in the mix? The answer was "just fine" as the Wolves closed the last 16 games of the season 9–7, a turnaround that finally put some good vibes into the organization after a woeful couple of seasons. Over that stretch came another key moment in Edwards's development, something that would foreshadow the kind of teammate he would be, and to Towns in particular.

It's no secret that Towns and Butler don't get along, but they haven't always been available to square off against each other when the Heat and Wolves meet twice per season. Sometimes Butler sat for rest or was injured; sometimes Towns would be injured. On May 7, 2021, Towns and Butler were both playing in Miami, and in a mostly empty arena because of COVID, microphones picked up the trash talk between the two. Among other things, Butler called Towns a "loser" and then said, "I already punked you once." Towns replied, "Go call Rachel," referring to

Butler's interview with Rachel Nichols after his maniacal tear through a Wolves training camp practice in October 2018. After the game, Towns and Edwards did their postgame Zoom press conference together and Towns was asked about the interaction. Edwards intercepted the question, and in that moment indicated he was going to be a much different teammate to Towns than Butler ever was.

"Man, they grown men, dog," Edwards said. "They was just talking, having a regular conversation if you ask me. If y'all come to see us compete, there's no competition if we're not talking shit to each other. Whatever, y'all can take that with a grain of salt."

Towns never replied to the question about Butler. Edwards handled it for him and he took the awkwardness out of the situation. It showed Edwards was going to stick up for his teammates, and he was going to be a loyal teammate to Towns in a way Butler wasn't.

"He's always fighting for his teammates in that way, sensitive to what's going on around people," Finch said. "He's always been protective of KAT. He was aware of the beef with Jimmy, for sure, like everybody is. But at that age, to be able to diffuse that for KAT shows a great amount of maturity."

Later in the press conference, Towns stumped for Edwards to be the Rookie of the Year.

"There ain't no other rookie in this league getting double-teamed. There ain't no other rookie putting up the numbers Ant is," Towns said. "There ain't no other rookie causing the havoc and mayhem before the game even starts with the scouting reports like Anthony is."

Voters didn't agree with Towns, and Ball took that award with Edwards finishing second. Ball finished the season averaging 15.7 points, 5.9 rebounds, 6.1 assists per game on a true-shooting percentage of 53.9 percent (true-shooting percentage weighs the value of three-pointers and free throws in a player's shooting efficiency). Edwards finished with 19.3 points, 4.7 rebounds, and 2.9 assists per game with a true-shooting percentage of 52.3 percent.

Despite the snub in the Rookie of the Year race, Edwards had come a long way from his slow start to the season. The Wolves ended that season with momentum internally going into that offseason, and Edwards was a big reason why. The NBA world at large may not have noticed anything was different about the Wolves, but they felt it. It helped that Edwards radiated good vibes on the team and for the fan base at large.

Part of the reason is that anytime Edwards stepped in front of a camera or a microphone, he had the ability to create a viral moment. One of his first came from an interview he did with Marney Gellner, the host of the team's podcast *Wolves+*, which was also turned into episodes that aired on the Wolves' local TV affiliate, Bally Sports North. Gellner asked Edwards about what sports he played as a kid, and they got on the subject of baseball.

"I coulda went to the MLB," Edwards said. "I played pitcher, shortstop, third base, and center field."

Edwards mentioned that he was "fourth, fifth hitter."

"You know what that mean?" Edwards said. "Straight cleanup on aisle three, come get it."

He then added: "Whatever you need me to play, I'm gonna go do it. If it's some money on the line, I'm gonna go do it."

Then closed with this gem: "I bet I be A-1 from day one."

Gellner said she did the interview with Edwards on media day just before training camp began, and the only thing she and the crew knew about Edwards was in that ESPN piece that ran before the draft. They didn't know what to expect in the studio.

"We had no idea what his personality was like," Gellner said. "And after our interview was over, the three of us in the studio all looked at each other like, 'Was he just fucking with us?' It was wild."

When it aired, the clips went viral and let everyone know just what kind of personality and humor Edwards was going to bring. There were other moments, like when Edwards told a reporter from Ireland he thought his accent was "tough." But one that hit another level of engagement was shortly after Marc Lore and Alex Rodriguez came aboard as owners of the Wolves. They agreed with Taylor to a gradual succession plan in which they would eventually become majority owners in a $1.5 billion sale of the team. After one game late in the season shortly after the news broke, Edwards, who had just claimed he was great at baseball in the interview with Gellner, said he didn't know who Rodriguez was. As he was fixing his hair on a monitor nearby, Edwards fielded the question from the Athletic's Jon Krawczynski.

"Who is he?" Edwards said.

"The baseball player? Alex Rodriguez?" Krawczynski said.

"Yeah, naw. I don't know who that is," Edwards said. "I know he's gonna be the owner, but I don't know nothin' about baseball."

These clips had an unintended effect for Edwards. As they entered the offseason, Edwards's teammate Juancho Hernangomez was cast to star in an upcoming movie with Adam Sandler called *Hustle*. Hernangomez would play Bo, an under-the-radar basketball prospect from Spain whom Sandler's character discovers and tries to get in the NBA.

As Bo navigates the draft process, he runs into a nemesis named Kermit, the projected top draft pick, who taunts Bo at every workout or scrimmage they have against each other. The filmmakers needed someone to play that villain role, and Hernangomez suggested they take a look at some of Edwards's press conferences. The film's director, Jeremiah Zagar, told *Vanity Fair* that Sandler suggested Edwards to him after watching those clips.

"He was just so charismatic," Zagar told the magazine in 2024. "He just has this innate, effortless charisma."

Edwards impressed them with his audition via Zoom, which Edwards woke up for about five minutes before it began, Wilkes said, and he got the role.

Edwards filmed his parts in the offseason after his rookie year, but it didn't distract him much from getting in the gym that summer. That summer was the first one in which Edwards would work full-time with someone who would help guide him over the next few seasons—Hines.

CHAPTER 8

CAN YOU GET IT DONE?

In the NBA, every player has an assistant or development coach they work with on a daily basis at practices and games. This staff member, no matter where they rank in the coaching hierarchy, helps guide the player through workouts and individual film sessions outside of team practice time.

Before each game, players go through on-court workouts with these staff members and usually sit off to the side to dissect film. Players and their development coaches can often form close relationships, and it's important to a young player's success that he end up with the right staff member.

During Edwards's first season with the Wolves, the team wasn't taking any chances with whom it had as his player development coach. That responsibility fell to David Vanterpool. With the No. 1 pick, the Wolves wanted their top assistant to oversee Edwards's growth.

But when Finch was hired and made changes to his staff in the summer of 2021, Vanterpool left for a job with the Nets. Finch had to decide who was going to work with Edwards next on an individual basis. But Edwards needed to be comfortable with this person, the one whom he could trust, who would come into the gym and put him through individual workouts while calling him out when he needed it. He had someone in mind.

Hines came to the Wolves during Edwards's first season as an assistant with the team's G League affiliate in Iowa. Hines barely knew who Edwards was when the team drafted him. He didn't watch much college basketball and only looked up film of Edwards after the draft was over.

Anthony Edwards in one of his Atlanta Vikings jerseys. His size, speed, and agility made him one of the most dominant offensive players of his age group.

Courtesy of Dana Watkins

Edwards and his friend Reign Watkins formed an unstoppable combination in their time playing for the Atlanta Vikings.

Courtesy of Dana Watkins

Edwards (*back right, facing the camera*) with his Atlanta Vikings teammates

Courtesy of Dana Watkins

Edwards (*No. 8, standing back left*) with his 10-and-under squad for the Atlanta Vikings

Courtesy of Dana Watkins

Edwards (*No. 10, back left corner*) with teammates on his Top Notch AAU team after a tournament

Courtesy of Dana Watkins

Edwards (*second from right*) poses in front of the White House on an AAU trip to Washington, DC, with teammates (*left to right*) Reign Watkins, Messiah Thompson, and Tre Clark III.

Courtesy of Dana Watkins

Edwards and his brother Antony (aka Bubba, *second from right*) spending some time on the holidays with Dana Watkins (*far left*) and his family

Courtesy of Dana Watkins

Edwards with former AAU teammate Christopher Hinton Jr. in the pool at the Hintons' former house on the northern outskirts of Atlanta

Courtesy of Chris Hinton

Edwards with Christopher Hinton (*right*) and his brother, Myles Hinton

Courtesy of Chris Hinton

Edwards with Christopher Hinton Jr., Chri Hinton Sr., and Myles Hinton at a football camp

Courtesy of Chris Hinton

Edwards met up with Chris and Mya Hinton after a game in Chicago in November 2024. He used to spend summers hanging out at the Hintons' house with their sons, Christopher and Myles.

Courtesy of Chris Hinton

Chris Hinton Sr. with the jersey Edwards signed for him and his wife, Mya, after a Timberwolves game in November 2024

Courtesy of Chris Hinton

Edwards and Peikrishvili asleep in the back seat of Rachel Little's car

Courtesy of Rachel Little

Edwards with his high school friend and teammate Buka Peikrishvili

Courtesy of Rachel Little

Edwards and Peikrishvili have stayed close throughout Edwards's NBA career.

Courtesy of Rachel Little

Edwards and Rachel Little in 2024. Little was the registrar at Holy Spirit and played a large role in helping Edwards navigate his way at the high school.

Courtesy of Rachel Little

Edwards with (*left to right*) Rachel Little's mom, Kathy; his teammate Buka Peikrishvili; friend Nick Maddox; and Little

Courtesy of Rachel Little

Edwards would frequently take naps on his lunch break in Little's office at Holy Spirit. This is one of those times.

Courtesy of Rachel Little

Peikrishvili and Little visiting Edwards when he was in college at the University of Georgia

Courtesy of Rachel Little

Edwards with his best friend, Nick Maddox, whom he met in high school, along with Little

Courtesy of Rachel Little

Edwards and his player development coach with the Wolves, Chris Hines, go through a workout before a game in Minnesota.

Courtesy of Chris Hines

Edwards has been working with Hines on a daily basis since his second season with the Timberwolves.

Courtesy of Chris Hines

Edwards and Hines celebrate Edwards being named to the All-Star team for the first time in 2023.

Courtesy of Chris Hines

Edwards with his grandfather, Ben, before a game against the Hawks on December 23, 2024

Courtesy of the author

The hoop Edwards used to play on when he was younger, in the backyard of his grandfather's house in Atlanta

Courtesy of the author

"Athletic, fast, great first step. It looks pretty coordinated. Shot didn't look too bad," Hines said. "Watched his turnovers, and I'm like, okay, well, got some work to do."

During the times he would be in Minneapolis, Hines would make sure Edwards was on time for his pregame court workouts and ran him through this drills. He'd do some film work with him as well.

"At the time, I didn't think or know I was going to have a relationship with him," Hines said. "Those players usually get pushed to more experienced coaches."

When Finch arrived, Hines wasn't sure what his future was going to hold.

"Finchy doesn't know who the hell I am, I don't know who the hell Finchy is," Hines said.

The Wolves' director of player development that Finch brought in, Joe Boylan, told Hines to keep working with Edwards while the Wolves figured things out. But Edwards expedited the process. He told Finch he wanted to work permanently with Hines. Finch called Hines the next day.

"He said you got the keys to the Ferrari," Hines said. "Don't run it into the ground."

After Finch tabbed him as Edwards's player development coach, Hines called Edwards into the facility to get together at 7 p.m. that night. Hines was dressed up to go out afterward; Edwards was dressed to work out. But Hines didn't want to work out this night. He wanted to have a chat.

"I'm literally going to dinner," Hines said. "He asked, 'What the hell are you doing, man?' And I sit down and say, 'Let's talk.'"

The question Hines wanted to ask Edwards was what he wanted out of his NBA career, and Edwards could be brutally honest in his answer. Did he want money? Did he want fame? Did he want to win? There would be no judgment if the answer was either of the first two. But Hines said Edwards told him, "I want to be the best to ever do it."

Specifically, Edwards wanted to be the best two-guard in NBA history. Hines had to remind Edwards there was steep competition for that title.

"There's a guy a little bit taller than you, about six-foot-six. His hands are a little bit bigger. Athleticism may be a great comparison. But he got six rings."

Hines said Edwards told him, "I need seven."

"I said, 'Say no more. We'll get to work, lock all the way in,'" Hines said. "'I'm gonna push you and there may be some things you may not like, but you got to trust me with your game.' He said, 'Bet, that's what I want.' We shook hands, came in the next day, and it's been history ever since."

As Edwards said about that talk, "I'm chasing my boy M.J., for sure."

Why did Hines think Edwards wanted to work with him, even after just a small amount of time they previously spent together?

"Honesty is huge with Ant," Hines said. "Don't sugarcoat anything with him. If you're really about it, come with it every day when he turns it on. Now, it's hard to turn him on sometimes, but when he is on, you got to meet him at his level, because if you don't, he'll expose you as a coach."

Hines learned early on to have answers and counters to everything he does with Edwards. If a coach helps Edwards see the reasons behind what he's doing—and gives him a voice in the process—he'll go with it. It's the same tactic Rachel Little used to get Edwards to do his homework and other things he didn't want to do back at Holy Spirit, and the same way Tom Crean built his relationship with Edwards at Georgia.

"He'll expose you because he's so talented at times that he's like, 'Yo, I'm not doing that no more. That didn't work for me,'" Hines said. "Or, 'Why am I doing that?' And if you don't have an answer, and it's a clean answer, he's gonna be like, 'Naw, that's bullshit.' He'll call your bullshit out."

Finch and Hines put together a "laundry list" of things they wanted Edwards to work on that summer, but if there was a theme, Hines said it was for Edwards to develop good habits. By good habits, the Wolves meant a consistent routine, showing up at the same time each day instead of always having different workout or court times, showing up for treatment, eating better, and making sure he was getting proper rest. These are the little things it often takes younger players years to figure out, because they're so accustomed to rolling out of bed and being so much better than their competition. That stuff takes time to sink in at the NBA level, but those little habits provide the margins for great players.

"He used to put the work in, but one night he would work at ten, and next night another time," Finch said. "We were always preaching, like, consistency is better. Get you on a routine. Then I realized, like, not just with him, and I've expanded it now to all young players. When you have Anthony's upbringing in his background and his life, like, what are habits?"

Like Ant's diet—if he was always on the go, moving from place to place, it's not about what he ate, it's that he ate at all. Finch called this another aha moment for him in coaching Edwards and other young players.

"Some of his youthful moments where he might be late or whatever, the easy knee-jerk reaction for any coach is: this kid doesn't care. That's not the case. He cares immensely," Finch said. "There were so many things beyond his control. So that helped me understand, like, Anthony doesn't have bad habits. Anthony has no habits."

The goal was to get him to develop those good habits those first few summers. As far as Edwards's game was concerned, the big thing he worked with Hines and Kierre Jordan on that summer was perfecting his Eurostep. Edwards can be a battering ram when he goes to the rim, and the combination of speed and physicality with which he attacks the hoop is rare in the NBA. But the more Edwards could slow down and remain under control, the more he could improve his shooting percentage at the rim and find open teammates easier. They also wanted him to clean up his shot. In his first season, Edwards's shot release had a lot more movement, which is typically not a good feature because it increases the number of things that can go wrong. So they worked with Edwards on honing his release, to make it a more compact motion from his waist to his forehead.

There was one aspect of Edwards's game that he wanted to work on more than Hines or Finch wanted him to—his midrange game. There has been a constant tug-of-war between the team, which wanted Edwards to shy away from these analytically despised shots (because of their low return per attempt), and Edwards, who insisted he needed to develop a fearsome midrange game to become a complete player. This made sense from Edwards's point of view considering that his favorite player, Durant, is one of the best midrange shooters of all time.

"I would try to figure out how to finagle the workout where we'd move past the midranges," Hines said. "Ant looked at me one day and said, 'Bro, you're not taking the midrange out of my game.'"

The team can show all the math it wants to Edwards and tell him that threes and driving to the rim are what he should focus on, but he would take at least a few midrange shots per game, so Hines tries to find a common ground where they will work on getting to the spots on the floor where it is most advantageous for Edwards to take those shots.

"I'd tell him, 'I don't want to take the midrange out of your game, let's just tone them down,'" Hines said.

Edwards shot a horrid 26.2 percent on 1.7 midrange attempts per game his rookie season. Over the next few seasons, his percentage would get better as the frequency of his midrange attempts went up. At the end of his fourth season in 2024, Edwards shot 35.1 percent on 3.8 midrange attempts per game, according to NBA.com. As a point of comparison, Durant shot 51.8 percent on 6.5 midrange attempts per game that same season.

Kierre Jordan said that summer he showed Edwards film of how Klay Thompson and Michael Jordan shot, and tried to get Ant to imitate the 90-degree angle of where their elbows were when they released it. He also worked on getting Edwards to square up to the basket and not turn so much when he shot.

"Shooting on the way up, keeping his body square versus turning . . . that critiquing started [that summer] where he understood and got what it looked like," Kierre said.

That offseason featured a lot of change for the Wolves, as Rosas made a couple of trades that altered the rotation. He ended the partnership between Rubio and Edwards with a trade that sent Rubio to the Cavaliers in exchange for Taurean Prince. In another deal, he acquired Patrick Beverley in a trade with the Grizzlies and provided a different kind of veteran mentor for Edwards. The strong-willed Beverley wasn't afraid to challenge Edwards, but he also imbued him with confidence.

"Pat Beverley was absolutely huge for Anthony, because he literally was like a hype man," Finch said. "He told Ant every day how special he could be. Coming from a player with that much energy, you could see Ant filling up with that."

Over the summer, Holland said Beverley "pretty much summoned" Edwards to Minnesota for a meeting with him and Finch. Beverley wanted Edwards to spend more time around the team's facility to set a tone for the rest of the team, Holland said.

"He said we're making the playoffs, and the way we're gonna make the playoffs is you're gonna lead this team, you're going to be in market because people are going to follow," Holland said Beverley told him. "When Ant knows somebody is right, Ant will just kind of concede."

Edwards altered his plans and spent more time in Minnesota that summer. Not only did the roster change, but the front office was changing too. That summer was the last one Rosas was in charge for the Wolves. Just days before training camp opened, the team fired Rosas for a combination of off-court issues, including a relationship he began with a woman who worked in the organization and for fostering what some who worked for him thought was an acrimonious environment. Rosas declined to comment on his dismissal in a 2024 interview. He said he looks back fondly on the work he did with the Wolves and will always have a "soft spot" in his heart for Edwards.

"I'm proud of the work that me and my staff did in Minnesota and really felt like we laid the foundation for a championship-winning team," Rosas said. "It's exciting to see that come to reality."

He would later land in the Knicks' front office, where he'd have a hand in affecting the Timberwolves and the arc of Edwards's career a few years later.

"Too Much Game"

The Wolves entered the 2021–22 season without a permanent president of basketball operations, as the team elevated Rosas's second-in-command,

Sachin Gupta, to interim POBO. Finch also helped Gupta in the day-to-day minutiae of running the team. Internal expectations were high even if the NBA world's were not. Beverley told the team and media he expected to make the playoffs, but that appeared like a long shot when the Wolves began 4–9, a stretch that included a six-game losing streak. After a 20-point home loss to the Clippers, Edwards let out some frustration that began an at-times-antagonistic relationship with the officiating.

The Wolves encouraged Edwards to attack the rim as much as possible, but it was hard for Edwards to accept the times he thought someone fouled him and officials wouldn't blow the whistle. Edwards was asked if it was "tiring" to drive to the rim so much; he said only at certain times. "It's tiring when you're getting fouled, you're missing the layup. That's tiring," he said.

A few games later, Edwards scored 48 points in a loss at Golden State in a performance Finch called "perfect." He was 16-for-27 from the floor, 7-for-13 from three-point range, and led a Wolves comeback that came up short. After that game, Edwards walked back some of his previous comments.

"What I said last week, I sounded like a loser," Edwards said. "When you are determined, I mean, you just gotta keep going."

Some early injuries contributed to the Wolves' slow start as Finch also tinkered with the lineup to find the right combinations. There were nights they'd have great wins and confounding losses. One of those good wins came at home against Miami the night before Thanksgiving. Edwards had an almost career highlight when he launched himself to the rim over Miami's Gabe Vincent in the fourth quarter. But the officials called an offensive foul, ruining what would've stood as one of Edwards's greatest dunks.

"The zebras, man. I don't know," Edwards said of the call. "If I'm refereeing that game and you dunk on someone like that, I'm not calling a charge. And you at home? I'm not calling a charge. I don't care if he was three feet above the circle, I'm not calling a charge. No way."

There was also another moment that displayed the difference between Edwards and Butler. At one point Butler went to grab the ball from Edwards's hands after officials stopped play. Edwards responded by shoving Butler in the back, and Butler ran up on Edwards to get in his face. The tense moment fizzled without any escalation, but Edwards wasn't afraid of Butler and made light of the situation afterward.

"Him taking the ball out my hands, I was like, 'C'mon, bruh. You ain't that serious,'" Edwards said. "The ball's going to get there. I felt like I had to let him know just chill. . . . He ain't finna fight nobody out there. All that walking up on each other, that's stuff for the birds, man. I ain't about to fight. I don't get into all that. That shit be fake."

It was a moment that encapsulated Edwards—he wasn't about to back down from anyone, and he wasn't going to stop having fun in the process. It didn't hurt his standing with the fan base that it came against the franchise's number one villain, Butler.

The Wolves were a mercurial team through November and December. They won seven of eight before dropping another five straight. In December, the Omicron variant of COVID-19 ripped through the league, causing mass absences everywhere, and it hit Edwards, who missed six games because of it shortly after he hit ten threes in a road win at Denver. All this uncertainty made it hard for the Wolves to find their footing before the calendar changed to 2022, but when it did, they began to take off.

Edwards was still having inefficient nights shooting. Some nights he might take over 20 shots; other nights he might go 2-for-11, as he did in a loss to the Suns that year. Finch would often preach that the key for Edwards—and for any NBA player to become great—is consistency. Young players often show flashes of brilliance, but can they get to that level when they play games every other night? Edwards was at a point where he'd put together great performances once every three or four games.

But once January hit, and the Wolves got their regular contributors back from COVID, the free-flowing offensive principles Finch was preaching, based on player and ball movement, clicked. He found a starting lineup—Russell, Towns, Edwards, Beverley, and Vanderbilt. Finch would joke about that group being the "greatest starting lineup of all time" after reporters found that their net rating on the floor was among the best of any five-man combination for as long as that statistic has been around.

From January until the end of the regular season, the Wolves had the No. 1 offensive rating in the league. Edwards's role was his commitment not only to attacking the rim, but to doing something the Wolves didn't know he was capable of doing at a high level when they got him—catch-and-shoot threes.

"Which allowed him to play great next to D-Lo," Finch said. "They actually had a pretty good chemistry, Anthony and D-Lo, playing at the top of the floor. I can remember running a lot of just simple drive-and-kick stuff, when there was help there on the two of them. The chemistry with KAT already existed."

Edwards was a 41.3 percent catch-and-shoot three-point shooter that season. That was much better than his 32.5 percent mark on pull-up threes. But there was always a challenge with that—catching and shooting required Edwards to space the floor and play without the ball in his hands, which tends to leave him less engaged than when he has the ball.

When he has the ball, Edwards can occasionally drive Finch crazy. There will be times Edwards pulls off moves, or doesn't make an easy pass that keeps the ball moving, that will turn Finch's hair grayer. But at the same time, the Wolves know they have to let Ant be Ant.

"Because if you don't, it limits him in terms of what he's going to give to the team," Hines said.

Hines often has to fight boredom with Edwards when they work out together; that Edwards can master moves and add things to his game rather quickly. Once he does, and the pair drills that for several weeks, Edwards is wondering what's next. So Hines teaches him counters and other moves to deploy off that. When Edwards enacts those moves in a game, and Finch would prefer Edwards to pass the ball, he'll turn around to Hines behind the bench with a common refrain: "God damn it, C. Hines, you're giving him too much game."

"That happens probably out of an eighty-two-game season, about thirty-two times," Hines said. "All the coaches will be just dying laughing."

By February and March the Wolves were clicking. Towns, Edwards, and Russell all were playing well in Finch's free-flowing system. Edwards and Towns in particular found success playing off each other. At this point, the Wolves were still Towns's team. He was the leading scorer, he made another All-Star Game, and was named to the All-NBA team thanks to 24.6 points per game. Edwards took more shots than Towns did per game (17.3 to 16.4), but Towns's efficiency was the key to the offense (he shot 41 percent from three-point range while playing 74 games that season). Towns even had a career highlight with a 60-point night in San Antonio on March 14.

The vibes were good. Finch often said the team seemed to really enjoy playing with each other and got along well on and off the court. Edwards, per usual, provided comedy in his postgame press conferences. He began the season expressing his bewilderment at Milwaukee's Giannis Antetokounmpo and how easily he could score.

"With a guy like that, you can't stress about him scoring, that's what he gonna do," Edwards said after a Wolves win on October 27, 2021. "Muhfucker's 7′2″, 280 pounds. Ain't nothin' you can do about him. Shit, we put four people on him, he still score the ball."

The Wolves were in Utah on New Year's Eve, shortly after the death of legendary football coach and broadcaster John Madden. Somehow (this reporter doesn't quite remember why) the subject of Edwards playing video games came up, and Edwards proclaimed himself the "best basketball-*Madden* player in the world."

When asked if he had seen Madden had died, Edwards said he had and added, "It was sickening, man. I was playing *Madden* when I heard the news. So I had to beat somebody by thirty, forty points to show my respect."

That quote went viral. As did a moment after a win in Detroit on February 3, 2022, when Edwards sat down for his postgame press conference and said, "What's up, nephews? Hold on, don't ask no questions yet. I'm tryna put an order in."

As he typed stuff into his phone, Edwards was asked where he was ordering from (McDonald's) and what he was getting.

"Hold on, I got one more thing, McChickens," Edwards said. "Wait, wait, wait, customize, no ice."

Order finished, he then said seemingly out of nowhere: "I love Minnesota, man. Hope y'all love me back."

Edwards had the personality of a star, but he was still learning the ins and outs of what it took to become one on the court. His habits were getting better, but they still weren't where the Wolves wanted them to be (like in ordering McChickens after a game). Before a game in Cleveland on February 28, Hines teamed up with Beverley to get on Edwards after he was again late for his workouts before the game. In the locker room, Hines asked Beverley a question before Edwards arrived.

"Pat, dude, in your experience, with these young guys, have you seen this type of behavior? Because I'm not used to it," Hines said.

Around such a young team, Beverley would talk about his experience playing with some of the elite players in the league, like James Harden in Houston or Kawhi Leonard with the Clippers, and would use their work habits to motivate Edwards and his teammates. Eventually Edwards walked in, and Beverley took it from there, Hines said.

"'Oh yeah, now it's time, y'all. We can start our shit, y'all. He's finally here.' And he's saying it loud," Hines said of Beverley. "'Put the red carpet out.' You know how Pat is. He's just antagonizing him. 'I know Michael Jordan wouldn't be late, I know the greats wouldn't be late. But for some reason, our guy wants to be late.'"

At first Edwards mostly ignored Beverley and wrote it off as typical Pat Bev bluster. He then went through his workouts by "piddling around," Hines said. So Hines poked Beverley to get him going again. This was a common tactic for Hines to get through to Edwards when he didn't want to listen.

"There were times that Pat would call Ant out. I couldn't reach Ant at times," Hines said. "It was a good dynamic because Ant respected Pat's work and I thought that was a unique relationship. I thought they bonded pretty well."

"I start gassing it with Pat," Hines said. "How was James when he was MVP?'"

Beverley replied: "It wasn't like that, C. Hines, I'll tell you that. It wasn't like that. His bag crazy. I don't know how you get a bag comin' late every day."

This finally got a reaction from Edwards.

"I don't wanna hear that shit. All that crap. It don't do nothing to me," Edwards said, according to Hines.

"'Well somebody got to do somethin' to you,'" Hines said Beverley replied. "'Because something's got to change, young fella.' They were going at it, verbally."

The Wolves won that game against the Cavaliers 127–122 to improve to 33–29 on the season. Edwards had 17 points on 7-for-13 shooting to go with 4 steals, and that night began a stretch of 10 wins in 11 games for the Wolves. Despite Edwards's frustration in the moment, the end result was what Hines and the team wanted.

"Ant started being a little bit earlier, and a little bit earlier," Hines said. "It was good for Ant to hear that from a vet that cared about him, instead of a vet that was trying to come at him. When they got into it, it was good, because it woke Ant up a little bit."

Beverley was only with the Wolves for one season, but it was an impactful one for Edwards. Holland said he didn't know if Edwards would have responded to Beverley's leadership style the same way a few years later in his career. But year two? Beverley's timing was spot on.

"Pat's form of leadership was what was needed at that point in his life," Holland said. "What I think Ant learned from it was actually being a leader was showing everybody around you."

Holland also said Beverley was an inspiration for Edwards to be more vocal, even as Edwards spent most of his life shying away from that type of leadership. It didn't come out right away, but Beverley left that mark.

"He would always say, 'I don't like to say much, I just show it with my game,'" Holland said. "Once Pat left is when he started to hold people accountable with his words."

Throughout the year, Edwards was getting better numbers-wise. Three-point shooting was up to a more respectable 35.7 percent from 32.9 percent, and his true-shooting percentage was .560. He was finishing at a better clip in the restricted area (62.7 percent compared to 59 percent).

The fans embraced Edwards's growth and growing pains. As crowds came to the Target Center for the first time since COVID, Edwards quickly captured their adoration. At home games they thrived off Edwards and he thrived off them. For as good as Russell and Towns could be, nobody could energize the crowd like Edwards could, especially when he ran hot. The sight of Edwards on a fast break would send a rush of anticipation through the arena. His smile, the way he played the fans, waving his hands in the air to encourage them to get louder—it didn't take long for Edwards to become one of the fans' most beloved players.

The Wolves were also good again, and a fan base that had been through so much disappointment finally had something to cheer. Edwards led that, but Beverley and his hard-nosed style earned a lot of goodwill with the fans. The Wolves were an average defensive team that year (13th in defensive rating), but they played a high-wall style of defense that required a lot of hustling. Instead of having the center drop on a pick-and-roll, the Wolves would jump out on it. If the ball rotated, the Wolves would rotate behind it, and that required a significant amount of running. Vanderbilt played a large role in making it work, as did McDaniels. The Wolves played with maximum effort on a nightly basis, and the fans appreciated that style of play.

They finished the regular season 46–36 and were the No. 7 seed, which meant they would host a play-in tournament game against the No. 8 seed Clippers for a playoff berth. This was the biggest game of Edwards's life up to that point, and they needed him to play like it was.

Postseason Parties . . . and Pain

Towns, repeating a pattern that has dogged him in his career, got into foul trouble and played himself out of the game with just 11 points on 3-for-11 shooting. He fouled out with 7:34 to play and the Wolves down 93–86. It was on Russell and Edwards to bring the Wolves back.

Seconds later, with the Wolves down 95–90, Edwards took Paul George off the dribble and sent him to the floor with a forceful drive and easy layup. Then a Russell pull-up three in transition gave the Wolves a 97–95 lead with over four minutes left. The next time Edwards found himself isolated on George, he went to a stepback three—and nailed it for a 4-point Wolves lead. Russell then dealt a body blow with a pull-up jumper and a 6-point Wolves lead with 1:56 to play. It was Russell's best game with the Wolves, as he had 29 points while Edwards had 30 in a 109–104 win. When time ran out, Edwards and Beverley embraced and Beverley nearly knocked Finch over as he jumped on the scorer's table, creating an instant meme in the process, usually set to the song "The Man" by Aloe Blacc.

This meant a twenty-year-old Edwards was going to play his first playoff series against the No. 2 seed Memphis Grizzlies and Ja Morant, who was a year ahead of Edwards in his career. The Grizzlies were set to be the next big thing in the NBA (though that was put on hold as Morant dealt with injuries and multiple suspensions for brandishing guns on social media in the next few seasons). But the Wolves didn't much care about that; they were expecting to win the series, and they put the NBA world and Memphis on notice with a decisive 130–117 victory on the road in Game 1. Edwards gave a full-throated declaration that the playoffs didn't scare him. He followed that excellent performance against the Clippers with a 36-point day in Game 1.

"I was extremely worried that he was going to go out and try to do too much," Finch said. "There's been a lot of players who have struggled in the playoffs early in their careers. Ant is not one of those."

The Game 1 performance was an eye-opener for Finch and the entire Wolves organization. It was also an eye-opener for Memphis, who was in for a competitive series regardless of the difference in seeding. On the Grizzlies side was someone who would become Edwards's teammate the next two seasons, forward Kyle Anderson.

"It was kind of like, okay, this is our game plan for him. Game one, it didn't work. Game two, that didn't work. Game three, we're going to do this—that didn't work," Anderson said. "Game four or five, just fight for your life and hope he misses it."

The Wolves' and Edwards's lack of playoff experience showed in that series. After Memphis handled them in a bounce-back Game 2 win, the Wolves led by as many as 25 in the second half of Game 3 at home, even with Towns playing himself out of the game with 8 points, 4 shot attempts, and 5 fouls.

One of the biggest weaknesses of that Wolves team was rebounding, and Memphis crashed the offensive glass all series. Wolves fans still have nightmares of Brandon Clarke grabbing offensive board after offensive board, and Memphis outscored the Wolves 37–12 in the fourth quarter for a stunning 104–95 comeback win.

After the Wolves eked out a Game 4 home win, they led Game 5 by 11 entering the fourth quarter on a strong night from Towns, who had 28 points. But Russell had just 12 points on 4-for-10 shooting. Clarke again dominated the offensive glass with seven offensive rebounds in the fourth quarter alone.

With the Wolves down three and under ten seconds to play, McLaughlin found Edwards in the corner for a three. Edwards buried it to tie the game with 3.7 seconds to play. But he undid what could have been a lasting highlight on the next possession. On the inbound play, Edwards gambled for a steal and went above Morant on a screen at the top of the key. He didn't get the steal, and that allowed Morant to penetrate the lane and hit a layup around Vanderbilt for the winning bucket.

"I had already had my mind made up that I was going to try to steal it. Dumb mistake," Edwards said afterward. "It's over though. Can't do nothing about it."

Game 6 was a microcosm for the rest of the series. Another second-half lead for the Wolves vanished. There were more problems on the glass, and inconsistency from the Wolves' star players. Edwards had 30 points on 24 shot attempts, but Towns was 6-for-19 and Russell had his worst game of what was already a miserable series for him. He scored just 7 points and was struggling so much that Finch benched him in the closing minutes for McLaughlin. Russell averaged 12 points on 33 percent shooting for the series. But for Edwards, the arrow was pointing up. The playoffs didn't scare him, and he was able to thrive under the pressure. He made mistakes, but he was the Wolves' best player in the series. He averaged 25.2 points per game. He shot 40 percent from three-point range for the series. Not bad for someone whose critics said eighteen months earlier that he could never develop a consistent shot at the NBA level.

"We noticed he was really figuring out the game," Anderson said. "He didn't quite have it yet in that Memphis-Timberwolves series. But once he gets it, it's going to get ugly."

After that season, fans figured the Wolves would stay on this trajectory with a mostly young roster that would grow together. But the front office was about to change again, and with that came a radical shift to the roster. Edwards's performance in that playoff series played a part in the major move the new front office was about to make.

"To be twenty and to be able to do that? It spoke to what might come," incoming president Tim Connelly said.

Added Finch: "There's different classifications of players that you're sifting through. 'Is this guy a franchise guy? Is he a starter? Is he an All-Star? Is he whatever?' But ultimately, all people really want to know is, can you get it done in the playoffs?"

CHAPTER 9

CHANGE EVERYWHERE

When Matt Lloyd was preparing to come to Minnesota as part of Tim Connelly's front office in the summer of 2022, the future Timberwolves general manager watched each game in the Wolves-Grizzlies playoff series, and as he did, it reminded him of when Lloyd was working in Chicago watching a then-rookie Derrick Rose nearly lead the Bulls to a first-round upset of the Celtics in 2009. Specifically, Lloyd thought to Rose's first-ever playoff game, when he scored 36 points on the road in a Bulls win.

"It was the precursor to this giant ascension over the next few years," Lloyd said. "He had no fear, and he was going to be able to stand up to playoff-caliber basketball in the NBA. So it almost changes your perspective to have a responsibility to him at that point. Coming in the door, I know Tim felt a responsibility to Anthony and the staff hired around Tim intrinsically felt that responsibility. . . . You can't be given this incredible gift and not try to maximize it as much as possible."

After going a season without a permanent basketball boss following the firing of Rosas, the Wolves aimed big for their next president in the summer of 2022 and were able to lure one of the most respected executives in the game from Denver to Minnesota in Connelly. Connelly's eye for drafting talent had built Denver into a perennial playoff contender around Nikola Jokic, whom Connelly took in the second round of the 2014 draft. In drafting Jokic, Jamal Murray, and Michael Porter Jr. and trading for Aaron Gordon, Connelly put the major pieces in place for a Nuggets team that won the title in 2023.

When he came to Minnesota, Connelly told ownership the Wolves needed to keep Edwards and his development at the top of mind in any decision they made. They also felt a responsibility to Towns to "put these guys in a position to see the deep playoffs."

"The team had gone through enough draft picks, gone through enough rebuilding phases. They'd seen all of that stuff," Lloyd said. "So how can we accelerate it a little bit, why not try to shift strategy-wise into a position where the time is now as opposed to constantly attempting to build, build, build."

Even though the Wolves were a playoff team the previous season, the new administration wasn't sure if that group was built for sustained success. It had a fair amount of "lightning in a bottle," Lloyd said. They also wanted more veteran voices around Edwards, and had discussed how best to maximize Towns's talents by slotting him next to another defensive-oriented big man.

"There were some pretty glaring issues: maturity, losing these monster leads," Connelly said. "I was concerned that maybe the team was too young to have sustained success, and I didn't want Ant going backwards."

As a result, Connelly and the Wolves got aggressive and surprised the NBA with a huge deal to get Jazz center Rudy Gobert. They sent out Beverley, Vanderbilt, Bolmaro, Malik Beasley, the newly drafted Walker Kessler, three unprotected first-round picks in 2023, 2025, and 2027, and a top-five protected pick in 2029 along with a 2026 pick swap for Gobert. The trade became an immediate lightning rod for criticism, with fans and media saying the Wolves gave up way too much. The Wolves didn't care. They got to keep McDaniels, who was important to them, and they brought in someone with a winning pedigree who could set the team on a new trajectory. He would also set an example for Edwards in the locker room with his diligent preparation and seriousness with which he approached the game.

"The Rudy trade was done with a complete emphasis on Ant and KAT," Connelly said. "KAT had been through so much here with different faces, different coaches, and the front office, and Ant had really started to taste it. I thought it was a chance for him to become addicted to the process that you need to win. Those two were the reasons we made the Rudy trade."

All of a sudden, the pressure and expectations ramped up, and the Wolves went from a feel-good story to wannabe contenders needing to justify the hefty price of the Gobert trade. The mood and pressure shifted around the team, and Edwards didn't do himself or the team any favors with something he did off the court that offseason.

During a night in September, he took out his phone and filmed a group of men on a sidewalk and commented on the way they were dressed. He referred to them as "queer" in a derogatory way before saying, "Look what the world done came to, bruh." His words hit hard for several LGBTQ+ fans of the Wolves, who aired their thoughts out to the *Star Tribune* for an article days later.

"It gave homophobes a voice," Eric Boogaard, a gay Wolves fan, said in an interview then. "It gave them almost a poster boy. 'Look at this big name, he feels that way. It's okay to feel that way.' It keeps the gatekeeping up of LGBT people away from the sport. It keeps that gate up of saying you're not welcome here."

Connelly's approach with players is to develop relationships organically, and he had done so with Edwards throughout that summer and onward. That extended not only to Edwards but to members of his inner circle, some of whom, such as Banks and Holland, he calls friends. He said he and Edwards have a similar sense of humor, and over the years Connelly said the bond they have built has allowed him to be "pretty hard" on Edwards.

"I don't want him to skip steps and don't want him to leave anything on the table," Connelly said.

This was one of the first times Connelly had to put the hammer down on Edwards. Connelly was in Europe at the time and called Edwards and essentially told him: *you were raised better than this.*

"You're a nice person. This is hurtful, that's not who you are or who we are," Connelly said. "Part of that upbringing is you're not mean to people. He can't stand bullies. He can't stand when you see people being mean, and this is hurtful to people. He was receptive and apologetic. It was a learning experience and it made him aware that as your star shines brighter, your words have consequences."

It may have also altered Edwards's relationship with social media. Before, he would post videos of himself on social media, like with his dog Ant Jr. After that his own social media posts became less frequent to the point that Edwards said almost all of his social media content is posted for him. He will still use DMs to keep in touch with people. But his future Team USA coach Kerr said he believes Edwards when he says he mostly stays off social media. When the team was in Abu Dhabi preparing for the Paris Olympics in 2024, they woke up to the news that a would-be assassin had shot at President Donald Trump during a campaign rally in Pennsylvania. Kerr said the news had been at least a few hours old at the time and he addressed it with the team. Edwards came up to him afterward to tell him he hadn't seen it yet.

"He said, 'Coach, I didn't even know that happened. I'm not on my phone and watching social media.'"

Edwards would apologize at media day in September 2022 for his homophobic video and the league fined him $40,000. Later that season, before the team's annual Pride Night, he donated an unspecified amount of money to Queerspace Collective, a Twin Cities organization that worked with LGBTQ+ youth.

"Just try to right my wrongs," Edwards told the *Star Tribune* about the donation. "You know, give back, show them that it's no hate. You know what I'm saying? It's all love."

Edwards had another lesson in fame the following season when a woman alleged Edwards pressured her to have an abortion and posted text messages of their conversation on social media. The screenshots of a tense exchange between Edwards and the woman made the rounds on social media the day the Wolves played a game in Miami. The woman also posted what appeared to be a wire transfer with a payment of $100,000 from Edwards. Edwards issued a statement on X confirming that the posted messages were with him. It wouldn't be the first or last time Edwards's personal life was fodder for gossip websites and publications.

"I made comments in the heat of a moment that are not me, and that are not aligned with what I believe and who I want to be as a man," Edwards said in the statement. "All women should be supported and empowered to make their own decisions about their bodies and what is best for them."

Edwards's relationship to his fame has been one he is reluctant to accept. Holland said that early in his career, Edwards would claim he wasn't famous, and Holland had to tell him that yes, he in fact was. With that came power and influence, and Edwards had to learn to use it wisely.

"It's self-realization," Holland said. "Realize the responsibility that you hold in your position. I hate when I hear people say I didn't sign up to be a role model. You didn't, but you are. I work with kids, so I have to be accountable for what I put on my social media. Did I ask for it? No, but my responsibility and the people who look up to me means a lot."

Edwards would become a father in 2024, when his longtime partner Shannon Jackson and he had a daughter, Aislynn. Edwards missed the second half of a game against the Kings to be there for this birth of their child, a moment chronicled in *Starting 5*. Holland reminds him of the impact he has on kids, whether he wants to acknowledge it or not, using his own son as an example.

"My son had thick, curly hair. The reason he cut his hair is because Ant cut his hair," Holland said. "I told Ant whether you realize it or not, this is my son. He watches everything you do. You have that responsibility. You have nieces, nephews. I think he internalized some of that, and I think he realizes his reach and sees the response from the kids. It's learning, learning through life experiences."

Vibes Are Off

When it came to what the team wanted from Edwards basketball-wise that summer, Connelly said it was to keep improving his habits, specifically his sleep. Connelly was telling the man who had been up until all hours of the night playing video games from the time he was kid that he had to cut it out now and get more rest.

"Sleep was a big issue," Connelly said.

There was also Edwards's diet, and the man who once ordered Mc-Donald's before beginning a press conference in Detroit started to give up food that was bad for him.

"I know I ain't got room to talk, but I'll be like, 'Listen, bro, I'm trying to see you play forever. Please don't do this to yourself,'" Maddox said he told Edwards about his diet.

In one of Connelly's first sit-downs with Edwards, Connelly showed him his two-guard "peer group," and there were only a few current NBA players in there, like James Harden. Others in that group? Michael Jordan, Kobe Bryant, Allen Iverson. Connelly showed Edwards how his numbers stacked up against theirs, but there was one key difference they had at an early age—good habits. Edwards had been a gym rat all his life, but Connelly saw Edwards in a different light than others.

"All those guys, they had unbelievable habits and were addicted to basketball," Connelly said. "Ant was addicted to competition. We were trying to get him addicted to basketball."

In the next two years Edwards would develop those habits to the point Connelly would call him "the most mature twenty-three-year-old I've ever seen." The Wolves knew they had a lot to work with in Edwards, and that it would just take some guidance to get him going in a better direction. Lloyd said that on the road, Edwards never misses an optional shooting opportunity when the team lands in a city. After the team checks into its hotel, the team will set up time at a gym nearby for those who want to go work out. It's completely optional.

"That guy is there every single time. Without fail," Lloyd said.

But Edwards still wasn't taking care of the little things in his life that older players valued. The same issues that were persistent in year two: diet, treatment, rest, overall care of his body.

They also noticed Edwards had a tendency to get complacent with success, and he might play down to the level of his opponent, which was something that unfortunately plagued him and the Wolves going into that season. The immediate results on the double-big experiment with Towns and Gobert in the front court (with Russell, Edwards, and McDaniels as the other three starters) were clunky.

"We were really excited about him being able to play with a rolling big [in Gobert] that should create some downhill ability," Finch said. "We also knew that the paint was going to be crowded in other ways, and that was going to impact him. I think that was probably the biggest frustration for Ant, was when he had played with KAT, or Naz [Reid] at the five, there was a lot of opportunities to always attack the paint. . . . Definitely a big learning curve."

The Wolves opened 5–8, a stretch that featured two losses to the Spurs and one to the Jazz, both of whom were not trying to win too many games that season. The ball movement was "sticky," as Finch typically refers to it, and it seemed like it was taking everyone time to learn how best to play with Gobert. Russell and Gobert were trying to get on the same page in their pick-and-roll game, as was Edwards. Minnesota's offensive efficiency was 23rd in those first thirteen games. The sight of Gobert fumbling a pass in part because players didn't know where he liked to receive the ball was a common one early that season. The same fans who were elated most of the previous season were now booing the team at home games. The frustration began to punch through following a road loss to another beatable opponent, Charlotte. Russell was asked by the *Star Tribune* how he felt his chemistry was progressing with Gobert, and he replied, "He catch the ball, he'll score."

A few days later, after a blowout loss at home to Golden State, the season kept spiraling when the Wolves lost to the Wizards in Washington, DC. Towns crumbled to the floor with a noncontact injury in the third quarter and needed help off the court. The injury was as close to a worst-case scenario as it could get—a severe right calf strain that was going to sideline Towns for multiple months. The team hit rock bottom after a New Year's Eve home loss to the lowly Pistons in a game that prompted the Wolves to have a team meeting afterward.

Not only were the Wolves off to a slow start, but now they weren't even going to find out if the Towns-Gobert pairing was going to work long term. Towns would miss 52 games, and in those 52 games, the dynamics of the Wolves franchise would change in dramatic fashion.

In hindsight, Towns's injury that season hastened the transition to the Wolves becoming Edwards's team.

And when Towns came back, he was more the 1b option to Edwards's 1a. Edwards's larger role also meant his voice and his leadership mattered more than it had.

"You could feel it. Even two, three years ago, before Ant took that jump [in 2024], I was there," Edwards's former teammate Austin Rivers told *The Bill Simmons Podcast* in September 2024. "It's not that Karl had any animosity toward Ant or did anything malicious. You could feel it in just the energy. . . . It's the way Ant moves. Ant walks in the locker room and it's immediately his. . . . It just happened."

Towns never had an issue with this, and Edwards and Towns maintained a very good relationship through Towns's tenure in Minnesota. This doesn't always happen in the NBA, when one star makes room for another, but Towns is as smart as he is skilled. He could see that Edwards was an ascending star, and instead of trying to block him from the spotlight, he made room.

"[KAT's] a nice guy and he's just the ultimate professional on top of that," Holland said. "Ant kind of put a little battery in him and gave KAT a little swag and KAT was like, I know what it's like when you're at the top, when they start coming at you, when you're at the top of the scouting report."

That's where Edwards was in the wake of Towns's injury, the top of everyone's scouting report, and Edwards was about to get a crash course in reading NBA defenses like he never had previously. It wasn't always a smooth process. Edwards's feel for the game is not as natural as players who may have grown up focusing primarily on basketball. Some players are like musicians who can sit in front of a piano and play by ear. Edwards needs the sheet music and to learn the chords first. He will become proficient; it will just take time and practice.

Edwards has to see things in order to process it for the future. The coaches need to drill what to do, and eventually it will stick. This is how Edwards matured as a player over the next season and a half. In that way, Towns's injury was like a new beginning of Edwards's career. Finch said it forced the team to become a "spread pick-and-roll" offense with Edwards handling the ball a lot.

"I thought Anthony's game lifted," Finch said. "I thought his awareness of pick-and-roll lifted. I thought his awareness to read different defenses—he saw a ton of different defenses every single night. So that was a hidden bonus when KAT went out was Anthony's acceleration with the ball in his hands."

Edwards's increasing knowledge for the game began to become a major asset for the Wolves. It had to, because without Towns's spacing—and spacing was already complicated with Gobert and Towns occupying the same floor—Edwards was seeing more blitzes and double teams than he had ever seen. The Wolves take a matter-of-fact approach with Edwards. As assistant Micah Nori said, the Wolves will go over how they expect a team to defend Edwards in shootaround or a pregame meeting. They'll explain to him where his options are in those moments. Then once they have footage from the game, they'll show him the next day what he did well, how to react to adjustments teams made to him, and where he could improve.

"It's just that cycle. The more you go through that wash, rinse, repeat cycle . . . over the course of four years, especially the last two years, he's seen most of it," Nori said. "There's pretty much nothing he hasn't seen now."

The constant struggle was convincing Edwards to make simple plays, to get off the ball when teams would send a double team his way. There was a hardheadedness about Edwards that would want to beat the double teams by himself, and his instinct to be aggressive might take over and cloud his decision-making.

"It's different than when you're in college or you're in high school, when they try to just blitz you, and you can just out-athlete everybody, right?" Nori said. "So that's where he starts having to see where the kickouts may be, where the next pass may be, or how he can get himself into space where he can attack. More importantly, he knows where the answers to the test are."

But it took plenty of studying to get to the point where he could ace the exams. It took lots of film work. Edwards had to trust that if he gave the ball up, it would create open looks for his teammates, and other times, he would get the ball back with a chance to drive or have an open shot himself.

"As an athlete, you think you're doing one thing, until you watch yourself on film and then you say, 'Oh, wow, I'm really not doing it like I thought I was,'" Anderson said. "So I think it was up to him to own it, to own that he wasn't really getting off the ball as much as he should and take accountability."

Edwards had the ball in his hands a lot more, and Russell also needed to have the ball in his hands to operate. Seemingly inevitable on-court fault lines began to develop that season as Edwards handled the ball more and Russell shifted his role. Russell would later tell the Athletic he felt like he was "held back" at times in Minnesota. He would clarify those comments on a podcast appearance with Beverley in which he said he appreciated and learned a lot from his time playing for Finch and his system.

"They opened my eyes to the game to a level that I didn't see the game from. I always give them credit," Russell told Beverley. "So, when I say held back, it was never held back, it was more or less like I didn't get to be who I wanted to be. I wanted to be more than they wanted me to be. And they allowed me to be and come and do things that I wanted to do, of course. But as far as finding a home in the NBA, it's a hard thing to do."

Russell, who was in a contract year, was averaging a career low 13.5 shot attempts per game as Edwards's shot up from 17.3 the previous season to 19.5. There wasn't any personal animosity between Edwards and Russell. They got along. Holland said Edwards and Russell would play cards together a lot. But Edwards would sometimes wish Russell's approach to the game would be different, just like the way he would get on Towns in the same way, Hines said.

"They have all the love in the world," Hines said. "Their bond was interesting too. D-Lo is so talented as a player and Ant is one of those guys who hates when guys don't get the best out of themselves in terms of who they are as players. He'll do that with everybody. . . . It was the same message to D-Lo, 'You're so talented. Be that. Don't bullshit the game.'"

There were times after Towns went down that Russell's hot shooting carried the Wolves to wins (Russell shot 39 percent from three-point range that season during 54 games with the Wolves). But there were nights when Russell's shot went cold, and if there was ever a time when Edwards didn't seem like himself during his Wolves tenure, it was during this stretch of his third season. The frustrations of the season and trying to make things work with Russell and Gobert—all without Towns—was taking its toll on Edwards's energy. If he couldn't see it, the organization could.

"For Ant to be his best, he has to have fun," Finch said. "There has to be joy in it. What I could tell as that season was wearing on . . . even though he was starting to play better, more consistent basketball and stuff like that, he wasn't really having fun."

All this came even as Edwards earned his first All-Star berth that season. His numbers were up across the board, and during the time Towns went out, he averaged 25.6 points, 4.7 assists, and 5.9 rebounds. He had a true-shooting percentage that season of .564, nearly identical to the prior season, while upping his shot volume. That All-Star announcement came shortly after the team decided to make another significant change. Thinking that the dynamic of Russell-Edwards-Towns-Gobert was not destined to work long term, Connelly pulled the trigger on a multiteam trade that sent Russell to the Lakers and brought Mike Conley and Nickeil Alexander-Walker in from Utah. The shot volume Russell was going to require was not going to be compatible with the emerging Edwards. Finch said it was on him and the coaching staff for not making it all work better.

"Anthony was growing up to the point where he knew he needed the ball more, and we knew he needed the ball more," Finch said. "With KAT getting the ball early in the offense, and D-Lo handling, it was just a natural pecking order that needed to be, like, rejiggered. That's on me, that's on the coaches, that's on the culture. D-Lo fought us a little bit on that because he obviously excels playing a certain way too. It was just everybody having to adjust to each other. But I never heard D-Lo complain about playing with Anthony. There were frustrations, I think, with Anthony just wanting the ball, but it never got to the point where I felt it was eating at the team."

Nonetheless, the Wolves wanted more of a complementary point guard alongside Edwards, and that's what the then thirty-five-year-old Conley was at this point in his career. Conley was also renowned for being one of the best teammates in the NBA. He would be the next Ant whisperer, the veteran mentor who would be in Edwards's ear when necessary, and he would be an example Edwards could follow. The Wolves were still an up-and-down team and were staying alive in the playoff race despite Towns's absence. The night they traded for Conley, they were 30–28.

"Mike, he's such an accomplished player, but he's so genial and friendly. He met Ant where he was. Mike loves to play video games," Connelly said.

And if there is ever a way for someone to gain favor with Edwards in a hurry, play video games with him.

"Some of these guys come in here like you're the big brother, but you don't have that relationship," Connelly said. "Mike came in as a colleague who's seen a lot. . . . His subtle, meet-Anthony-where-he-was approach—there's no moodiness to him."

After the trade, Edwards's mood improved, and his energy was back at the facility every day. He was again himself, and the team could see it. Joking, shit-talking, and throwing around his patented one-liners.

"You know how your grandma has all the sayings? How your grandpa has phrases for days?" Alexander-Walker said. "Ant's got phrases on phrases."

Edwards doesn't unleash these one-liners often in his public interviews, but he certainly says them in the locker room and during practices. Some may make more sense than others. Alexander-Walker said his favorite is "What you eat don't make me shit."

Anderson's is "You ain't gonna catch no fish watching my pole."

"I thought my dad was king of the one-liners. That's one of the best one-liners that I'm able to use almost every day," Anderson said. "That's my favorite hands-down Ant one-liner."

Naz Reid's favorite? "The same cow that gives milk gives butter." He isn't sure what it means.

The humor, the authenticity to be himself no matter if a camera is on him or not, that is what attracts fans to Edwards, and it makes those in his hometown swell with pride when they see somebody who is one of their own, unapologetically, shining on the national stage.

"Man, listen, after we'd play . . . we wear our hats like him, cocked to the right, cocked to the left," Moye said, referencing how Edwards dresses sometimes in press conferences. "I'm forty-two years old, I still wear my hat like that. I'm educated, college-decorated, and I still talk like I'm from Atlanta. . . . He's from the South Side of Atlanta, and he got Atlanta character. . . . Atlanta dudes think we can do everything. Ant is Atlanta, man, and we love him."

Reign Watkins said as Edwards became bigger in the NBA, he noticed "Timberwolves fans coming out of nowhere in Atlanta." His Adidas shoes would be hard to find across the area, especially in the postseason.

"Ant is true to himself at all times," Sturdivant said. "That's why people draw to him, because they know it's not a thing he's trying to put on, and that's why I think Atlanta loves him so much. Because that's Atlanta, like he represents it. Authentic, and that's what Atlanta loves. Like he's putting on for us nationwide and globally, even in the Olympics. That's never changed about him."

That Edwards was back after the trade, and Conley was going to help Edwards change the collective mood of the organization going forward. The night of the trade, they just so happened to be playing Utah. It made for a surreal scene inside and outside of both locker rooms. Conley went home to begin the process of moving to Minnesota. Alexander-Walker stood outside the Wolves' locker room after the game to greet his new teammates. Gobert spoke with reporters to say how happy he was Conley was coming to join him. Other players from the Jazz found out they were getting dealt as they were going through pregame warm-ups. Conley wasn't quite doing backflips at getting dealt to Minnesota at this point in his career, but he soon realized the Wolves had a serious chance of contending with Edwards.

"He's a guy you want to go to war with," said Conley, who is thirteen years older than Edwards. "He's like that every night. He's like that every practice. He's like that in every film session. The intensity that he just lives with, that he walks with, that he talks with—you can just feel that."

Conley had heard about Edwards's competitive drive; now he saw it for himself.

"His aura, his way of saying things without having to say it with his body language, the way that he's approaching practices, his competitive nature. He believes he's the best in the world . . . you can see that," Conley said. "I saw that from the first few weeks being there, and I think the Timberwolves already knew who they had in Ant. But I was kind of like stamping it: Y'all got a good one. He could be really, really good."

Conley followed in the legacy of Rubio and Beverley as Ant's veteran mentor, but he would be there across multiple seasons. Some younger players might bristle at the thought of so many veterans mentoring them, but Edwards's willingness to embrace these kind of friendships with older teammates is in line with who he is, considering who Edwards keeps in his inner circle. There are his family and friends like Maddox who are close in age to him, but there are also friends and mentors in that circle who are older than he is by a decade or more, who are around Conley's age. There's Banks, Holland, and his uncle Chris, and now Edwards had someone in that age range on this team who could still hoop with him.

Conley fit right in this mold, and the two hit it off from the moment they met aboard the team bus. Conley greeted the team at their hotel for their flight to Memphis—the place where Conley made his legend with the Grit and Grind Grizzlies. Edwards was in the back of the bus and when he met Conley, Conley said Edwards did most of the talking. When they got on the plane, their seats were next to each other, and their connection took off.

"I got to talk to him a lot while on the plane just about the team and what direction he thinks we're going," Conley said.

Film and Finch

Conley would get used to Edwards sitting next to him. Before Conley arrived, Edwards sat in the back row at film sessions, Finch said. He would still be engaged in the sessions, but he said Edwards would be like "the typical kid that sat in the back row in class." The first session Edwards had with Conley, however, he sat in the front row right next to him. Neither Finch nor Conley said they had anything to do with that.

"I didn't say a word to him," Conley said. "That was him taking that initiative."

Added Reid: "It played a big part in leadership to see him in the front row, and that Mike was somebody he wanted to mirror as a young guy."

Whether he meant to or not, Edwards's moving up to the front row in those film sessions was a subtle sign to the franchise—he was back to being Ant. Whatever residue there was from the on-court friction with Russell over who was commanding the offense was gone almost instantly. Edwards's joyful attitude returned on a regular basis, and the change in his demeanor was noticeable to those around the organization. He was again locked in during practices and film sessions, and that lifted the rest of the team.

Conley was going to be a more complementary fit to Edwards on the floor since he didn't require as many shots as Russell did. In fact, while Towns was still out, Finch had to urge Conley to take more shots and alleviate some of the defensive pressure on Edwards.

Conley helped Edwards break down defenses, and he also served as a mediator at times in film sessions with Edwards. Normally, Conley said, Edwards is "observant" during film sessions and tends to keep quiet, but there are times when he senses Edwards wanting to speak up when Finch gets on him for a few bad possessions.

"He'll start shaking his leg back and forth," Conley said. "Coach is getting on him about something . . . and I can just see his leg start to move, as if he's getting ready to blurt out something. Both legs. You know how people do when they have to go to the bathroom? Just very antsy."

Finch may get on Edwards as many as three times in a row over his decision-making, and that's when Conley sees Edwards ready to "jump back at him." Conley reminds him that he needs to hear this, that what's happening on the screen is actually his fault and Finch has a point.

"I'll be like, 'Hey, chill. You need this. This is good. Just let it happen.' He'll be quiet and let Coach continue to do what he does," Conley said. "But for the most part, he's observant, but he will speak up and he's ready to fight back if he feels the need."

Reid said he also sits in the front row, and he can tell when Edwards is feeling like he wants to speak.

"I've been with both of them [Finch and Edwards] for so long, I know what's about to happen," Reid said with a laugh.

Conley quickly learned that, much like Hines, he was going to serve as a mediator between Edwards and Finch. He will tell one or the other they went too far in a given interaction.

"They go at it. Honestly, they do. They go at it," Conley said. "They have days where they're getting ready to fight, and then after the game they hug each other. Finchy apologizes, or just says, 'Man, I just got caught up.' Ant's the same way: 'Like, man, you're right. I got caught up too.'"

Conley admitted that Hines's job was "ten times harder than mine."

"I'm in the middle, like always the string holding it together," Hines said. "Or I'm pushing away like y'all need to back up, give each other space. 'Let me handle that, Finchy, I got him.' I get to see this tug-of-war, and it's the funniest tug-of-war that I've ever seen."

Reid said even when Edwards and Finch have these heated moments, "We know they're fine." He compared it to moments when Edwards appears to get hurt during a game. Edwards could be writhing in pain on the court, and sometimes he will head back to the locker room, only to emerge a few minutes later seemingly fine. A verbal tussle between Finch and Edwards gives Reid the same feeling.

"Nobody ever really worries," Reid said. "Literally laughing [afterward] like nothing happened. That's two alphas. They both want it bad."

Hines said there was a game the Wolves weren't playing well, and Edwards in particular was making some bad decisions that were driving Finch crazy on the sideline. He was letting Edwards hear it. But then Edwards went on a hot streak that featured shots of dubious selection.

"He did something dumb and we're like, do not shoot that, and then he made it," Hines said. "Finchy said, 'God damn it.' . . . Ant then turns around, slaps Finchy on the ass, and keeps going. I'm like, 'Dude, you're nuts.' That's the relationship, though."

There was another time Finch tried to sub out Edwards in a game on December 30, 2023, only for Edwards to refuse to come out. Edwards later apologized.

"I'm just competitive. I don't take it personally if he gets mad at me, and vice versa," Finch said. "I'm honored to be able to coach a guy like him in so many ways. It's fun because he makes it fun. And, you know, there's been . . . times where he didn't even realize it was wrong."

Anderson enjoyed watching the dynamic between Edwards and Finch, whom he called two of his favorite people in basketball. Their relationship, he said, showed just how close they were on and off the court.

"I love them both as people, forget basketball," Anderson said. "They have such a great relationship, those two. . . . In order to get along, you have to get along off the court, and both of them are just great people. I'm that type of person to where we can MF each other and then later, let's go to dinner and talk it out. That's a testament to both."

Edwards doesn't have a problem with that kind of coaching from Finch, where some young NBA superstars might. That's because Edwards has always had that kind of coaching, dating back to his Atlanta Vikings days and through his time at Georgia with Crean. Edwards also respects it, because it's a sign a coach cares about him and about winning as much as he does.

"Both of them are no-bullshit guys," Hines said. "Tell you what it is, very stern. You know what you'll get out of Finchy. You know what you're gonna get out of Ant. Ant allows Finchy to coach him hard. Finchy allows Ant freedom out there, but freedom within playing the right way. So there's a love and respect of each other for sure, and I think Ant thinks Finchy's brilliant. 'My coach is smart, and he knows that going into the game.'"

Before a win over the Suns on January 29, 2025, Alexander-Walker said there was a film session in which Finch "woke up choosing violence." Edwards joked that Finch must not have slept well. But Finch didn't hold back in his critiques of the team, especially Edwards.

"The way he did us in film today, particularly me, it was a tough day for us," Edwards said.

In that interview session, Edwards provided a glimpse into how he processes the coaching he gets from Finch in these moments; how his mind goes from wanting to answer back at Finch to accepting the coaching; and how the clips help him see just what kind of effort he gives or doesn't give.

"When he was getting on us, especially to me, as you're growing up to be a young adult, you always want to think about, 'Aw, he trying me. I want to say something back. He trying my manhood.' But when you think about it . . . I would've been a fool in film to say something back," Edwards said. "He ain't trying my manhood, because the clips on there, they look bad.

"I definitely felt some type of way about it. I told my best buddy, 'Finchy got on my butt today, but he was right.'"

Some of the best teams in NBA history have had this dynamic between star players and their head coach. Nori pointed to the Gregg Popovich–coached Spurs as an example where a coach could call any player out, regardless of stature, and that benefited everyone involved. Some NBA coaches may think they can only do this with a star player a few times per season, Nori said, whereas Finch doesn't care.

"I think when coaches not only hold the best players accountable, but those best players allow those coaches to do so, that's when teams are dangerous," Nori said. "The by-product of that is, when we're in a film room and Finchy is motherfucking Ant and Ant might motherfuck him, all those other guys in that room are going, 'Holy shit. If he's motherfucking the best player, we better get our shit together too.'"

Whether he knows it or not, Finch has some of the same qualities in dealing with Edwards that a lot of people in Edwards's life previously had. Banks wanted to hold him accountable without being a father, as did Holland, as did Little, who wasn't trying to be his mother at Holy Spirit. Nori said Finch was the same way with Edwards. He wasn't trying to get Edwards to like him.

"If Ant knows you are real, if Ant knows you care about him and others, then he's fine with it," Nori said. "And Finchy is not doing it as self-serving. It's genuinely coming from a place to ultimately help us be a better team."

Holland said Finch's holding everyone accountable from the first day garnered Edwards's respect, and their bond only grew from there.

"Those guys really love each other," Holland said. "After meeting all his old-school coaches back from home, that's what Ant is used to. He's used to people shooting him straight, like not bullshitting, not taking it easy on him."

"Fire" Potatoes

As he grew to be the focal point of the team, Edwards began finding his voice as a leader, a trend that would continue into his fourth season. The Conley trade didn't solve everything for the Wolves that season. They still were prone to immature moments and went 6–10 against the bottom teams of the league. Then the hits, figurative and literally, kept coming. In addition to Edwards's growth, another silver lining of Towns's absence was that Reid had developed from a player who might not play on some nights to someone Finch could not afford to keep off the floor, even as Towns made his return late in the regular season.

But just four games after Towns had returned, Reid took a hard fall in a game against the Suns and suffered a broken wrist that ended his season. The Wolves were fluctuating in the playoff seeding, and by the time they got to the final day of the regular season, they faced the Pelicans knowing the winner would end up as one of the No. 7 or 8 seeds and the loser would be No. 9, a big difference in the odds of making the postseason under the league's play-in tournament format.

Chaos was the theme of that first half for the Wolves. McDaniels, ever the fiery competitor, left in early foul trouble and went to a darkened tunnel near the bench. He punched the wall in the tunnel, but there was no padding on it. So McDaniels broke his hand, ending his season. Then, during a time-out, Anderson, never one to shy away from speaking his mind, called out Gobert in a huddle. Gobert took offense and a swing at Anderson. He left the game and the team suspended him for its first play-in against the Lakers even as Anderson and Gobert squashed the beef quickly after the game. Both players spoke fondly of each other from that point onward, and there were never any issues the following season they played together.

On one of the craziest days in recent Wolves history, they still beat the Pelicans despite the drama. Edwards had 26 while Towns had 30. Conley pitched in 17 while Taurean Prince had 18 off the bench. That meant the Wolves were headed to Los Angeles for a play-in game against the Lakers, but they were without Reid, McDaniels, and Gobert, two starters and another important piece of their rotation. Towns played brilliantly, but he got into foul trouble in the second half while Edwards couldn't solve the coverages the Lakers were throwing at him. The Wolves squandered a double-digit fourth-quarter lead and lost in overtime 108–102. Edwards had nine points on 3-for-17 shooting.

With Gobert back, the Wolves rebounded with a 120–95 blowout of Oklahoma City a few nights later to make the playoffs as the No. 8 seed, but that blown lead over the Lakers loomed large. Instead of drawing the vulnerable Grizzlies, whom the Lakers beat in the first round, the Wolves got the Nuggets, who appeared to be a juggernaut behind Jokic. Not only that, but the Wolves were still down Reid and McDaniels.

In Game 1, the Wolves were running on fumes after their travel-intensive play-in week, and Denver blew them out by 29. Edwards's performance (6-for-15, 18 points) mirrored that of the team. But in Game 2, he got his legs under him. His former head coach Saunders was now an assistant with Denver and had the responsibility of scheming a defense to stop Edwards.

"He's in the bucket of star, elite players that your game plan is going to be different for him compared to ninety-nine percent of the league," Saunders said. "He's a heck of a talent. . . . [That series] was really a coming of age for Ant. He was close to unstoppable as he moved forward."

He was unstoppable in Game 2, even as Denver squeaked out a 9-point win. Edwards carried the Wolves as Towns struggled (3-for-12, 10 points, 5 fouls). He stuffed the stat sheet in all good ways: 41 points on 14-for-23 shooting, 4 assists, 2 steals, and 3 blocks. Edwards hit 6 threes and Denver wanted no part of him anytime he attacked the rim aggressively.

"I had seen flashes of it all year, but wow, he really turned it on in that series," Anderson said.

On one sequence, you can hear Edwards yelling midshot before the ball went in after taking a fadeaway over Bruce Brown. But in taking Towns out of it, Denver did enough defensively to win 122–113 despite Edwards's night. Without McDaniels there to guard him, Jamal Murray went for 40 points on the other side while Jokic had 27 points and 9 assists.

When the Wolves returned home for the next part of the series, Gobert had Edwards over to his house for dinner. Gobert is heavy into organic foods and French cuisine, and his personal chef can make a wide variety of meals. When they met for dinner on the road, Gobert would try to get Edwards to deviate from his usual palate.

"Trying to get him to try some different foods," Gobert said. "I'd try really hard and he's like screw that, I'm not eating no escargot," Gobert said.

So when Edwards goes over to Gobert's house, he reminds his chef not to make "anything too complicated."

"Do it right, but do it simple. So my chef would do some roasted potatoes and chicken," Gobert said. "Always organic and all that stuff. I was like, he's gonna eat what he loves, but at least it's going to be healthy, and he always tells my chef, 'These are fire potatoes. These are my favorite potatoes.'"

Since Gobert arrived, his was two slots over from Edwards in the team's locker room. So there were plenty of times reporters could see Gobert and Edwards interact in there after games. Gobert has adopted one of Edwards's favorite words, "sac," a term of approval Edwards has when addressing someone to indicate they are solid. Gobert will often refer to Edwards as "sac" with a heavy French accent. Edwards isn't shy about poking fun at Gobert. In November 2024, while making an offhand remark with reporters present, Edwards jokingly told Gobert how he likes Gobert a lot better than anybody did when Gobert was in Utah. That's where Gobert's relationship with the franchise's young star guard Donovan Mitchell had diminished over their final seasons there.

One reason the Wolves traded for Gobert was his reputation as someone who prioritizes winning above all else. Few in the NBA take more diligent care of their body than Gobert does, down to his stretching and lifting schedules, to his diet. Connelly said having that example around Edwards was a motivating factor of trading for Gobert.

"We thought it was a chance for him to really become addicted to the process that you need to win," Connelly said.

Hence the organic meals when Gobert invites Edwards over for dinner.

"He was really someone that I think doesn't care about the flashing lights and all that stuff. It's just about having fun. It's about winning," Gobert said. "So for me, I took it upon myself to really try to be the best mentor I could be for him. How can I help him be the best version of himself? Help him take care of his body. Help him just try to lead by example. We went through a lot of adversity over the years. Every year, it's made him better, stronger, more mature."

One of the things that Gobert said he noticed right away about Edwards was how much he absorbs from the world around him. He may not say much about what he's seeing, but he's processing how people move. So Gobert was always cognizant to set a good example with his actions around Edwards.

"My goal wasn't to be the guy that just tells him what to do, but this guy that shows him everyday things that I've been doing," Gobert said. "Being able to handle the season, how to take care of yourself, how to work. I think him seeing that it's easier to listen to someone when you know that is about it and not just saying things."

These dinners were how Gobert got to know Edwards, how he came to understand his story and what motivates Edwards to say and act how he does. They helped Gobert not take it personally if Edwards has something critical to say, and they helped Edwards get to know Gobert beyond what he may have heard about Gobert from his Utah days.

"He really helped me understand better how to communicate with him and when you know someone deeply, then you understand more their way of thoughts, their reaction to events," Gobert said. "When I was younger, I didn't understand that as well. But now it really helps me to get to know my teammates on the deeper level, understand what they've been through, understanding their battles in life that they have to go through."

Edwards had some of those "fire" potatoes prior to resuming the series in Minnesota, and Gobert joked they were the reason Edwards played so well.

Towns got it together in Game 3 (27 points) as Edwards continued his tear, this time getting to the free-throw line 15 times on his way to another 36. Unfortunately for the Wolves, Denver was operating on all cylinders offensively. Michael Porter Jr. had 25, Jokic had 20 points and 12 assists, and the Nuggets shot 57 percent in a 120–111 win. There were few losses Edwards took as hard as this one.

After the game, he sat at his locker with his head down for several minutes and left without speaking to the media. It was one of the most outward displays of disappointment Edwards had made in his career up to this point. It just so happened to be in view of the media that day, but it was something the team saw often.

"Does he want to win or does he hate to lose? He genuinely hates to lose," Nori said. "But the difference between him and most is he can have a more impactful outcome to winning."

Nori, who's been in the NBA over two decades, said he has only coached two players—Edwards and Vince Carter—who could make a team feel like "as long as they are healthy and as long as they're on your team, you'll be playing basketball when the regular season ends."

Edwards vowed to the team that the Wolves wouldn't get swept in Game 4, and with another 34-point performance, he backed that up. The Wolves won in overtime to send the series back to Denver for Game 5 with the Wolves down not only Reid and McDaniels, but also Anderson, who suffered an eye injury in Game 4.

Even with that attrition, the Wolves were an Edwards three from sending Game 5 to overtime, but his final shot clanged iron. Edwards sprinted off the floor and threw a chair as he went down the tunnel, which drew a fine from the league. Denver won 112–109 and went on to win the NBA Championship.

It didn't matter that the Wolves were playing the No. 1 seed Nuggets and down three significant rotation players. Edwards wanted and expected to win.

"I can remember him just repeating, 'We're not getting swept. That's not happening. We're gonna come back and win,'" Conley said. "He still had all the confidence, like we figured them out. That kind of mindset, which is contagious."

The way the Wolves hung tough with Denver in that series set the tone in the playoffs the following season. If they could get Reid, McDaniels, and Anderson on the floor—and Edwards would keep ascending—they liked their chances of matching up with Denver. A big part of that was how Edwards responded in that series. To Alexander-Walker, Edwards never flinched, no matter the odds.

"Up close and personal in a situation like that, it showed, for a guy his age, his mindset when it comes to, quote, unquote, 'pressure,'" Alexander-Walker said. "I could truly feel he was someone who does not feel pressure because he doesn't believe in the dynamic of what pressure is."

Even though that first Denver series hardly registered across the league, Connelly called it a "watershed moment" for Edwards. Connelly and his front office had come into the season thinking Edwards had the intangibles to rise to the moment in postseason. The Denver series, as short as it was, was still more evidence that Edwards was the kind of player who wouldn't be stuck in the first round for long.

"We were super banged up," Connelly said. "So the burden was monstrous on his shoulders . . . and he ran to it. He didn't run away from it."

CHAPTER 10

HEAD OF THE SNAKE

Even though the 2022–23 season didn't go at all like the Wolves wanted, Connelly and Finch both felt confident that the Gobert-Towns combination could work moving forward. The team wasn't about to make any drastic moves and was going to run it back. This was in line with how Connelly ran Denver, where he rebuffed calls to reshape the roster in favor of letting a core of players gel together. That played a large role in Denver winning the championship that season, even if Connelly was in Minnesota at the time. Running it back with Towns and Gobert was not an obvious call, but one Connelly made in the face of pressure to punt on the experiment. One of the most obvious decisions he's ever made as a basketball executive was to hand Edwards a maximum contract offer that July for five years and up to $244 million. Edwards had made $44 million on his rookie deal, but this kind of money put him on another level. It represented generational wealth for his family, a promise fulfilled, millions of times over, to make it out of Oakland City and take care of those around him.

It also meant he could branch off into new endeavors like funding an entertainment company called Three-Fifths Media. This was one reason Edwards switched agencies that summer from Klutch to WME and NBA superagent Bill Duffy. Edwards also began a charitable foundation with a focus on helping kids.

Edwards celebrated signing the lucrative deal by playing twenty-dollars-per-hand blackjack while the team was at Summer League in Las Vegas. Kyle Theige, a lifelong Wolves fan turned podcaster, was at the table with Edwards and said Edwards kept referring to the dealer, whose name was Victor, as "Wemby," after incoming San Antonio center Victor Wembanyama.

There was something else that was on Edwards's mind as he was working out with Kierre Jordan that summer. Edwards had told Hines a few years before that he wanted to be the best two-guard of all time. But headed into his fourth year, he wasn't considered the best two-guard in the league. It annoyed Edwards to see a name who was ahead of him on that list: Phoenix's Devin Booker.

"'I'mma show motherfuckers he not the best two-guard in the league,'" Kierre said Edwards told him. "Every time I play him I shut him down. So, he was like, watch, Ki, watch. When they played Phoenix [in the playoffs], I knew. Just because of that conversation in the gym. No cameras. Nobody to really hear it like that but me, him, Nick."

Booker is four years older than Edwards and had a finals appearance on his resume. That gap didn't matter to Edwards.

In order to become the best two-guard in the league, Edwards had constantly tweaked his shot since his rookie year. Looking back, there's a noticeable difference in his release. By year four, a lot of the extra movement was gone. He also had a cleaner release from his waist to above his forehead, his shot "pocket," even if that's something Hines has to tell him to maintain over the course of a game. If Hines says "pocket" to Edwards in a game, Edwards knows his release is meandering. If Hines yells "box" it means for Edwards to stay within a certain "box" when he jumps and lands. If he is landing to the right or left from where he should be, he is off balance. "Base" means Edwards needs to generate more power in his legs, while "elbow over eyebrow" means to watch how he follows through on the shot. Don't bring the ball back over his head. Keep it in front.

Hines and Jordan had also been working over the years on Edwards's post-up game for a few summers. Jordan laughed when thinking back to a time when Finch came through Atlanta and saw them working on that.

"Finch was like, he's not gonna be doing this," Jordan said. "Finch said, 'I wanna see him moving off the ball relocating, coming out of the corners.' So Ant was like, 'All right, like, we're going to do this right now because that's what he wants. But then we're also going to do this [the post-up game] because I know that I'm gonna need it.'"

That's a microcosm of how Edwards attacked his offseasons. Those workouts tend to be a mix of what the team wants and what he thinks he needs for his game, hence his insistence on developing his midrange jumpers and a post-up game despite hesitancy from the team. Jordan and Edwards will do separate workouts that are team-focused on what the Wolves want and other ones for what Edwards wants. Edwards also mixes in strength and agility workouts throughout his offseason plans, which can bring his total number of workouts per day to four. Edwards often credited members of the Wolves strength and conditioning staff like Javair Gillett and David Hines for pushing him each season.

In those post-up workouts, Jordan incorporated some of the work he did with the Pelicans' Brandon Ingram. He instructed Edwards to give his defender a bump as a way to create separation. This showed in a playoff game later that season when Edwards used the bump to create space against Kentavious Caldwell-Pope and knock down some jumpers late in a Game 1 win against the Nuggets.

As Edwards entered year four, his habits were where the team wanted him. Rest, diet, taking care of his body, all these things were much better than they had been previously. It also helped Edwards that he spent part of his offseason playing for Team USA in the FIBA World Cup. There, head coach Steve Kerr had designs on Edwards being a bench player as he mixed in with the likes of Tyrese Haliburton, Mikal Bridges, Ingram, and Jalen Brunson. That lasted all of one scrimmage. Kerr imagined Edwards being like Dwyane Wade on the 2008 Olympic team when Wade sat behind Kobe Bryant. Edwards told Kerr: "We don't have a Kobe."

Edwards was in the starting lineup and was the best player for Team USA that summer, even as the team underwhelmed with a fourth-place finish. Edwards's performance lit up an otherwise slow time of the basketball content calendar. All of a sudden, outlets like the Athletic were posing questions wondering if Edwards was going to be too big for Minnesota eventually (Edwards's former teammate Beverley had said on a podcast Edwards would leave down the line). That USA experience was foreshadowing for Edwards's bigger place in the league. Whereas Kerr might have thought Edwards was more on equal footing with a lot of Team USA members that summer, he was about to zoom past most of them on the NBA pecking order. All the little things the team wanted Edwards to focus on were locking in place. The questions for the Wolves in Edwards's fourth season were more with how the team would do as a whole. Nobody had superhigh expectations for the Wolves.

The Wolves came into training camp with an emphasis on maximizing their defensive abilities. They had an all-time defensive player in Gobert, one of the league's best perimeter defenders in McDaniels, and a weapon in Edwards, who was also an excellent on-ball defender. If the Wolves were going to win, they would do it with defense.

The offense? That was still a work in progress. Finch came into training camp still trying to figure out how best to make the combination of Edwards and Towns work with Gobert. The trade, which required Towns to move to the four, and Towns's injuries had fizzled the chemistry Edwards and Towns once had in Edwards's first two seasons.

"There was just this natural collateral damage to that," Finch said of Towns and Edwards. "We worked to rebuild that and get those guys to recapture some of those things they did so well early in their career."

This was also the offseason when the chatter of "Whose team was it? KAT or Ant's?" grew louder in the narrative-driven NBA consciousness. Both played it off as nonsense and said none of that could affect their relationship. When both were playing in the World Cup (Towns with the Dominican Republic), they hung out a lot in the Philippines, Holland said.

"They spent so much time together," Holland said. "Even when the 'trade KAT' rumors started coming, Ant was like, 'No, we need to work together. I need KAT to help space the floor. I help KAT, KAT helps me.' They made an intentional effort to get together and try to figure things out that summer."

The Wolves were staring at a steep financial cliff the following season when Edwards and McDaniels would be on new contracts. Were Towns's days with the Wolves numbered as the more movable of the two max contracts between him and Gobert?

Connelly stuck to mostly the same roster as what ended the previous season. The Wolves had interest in guard Donte DiVincenzo in free agency, but DiVincenzo opted to sign with the Knicks.

That summer before Edwards's fourth season, Towns and Edwards wanted to get on the same page, to figure out how best to rekindle that chemistry. One thing Towns said he and Edwards discussed during that visit to the Philippines was just how much Towns was sacrificing, given Towns was playing the four position and ceding shot volume to Edwards. Edwards could see what Towns was like when he was the focal point of a team the way he was with the Dominican Republic in that World Cup.

"We were laughing and having a good time, and I told him, 'Now you see how much I sacrificed so that we both could look great,'" Towns said.

They grew close enough that Towns joked that Edwards knew whatever security codes he needed to come by his house when he wanted. It didn't matter when or what Towns was up to; Edwards might drop in anytime. Edwards might be playing cards with friends, shooting pool, shooting some hoops on Towns's court, all with Towns in another part of the house.

"He knew how to use the app if he needed to get in there," Towns said. "He could be there all night. There's been times he's been at the house and me and [Towns's girlfriend] Jordyn [Woods] are upstairs watching a movie, and we fall asleep on the couch, and he has free rein to stay or leave as he pleases."

Said Maddox: "Man, we'd spend so many nights at KAT's house just chillin'. . . . That cohesiveness they had throughout this run was a giant step in the right direction."

To Towns, Edwards was a brother that he never had. The feeling was mutual.

Edwards could sense Towns's authenticity in wanting to help him. As a result, there was always a good relationship between the two, and they'll always have the 2023–24 season.

Blitz at Your Own Risk

The Wolves opened 1–2 but went on a seven-game win streak that set the tone for the rest of their season. They blew out Denver at home 110–89, and in one of their most exciting games of that year, they beat eventual champion Boston 114–109 in overtime with Edwards and McDaniels playing tough defense Jayson Tatum and Jaylen Brown late in the game. At the end of that win streak, the Wolves won a pair of games in Golden State, the second of which featured McDaniels and Klay Thompson getting into a tussle that escalated to Draymond Green putting Gobert in a headlock.

Through the first quarter of the season, the Wolves had the No. 1 defensive rating in the league and they wouldn't move from that spot the rest of the season. All the benefits of the Gobert trade were locking into place. Conley was a better fit to run the offense with Gobert than Russell was. The Wolves had a year of figuring out how best to play around Gobert on both ends of the floor, and it showed. They were on a string defensively as they asked Gobert to step out of his comfort zone a bit and guard more along the perimeter. Gobert had fewer fumbles of passes on the other end. Towns was his efficient self, and his numbers (21.8 points per game while shooting 50 percent from the field, 41 percent from three-point range, and 87 percent from the free-throw line) nearly had him in the coveted 50/40/90 territory that only a few players have reached in league history.

This earned KAT his fourth All-Star Game appearance and the Wolves contended for the top seed in the league all season with Oklahoma City and Denver. In spite of the heavy criticism the trade received the previous year, it was finally having the effects the Wolves thought they would see. Edwards joined Towns on the All-Star team, as did

Finch, who earned Western Conference coaching honors. That weekend in Indianapolis was a special one for all involved. Finch has a picture on his desk of him, Towns, and Edwards with the rest of the team's coaching staff from that weekend. Towns and Edwards both signed the picture.

Edwards's ascent continued. He was getting to the free-throw line more than he ever had (6.4 attempts per game), getting more assists (5.1 per game), and averaged a career high 25.9 points per game. He was also reading defenses and processing the right plays at a higher rate than the previous season. One of the most noticeable differences was Edwards giving the ball up when teams would double-team or blitz him.

"We knew that was a problem from the season before," Anderson said. "However, within a few games, he really started to dial into watching himself [on film] not get off the ball, taking accountability and looking in the mirror and making it a point to go out there and get his teammates involved."

Anderson pointed to Edwards's increase in assists as evidence of that, and Edwards also put up a lot of "hockey assists" where a pass he made led to another pass that created an open shot.

"Guys weren't making shots at the start of it, but he stuck with it and trusted his teammates, and that's a credit to him," Anderson said.

Even as Edwards continued to expand his skills, Finch kept reminding him not to abandon his "superpower," even as he said the offensive puzzle with Towns and Gobert was more "complex" for Edwards and Finch to solve.

"He has a ton of game, and he works hard on adding things to his game and wanting to show all those things," Finch said. "But sometimes he'll forget—his superpower is getting to the hoop and spot threes and drawing fouls and that kind of stuff."

As always, Finch would not hold back in his blunt assessment of Edwards's game on a night-in, night-out basis in film sessions.

"If you want all the responsibility it comes with all the consequences, you know, and they're not always good," Finch said. "So you're going to take all the shots and you want the ball in your hands, and you're going to end up on tape a lot. That's just the reality."

Even as Finch was there to remind Edwards where he could still be better, he said Edwards had made significant growth in the consistency of his effort each game. Finch has a "rule of threes" when it comes to evaluating players—as in, how often out of every three games will you get a player's maximum effort and peak performance? Prior to that season, Edwards was hitting that two out of three games. By season four, he was on a three-of-three level.

"He might have a bad shooting night, or let's say a bad scoring night, but you knew what you would get in terms of approach, energy, game plan, execution," Finch said. "Every three you were getting three good games. . . . And it was high-level stuff. Then there's just these transcendent moments where you're just like, wow, what did we just watch?"

No stretch of Edwards's regular season encapsulated that wow factor more than a road trip the Wolves had shortly after Towns went down because of a meniscus tear in his left knee. After Towns suffered the injury on March 4 against Portland, the Wolves embarked on a six-game trip that began in Indiana.

Early in that game, the Wolves season looked like it was headed for disaster. Towns was already out, then Edwards had to leave the game twice in the first half because of apparent injuries. But this is the same Edwards who often made like he was injured so he could get out of running in Vikings practices. He typically makes injuries seem catastrophic—only to emerge a few minutes later seemingly fine. His teammates came to expect this, and it happened twice in this game against Indiana, once after Edwards stepped on guard Aaron Nesmith's foot and appeared to roll his ankle. The second time he exited after a hard fall.

"If he's not being dragged off the court, he's probably coming back," McLaughlin said. "Maybe it happened three or four times and after that, he'd go to the locker room and everybody will look at each other and be like, 'Oh, he'll be back.'"

Edwards had 44 points, and he had a chance with the second of two free throws to put the Wolves up three with 7.2 seconds to play. He missed, and Indiana opted not to call a time-out. Nesmith went down the floor, as did Edwards, who leapt over McDaniels and blocked the shot as time expired. Edwards leapt so high—and used McDaniels to propel himself up even more—that his head hit the rim.

"I ain't never jumped that high in my life," Edwards told the post-game broadcast.

He would get pretty high on the final game of the road trip in Utah as well. In the third quarter, guard Nickeil Alexander-Walker poked the ball away from Keyonte George and Edwards gathered it. Edwards passed it upcourt to Alexander-Walker, who dribbled to the right wing. Edwards raced down the floor and got the ball back. In his way was forward John Collins. Edwards leapt from a step inside the foul line, and he just made it to the rim. He threw the ball through the hoop with such force, he whacked Collins in the head on the way up and Collins had to be checked for a concussion. Edwards hit his hand on the rim and dislocated a finger. He ran back to the locker room as the crowd and his teammates tried to process what they had seen.

The Wolves' locker room was beside itself afterward, and their re-action mimicked that of social media, with Edwards eventually winning Dunk of the Year in an NBA fan vote. He would also win Block of the Year for that moment in Indiana. All his teammates were talking about it, and everybody was saying where they were when it happened. What their angle was and what their reaction was. Alexander-Walker boasted that he can tell his kids and grandkids that it was his assist.

"I don't think people understand what they just saw," Alexander-Walker said. "That was probably the craziest thing I've ever witnessed, by far."

Anderson was asking everyone if they had ever seen a dead body. McDaniels couldn't believe any of it, while Conley, who never received a technical in his career, said he nearly came off the bench.

"When you see him jump, a lot of people don't continue to go higher. They don't continue to go forward," Conley said. "He's like a cat—he keeps going forward, lands on his feet."

Edwards had taken his game to new heights in Towns's absence, and he kept the Wolves from sliding down the standings while Towns recovered in time for the end of the regular season. He put the Wolves on his back and they were in the race for the No. 1 seed until the final day, when their third lopsided loss of the season to Phoenix put them in the No. 3 slot. By coincidence, the win put Phoenix in the No. 6 seed. So the Wolves entered the playoffs in a weird place—with an opponent that had owned them during the regular season.

For Edwards, it was a matchup against Durant and Booker, the player he wanted to replicate and the one he wanted to replace.

Victory, at Last

The Wolves were ahead 76–68 near the end of the third quarter in Game 1 when Edwards made his declaration that this playoff was going to be different.

Ant began by hitting a one-handed runner on Booker in the lane, made a fadeaway from the left elbow, faked out Durant for a midrange jumper, and then launched a three over Durant for a 16-point Wolves lead. The crowd, which included Minnesota Vikings receiver Justin Jefferson, was in a frenzy.

After hitting the three, he immediately started talking crap to Durant. Durant, who had been having a great game of his own (31 points), couldn't help but smile and laugh. As Edwards said after the game, it was one of the "best feelings" of his life to experience that against his favorite player growing up. It was special for Durant too.

"That matchup just trumped all of the implications of the game that day. It was just all about the purity of basketball at that point," Durant said during an interview in October 2024. "I think a lot of people on TV seen that, and in my smile, his enthusiasm. That's truly what it's about.

"Obviously we want to compete every day and try to win championships, be the best we can be, but when you guys share that moment, the competition, love for the game together like that, I thought it was cool."

That moment launched a solid month-plus of Edwards being everywhere on social media. The Instagram accounts for ESPN and Bleacher Report couldn't pump out enough Edwards highlights on the court or press conference quips off it, like when Edwards did a DX taunt at the end of Game 3 or told Towns to "stop fucking fouling" when the Wolves won Game 4. Towns, who was seated next to Edwards, told him, "You right."

There are times Towns may exaggerate a bit when he steps in front of a microphone, and social media likes to get laughs over something Towns says or the way he says it. Edwards never cared, and he would laugh off things Towns said that sounded outlandish. Yes, he might get annoyed with Towns sometimes, like any other teammate.

But he was also Towns's biggest supporter. He said at media day before that season that Towns could win the MVP Award. As with his teammates of all levels, Towns was Edwards's guy. That was his teammate, and he sensed Towns had his best interests at heart. Towns knew what that looked like when another star didn't.

The age difference between Towns and Butler is roughly the age difference between him and Edwards. Towns said his previous experiences shaped how he wanted his relationship with Edwards to be. He wanted to be the friend and support system he wished he had at different points in his career.

"I think Ant, in his eyes, he saw the things I told him, how I was going to protect him and respect him and I was always going to be by his side for everything and anything that could go wrong," Towns said. "I showed him time and time again I would do it and that garners trust. We had a tremendous amount of trust in each other. . . . The man I see now, I couldn't be prouder because I know what it took to get there. I never wanted him to not be himself."

He added: "I'm never going to be here to say I was the one that gave him the blueprint. But all I did was just help him hold the paper and see the blueprint."

Anderson said Edwards was one of the best teammates and people he has been around in the NBA. If there was one thing he wanted to communicate about being Edwards's teammate, it was how welcoming and energetic he was toward everyone on the team. He would always invite people out to dinner or to hang. He didn't want anybody to feel left out.

"He's tight with everybody on the team. He doesn't like outcasts,"

Anderson said. "If you're on the team, you're his guy, and he makes you feel like it."

Alexander-Walker said Edwards's "young spirit" shines through in how he approaches his days in the Wolves' practice facility, whether he's working out, competing against teammates, or just hanging around the building.

"He's lighthearted. Even when he's working out he might take his approach seriously, but he's not upset," Alexander-Walker said. "He has this genuine kindhearted spirit to him. He can be intense where he's passionate and cussing you out, but he can also be passionate in hyping you up."

For instance, during one memorable exchange within earshot of reporters the previous season, Edwards told Alexander-Walker he had "gorilla nuts" for the job he was doing defensively for the Wolves that postseason. So Edwards could tell Towns to "stop fucking fouling" and Towns would accept it without feeling like there was any animosity on Edwards's part because Edwards would also hype him up a lot more frequently. When Towns didn't get in foul trouble, good things happened for the Wolves.

By the end of April, the NBA communications staff announced that Edwards had generated more than 100 million video views across NBA social and digital platforms since the start of the playoffs. That trailed only LeBron James. One of the clips that went viral was an interview Edwards gave the previous season when someone asked him about the Suns acquiring Durant. Edwards's response of "They got KD, but we got Jaden McDaniels" was very him. He'll never miss an opportunity to hype up his teammates, especially McDaniels. Casual NBA fans may not know McDaniels's name, but he was an unsung hero in the Wolves' resurgence. Edwards, Towns, and Gobert attracted a lot of the attention and accolades, while McDaniels had to settle for second All-Defense that season. But the Wolves don't make it as far as they did that season without his contributions and sacrifices. He didn't publicly complain when he might only get a handful of shots. Meanwhile, he was always willing to guard the other team's best perimeter scorer. Game 2 was one of his best in a Wolves uniform because not only did he provide his usual stringent defense, but he scored a team-high 25 points on 10-for-17 shooting in a 12-point Wolves win.

The Wolves had Phoenix figured out. They put Towns on Durant one-on-one for stretches and lived with Durant taking long twos over him if he wanted. They wanted to limit Booker and Bradley Beal, who had an up-and-down series thanks to the defense of McDaniels, Edwards, and Alexander-Walker. At times the Wolves would bench Towns and play a smaller lineup with those three matching up on Booker, Beal, and Durant. It worked.

When Edwards was at home, Maddox said Edwards was still locked in on the matchup, and Maddox was in his ears reminding Edwards of the scouting report and what Edwards had to do in his individual defensive matchups.

"I'm paying attention and I'm asking questions just in case," Maddox said. "I gotta remember and keep on him for everything. . . . 'Cause you know, hey, listen, man, I'm tryin' to get me some gold too. I'm tryin' to put on that ring."

On offense, a lot of what the Wolves had been preaching to Edwards about getting off the ball when teams would double him finally stuck. He was making the right decisions, trusting his teammates and trusting that the ball would get back to him.

No sequence encapsulated that better than the one that gave the Wolves a 113–109 lead late in Game 4. Edwards had the ball on the right wing with Beal on him, and Royce O'Neale came to double-team him. Instead of fighting it, Edwards made a simple pass to Conley at the top of the key. He passed to Towns on the left wing, and then Towns hit an open McDaniels in the left corner. O'Neale was late recovering, and McDaniels buried the three. Edwards put the exclamation mark on the series moments later with a soaring dunk over Durant, who just wanted to get out of the way and not suffer the same fate as Collins in Utah. Edwards had 40 points in the clincher.

Late in that game, Conley collided with Finch during a sequence near the Wolves sideline. Finch had to leave the game after suffering a ruptured right patellar tendon. Nori finished out the game on the

Wolves bench. After that frantic ending, Durant heaped praise on Edwards.

"So impressed with Ant," Durant said. "My favorite player to watch. Just grown so much since he came into the league. . . . Love everything about Ant. Everything."

After a lot of people had left the arena, Edwards remained in the back hallway sharing a moment with Holland and Banks. They stayed in the arena for a while, seemingly just talking. As they did, Finch came rolling by on a cart. Everybody smiled, even Finch, amid all the pain (and possibly painkillers) that were in his body at that moment. They exchanged a few words and the cart whisked Finch away. Edwards, dressed as usual in a white T-shirt tank top with a hoodie on his shoulder, stayed in the hallway with Banks and Holland for a while as Netflix cameras caught the interaction. Car rides to and from school in Atlanta traffic, late-night and early-morning workouts, a prolonged and excruciating draft process, and two playoff disappointments had finally led here, Edwards's first playoff series victory.

"I couldn't believe what I was witnessing," Banks said of that moment. "I know Ant was a bad MFer since he was five years old when it came to sports, and seeing it play out with him twenty-two, I knew he was one of the best players on the planet."

Now a rematch with Denver awaited.

The Rematch

For most of his life, Edwards had been a reluctant leader. There was something about using his voice in that manner that came off as inauthentic, and authenticity is one of Edwards's superpowers. He is himself, at all times, no matter the circumstances. He'll show up to a Netflix movie premiere in sweatpants and a hoodie, his preferred sartorial choices. He'll curse in interviews without hesitation, despite the league fining him hundreds of thousands of dollars for doing so. He'll trash-talk. His realness is one of the things that draws people to him.

Beginning in his third season, Edwards began finding his voice gradually. The Russell trade had unlocked part of it. Towns going out another, and Conley coming in helped it too. Everyone on the team noticed it.

Overall, the Wolves culture under Finch was one of "hard truths," as Conley put it, no matter who was speaking to whom. Edwards found his voice within this space. When he has something to say to a teammate, it's usually delivered with a dose of humor.

"It's almost borderline where he's always funny and making jokes to where that joke has that truth in it," Conley said. "It's like, 'Oh, that is funny, but damn, you're right. Like, I was getting torched one-on-one, and I'm supposed to be the best at this.' I think it's accepted well because of his overall demeanor."

Finch said there are times he and Edwards will discuss what the team needs to be doing better at a given moment in the season, and he will encourage Edwards to say that in front of the team.

"Don't worry about how it goes. I got your back," Finch would tell him. "The team needs to hear you say that. So it was like these little platforms that he can stand on safely. He figured those out a bit. Now he does it without as much prompting."

To Anderson, Edwards's natural charisma makes what he has to say go down easy for everyone. As Edwards discovered that his teammates were receiving his messages, they empowered him to say what was on his mind.

"I don't think he knew it at first, but people gravitate to what he says," Anderson said. "There's only so much me and Mike Conley can say. But when the head of the snake is getting on you, then you're gonna respect it."

Edwards would use his voice in a key moment in the team's series against Denver. The Wolves surprised almost everyone in taking the first two games of the series on the road. Game 1 for Edwards was a master class—43 points on 17-for-29 shooting. He hit a number of key jumpers down the stretch as his fellow Georgia alum Kentavious Caldwell-Pope tried in vain to make his life difficult. That post-up game

Edwards wanted so bad? He put it on full display against Caldwell-Pope late when he hit a few clinching buckets.

In Game 2, Gobert was out for the birth of his child, so it was a bit ironic that without the Defensive Player of the Year, the Wolves turned in one of the most dominant defensive performances in recent post-season history. They swarmed and frustrated Denver to the point that Murray threw a heating pad onto the court during play. The Wolves won 106–80, but another sweep wasn't inevitable. Denver figured some things out; they alleviated some of the pressure on Murray and blitzed the heck out of Edwards. They won the next three games of the series to set up a Game 6 in Minnesota.

During the series, Nori was coaching on the sideline while Finch was behind the bench offering his input as he could. This changed the dynamic between Edwards, his teammates, and Finch for the series. Typically during time-outs, the coaches will huddle near the free-throw line while the players have time to catch their breaths and talk to each other. Finch could now be a part of that conversation with them during that portion of the time-outs. Finch's spot also allowed him to zero in on what Edwards was doing and communicate with him when he was out of the game.

"Finchy wasn't up on the sidelines and having to always think, just like he does as a head coach," Nori said. "He had more time to talk to Ant when Ant was sitting out."

With a chuckle, Nori added: "That could be a good thing and a bad thing."

Edwards wanted to make Nori's life as easy as possible as he took over the sideline coaching duties in game.

"He said, literally, in the first quarter [Game 1], 'Micah, don't worry about calling shit for me,'" Nori said. "'I will find a way to get mine and then we'll work our way back to me,' which goes to his leadership."

His confidence never wavered, even as the version of the Wolves that had taken the floors in Games 1 and 2 seemed to vanish. Denver had solved Minnesota's swarming defense in part by having other players besides Murray bring the ball up to initiate the offense. But Finch had a saying he kept repeating throughout the series: "Our best is better than their best." Edwards's focus remained lasered in, Maddox said. Back in Minnesota, Maddox said there was a mood of quiet confidence in Edwards's house.

"I'm getting goose bumps right now," Maddox said. "He didn't really say too much. We got a saying from one of Bubba's songs, 'Ain't got to say too much, because you already know how it's gonna go.'"

Game 6 wasn't close outside of the first few minutes. The Wolves had their energy back, and they put on another defensive clinic in a 115–70 mauling of the Nuggets to set up Game 7 back in Denver. After the Game 5 loss, Edwards was finishing getting dressed while chatting with some of the locker room attendants from the Nuggets. Before he left, he told them, "We'll see y'all motherfuckers for Game Seven," a quote he repeated verbatim in a press conference after the Wolves won Game 6.

Edwards was in full Atlanta mode in that moment. No bullshit, all confidence, no filter.

"Hell yeah, they know, y'all was in there," Edwards said, pointing toward some of the media. "I said I'll see y'all motherfuckers for Game Seven."

With that deadpan delivery, Edwards nodded his head and gave a little "yeah" into the microphone as the room erupted in laughter. A Wolves public relations representative said, "Thanks, Ant," to end the session after the MF bomb.

The Wolves were on to Game 7.

The series featured a lopsided result in either direction in most of the games. It was a dramatic series, but the actual games themselves didn't hold much tension.

Maddox and the Edwards crew boarded their flights for Game 7 back in Denver. Holland sat courtside while others sat up in the lower bowl with hundreds of Wolves fans who made the trip—and made their presence known in Ball Arena that night.

"I just felt chills getting off the plane," Maddox said. "I like this feeling of everybody against us. I'm walking proud through the airport with my AE gear on. Letting them know. I want somebody to say something to me."

Well, there was somebody saying something throughout the game: a gray-haired fan seated near Holland courtside who was trash-talking Wolves players every chance he got—and he had opportunities to let it fly early in the game. The first half could not have gone much worse for the Wolves. Denver raced out to a double-digit lead, and a series that had featured all these blowouts looked like it was headed for another one.

Edwards struggled in the face of constant attention from the Denver defense. He was 1-for-7 for 4 points at halftime. The Wolves weren't down more than 53–38 at the half because of McDaniels and Towns. McDaniels had 10 points while Game 7 was perhaps Towns's greatest in a Wolves uniform. He had 13 points on 5-for-6 shooting in the first half to keep the Wolves in it. Murray had 24 for Denver.

What happened next in the Wolves' locker room was a moment years in the making for Edwards. He had always been a positive teammate, never one to bring the energy or mood down, but he had been reluctant to use his voice in moments that called for leadership. He would defer to veterans like Conley or Anderson. In this moment, the Wolves needed as much positivity as they could muster.

Where You At?

Edwards didn't wait for anyone else to speak. He was the first one to address a frustrated locker room. This had rarely happened before.

"You can see what he's shaping up to be," Reid said. "He came out and gave the speech himself and just told us, 'I don't want to go home. I know you don't either. I got a lot more basketball in me.' In that moment you could see the transition he was making in the kind of player he's going to be in the years to come."

It wasn't a rah-rah moment like some grand or epic speech that a Hollywood scriptwriter might try to re-create for an Oscar one day. It was a direct and short message, very much to the point. It was uplifting and didn't reflect on all the bad that had happened, but rather on what was still in front of the Wolves. It created a "domino effect" in the room, Reid said.

"Kyle, Rudy, KAT, so on, everybody [spoke up]," Reid said. "But it's just like, as one of the youngest in the room, for him to be able to speak up, understand the situation, what could be at stake, it was huge."

From a basketball standpoint, Edwards's message was for the Wolves to lock down defensively, that he would take care of the offense, Anderson said.

"He came in the locker room and let us know the game's not over," Anderson said. "In that situation, as one of the other players, you can hear me and Mike Conley say it and it's very cliché. But once you hear Ant's voice having faith in us, still having a chance to win, it brings a spark. It does something to you."

Finch came in and matter-of-factly showed the Wolves what they needed to do better without much emotion.

"He wasn't really mad today," Edwards said after the game. "It was more like, 'I know we going to win this game, we've just got to do this to win the game.'"

This was the formula in the halftime locker room for the largest Game 7 comeback in NBA history.

Denver grew its lead to 20 early in the third but then it almost seemed inevitable that the Wolves were going to win. The team heeded Edwards's advice at the defensive end of the floor. The Wolves turned Jokic into a scorer, and he had 21 points in the second half. But they clamped down on everyone else and took away Jokic's true superpower, his ability to set up teammates. He had just 2 assists.

The Wolves held Denver to just 26 percent shooting in the third and Edwards did a commendable job setting up his teammates that quarter. He hit McDaniels for a pair of open threes, and he got off another double team that set up a Conley three. The Wolves had cut Denver's lead to one entering the fourth quarter.

Edwards continued seeing double teams, and he continued passing out of them. That led to big nights for McDaniels (23 points) and

Towns (23 points) and a big fourth quarter for Reid, who had 11. With the Wolves up 7 late, they were in transition after a Conley steal, and Reid decided to hit an open Edwards in the right corner with a pass. Edwards took his time, dribbled behind the three-point line, and buried it for a 10-point Wolves lead with 3:05 to play. Denver called time-out and Edwards turned around and celebrated with Holland, who was right behind where he shot it.

Then Atlanta came out, and Edwards pointed to the gray-haired fan seated near Holland and appeared to yell, "Where you at? Huh? Where you at?" among other things.

"[That fan] was talking shit to everybody walking into the gym, the whole thing," Holland said. "Ant didn't say anything to him the whole game until that moment. He deserved every bit of whatever he told him."

The Wolves won 98–90 and advanced to the Western Conference Finals for just the second time in franchise history. Edwards typified the example of Finch's "three out of three" philosophy on a night when he wasn't scoring at a high clip. Edwards finished with 16 points on 6-for-24 shooting, but he made his presence known in every other area. There was his energy, his leadership, and his defense (2 steals). The scoring wasn't there, but he didn't let it affect his overall game, and he had a positive impact on the outcome.

"That is, like, the collection of a great player," Finch said in his own coaching vernacular.

After the game, Edwards and Towns had another dual press conference and shared some laughs over Gobert hitting an improbable fade-away jumper in the fourth quarter. Think of how far they had come from when they did a press conference in Miami in Edwards's rookie year, and Edwards stuck up for Towns after his confrontation with Butler. They seemed like they were auditioning for a buddy comedy after a reporter asked them if they felt like they had lost enough and earned enough play-off battle scars to make a deep run.

Towns: "We lost last year."

Edwards: "We lost the last two years. Goddamn, how many times we got to lose? How much you want us to lose?"

Towns: "We've been losing for twenty years!"

Edwards: "That's just the truth, dog."

Then Edwards had some high praise for Finch.

"It starts with our head coach, Coach Finch," Edwards said. "He's just a great coach. And he don't sugarcoat anything. . . . He going to get on anybody that's messing up throughout the game, and I think that's what makes him the best coach in the NBA, to me. Because, no matter who it is, no matter how high up on the pole, he's going to get on you from start to finish. And it starts with the head of the snake, and he's the head of our snake."

From one head of the snake to another.

Having just beat the defending champs, the Wolves felt like they had punched their ticket to the finals and were riding high headed into a matchup against the Mavericks. It was a series they felt like they should win. On TNT, Edwards told Charles Barkley of *Inside the NBA* to "bring ya ass" to Minnesota, and the city ran wild with that new slogan. Even Governor Tim Walz released a proclamation in honor of the Wolves with each sentence of the proclamation spelling out "Bring ya ass."

But everyone got humbled quickly.

Goodbyes

The first two games of the series were in Minnesota, and the Wolves felt like their defense was well equipped to handle Luka Doncic and Kyrie Irving. What they underestimated, though, was Dallas's defensive ability to cause them fits.

Edwards had spent the first two series playing mostly the same way. Constant doubles and big men who defended along the perimeter. He got into a rhythm this way. Dallas defended him differently. They played largely a drop coverage scheme with their big men, where they'd retreat to the paint on screen and rolls. Then they filled the gaps with other defenders. Edwards had 11 assists in Game 1, but he and Towns combined to shoot 12-for-36, and the Wolves lost a winnable game 108–105. Nori said the change in defensive scheme had an impact on how Edwards processed that series.

"He was so used to bigs being up, like in the other series, and people literally trying to get the ball out of his hand all the time," Nori said. "And so when you play in the drop, it's more of like facing a zone, like in football or something, and there's just more reads to make, and there's more things you can do, and when teams are in drop, you can always shoot the pull-up. . . . We just couldn't execute or make enough shots against it."

The drop coverage concedes open, inefficient midrange shots to opponents, and those were the shots the Wolves didn't want Edwards taking. He and Towns could never get going scoring-wise, even as the Wolves nearly won the first two games.

"We never clicked all together as a team in this series," Edwards said after the Mavericks closed it out in Game 5. "Not even one game. That was the main thing. The last two series, we was all clicking at one time, making shots and stuff. We wasn't clicking at one time."

Game 2 featured a moment of schadenfreude for Gobert's critics as Doncic knocked down the winning three over him with 3.8 seconds remaining. It didn't matter that Gobert's defense was a primary reason the Wolves were in the Western Conference Finals, or that he had acquitted himself well on the perimeter the rest of the season. This was a field day for his critics on social media and on *Inside the NBA* after the game.

The Wolves heard the criticism, and after their Game 4 win in Dallas, the Wolves refused to have someone join the postgame set of *Inside the NBA* as a way to protest how they had been speaking about Gobert on the program, according to the Athletic. That included Edwards. Gobert was his teammate, and he was always going to stand up for them. The Wolves lost three consecutive close games that they could have won, and all acknowledged after the series that the Denver matchup had taken a lot out of them physically and emotionally. Their execution late in games wasn't up to what it was in the previous two series, and that's where Edwards had grown in the last two. Edwards was also physically exhausted, and said he needed to train himself differently to tackle long playoff runs.

"I've never played this deep into a basketball season," he said. "So now I know, okay, in order for me to be dominant in the third round and if we get past this and finally go to the finals, I've got to train like I'm going to go to the playoffs. So I can't be missing training days, I can't take days off."

He would get world-class tutoring sessions on this and other topics from some of the game's best players in the Paris Olympics that summer. But when Edwards returned with a gold medal and started preparing for his fifth season, Connelly pulled the trigger on his biggest move since acquiring Gobert. The Knicks had long coveted Towns, and they kept lines of communication open on Towns's availability. There was a heavy connection between the Knicks and Creative Arts Agency (CAA), which represented Towns and multiple players on their roster. Leon Rose ran the team, and he was Towns's former agent at CAA. Josh Hart, Jalen Brunson, and OG Anunoby all were clients. To further the connections, Gersson Rosas, the man who drafted Edwards and once envisioned Towns as a foundational piece of the franchise, worked in the Knicks front office.

When Rosas wanted to pursue Russell while he was president of the Wolves, he never gave up, even after not signing him in free agency. The Knicks never gave up on their pursuit of Towns. When the Knicks made DiVincenzo, whom the Wolves had wanted to sign as a free agent, available in the trade along with Julius Randle and a protected first-round pick via Detroit, the Wolves made the move. They coveted DiVincenzo, and Randle had found success playing under Finch in New Orleans. Plus, it gave the Wolves additional flexibility in the long term to keep reshaping the team around Edwards in this NBA era of the first and second apron. Towns had four years of a supermax deal upcoming, and he will make $61 million in the final year of that deal. The Wolves had made the Gobert trade before the punitive luxury tax "aprons" that came with a new collective bargaining agreement in 2023.

With extensions coming on board for Edwards and McDaniels beginning in the 2024–25 season, the Wolves would eventually have to make some moves to avoid paying massive luxury tax bills and escape the roster-building restrictions of the second apron, like the inability to use midlevel exceptions and freezing draft picks the team could potentially trade. The most surprising thing about the Towns trade was the timing. The Wolves went almost the entire offseason with Towns on the roster and it seemed like they'd run back the previous season's team (minus Anderson, who signed with Golden State). But just before training camp in October 2024, after the Knicks lost center Isaiah Hartenstein to Oklahoma City in free agency—and they learned their other center, Mitchell Robinson, would be injured the first few months of the season—they upped their offer for Towns, and the Wolves accepted. Connelly drove to Towns's house to deliver the news personally.

"KAT's an excellent basketball player—he's a better person," Connelly said. "There's certain realities that when we made the Rudy trade, the CBA wasn't even there, right? There were new parameters that were given to us midflow, and we think that with these new restrictions, and with this much more difficult deal-making environment, depth is more important than ever."

During one of the recent offseasons—Connelly wasn't sure which one—he said he sat down with both McDaniels and Edwards together and gave them a rough sketch of their futures in the organization. Then they had a similar chat before the 2024–25 season began.

"Hey, you guys are gonna be here a long, long time, and you're gonna see different iterations of teams," Connelly said he told them. "It's going to be Rudy, KAT and you guys are young guys. The same thing [I told them] this summer [in 2024], as much as we love Mike Conley, there's going to be a day in the future where this Mike Conley–Rudy team, it's not going to be there anymore. . . . We hope they retire [here]. It's just inevitable. Ant is fourteen years younger than Mike, nine years younger than Rudy. That's just how life is, right?"

Connelly often says the idea of trading players is "gross." But that's just how life is sometimes in basketball. For four years, Towns and

Edwards were a successful pairing. A franchise that had experienced so many years in the NBA wasteland became relevant again on their watch. In his nine years in Minnesota, Towns learned a lot about the business of the NBA—from seeing coaches and front offices come and go, to experiencing his own drama with teammates. The experiences didn't make him jaded, but he knew a day like September 27, 2024, might come, when the Knicks and Wolves agreed to a trade.

"I never wanted him to have the experiences I had," Towns said of Ant. "I made damn sure that every time he could be amplified, I was going to be the one to do that and never going to destroy him for my benefit. That's not what you do."

That happens more often in the NBA than fans might know. Towns had spent four years trying to help Edwards navigate the choppy waters of NBA life, to prepare for what might come his way and prepare him for his ascent as a superstar. With the trade, he was giving Edwards one last lesson; it just came at his expense.

"I told him since day one, I'll sacrifice for his benefit," Towns said. "I definitely had came through on my word until the last day."

At media day a few days after the deal was reported, a dejected Edwards didn't feel much like discussing Towns's departure.

"I mean, I think everybody knows KAT's my brother, so that definitely hurt," Edwards said.

Towns, in speaking for this project, noted the trade carved out a "new chapter" in the career of Edwards, and that's where the Wolves were in the fall of 2024. This was a new era, and the trade was something the Wolves did only because Edwards possessed the kind of talent of a potential MVP candidate, one they had to build around and hold on to by keeping the roster around him competitive well into the future. Holland had told Edwards for a few years that he wasn't ready to make that leap to "carry a franchise." But after year four?

"I know he's ready now," Holland said. "Yeah, he's definitely ready now."

CHAPTER 11

ALWAYS MEET YOUR HEROES

In July 2024, Team USA gathered in Las Vegas for their first practices in preparation for the Paris Olympics, and each day a different set of players did postpractice media obligations on the balcony at the practice gym of the University of Nevada, Las Vegas (UNLV). Edwards was up on day two, and he offered a quote that spread through the desert air across social media almost by the time Edwards was done talking.

The question: Would there be any adjustment for Edwards going from being the No. 1 option on the Wolves to playing alongside a team full of them?

"I'm still the No. 1 option," Edwards said. "Y'all might look at it differently. I don't look at it no differently. . . . They got to fit to play around me."

His Olympic teammates saw the wide smile with which he delivered those words.

"That was the most unsurprising comment, knowing his personality," Curry said.

There was more nuance to Edwards's other answers that others didn't see.

"They mentioned some guys you might not play some games, might not play that many minutes. I don't mind. I'm playing alongside Hall of Famers," Edwards said.

Then when he was asked who the alpha on Team USA was, a question that was set up on a platter for him to say himself and create another viral moment, he turned more genuine.

"I think Kevin Durant," Edwards said. "He better be. That's who I came to see."

The Olympics can be a place where the greats of the game learn from each other—they steal routines, regimens, tricks of the trade. LeBron James famously learned from Kobe Bryant when both were on the 2008 team. All his life, others had motivated Edwards by telling him what other great players would do. He'd hear from Crean at Georgia about how Dwyane Wade worked. He'd hear from Beverley what Kawhi Leonard and James Harden did to become superstars. This was one surefire way to motivate Edwards. Now Edwards was finally going to see them for himself. He could absorb what James, Curry, and his childhood hero Durant did on a daily basis. He could pick their brains as much as he wanted.

"It's funny, because Ant has this dominant personality where he doesn't bow down to anybody," Holland said. "But he also has this childlike innocence where he's receptive to things that he knows will make a difference.

"So in one moment, it's 'I'mma bust y'all ass next year' and he's talking to KD, Steph, and Bron. Then we go to dinner and Bron and KD are like, 'Young fella, you need to do this and this.' It was a nice balance."

This was typical of the energy Edwards brought. In one breath, he'd talk about being the No. 1 option, then in the next say he'd accept a bench role or not play at all considering the company he was keeping. Just like at every stage of his basketball life, his upbeat personality added to the chemistry of the team around him. It was the same at Holy Spirit High School as it was playing for Team USA.

"We needed some youthful energy," Curry said. "Obviously, that's not just what he brings. He's a guy who was superconfident in his abilities and why he was there, but also aware of what the moment meant for everybody on that team. He spoke to it from the beginning of the first practice that I was with him. He's like, 'I used to watch all y'all growing up, now I'm here with y'all.' He was at my camp to now playing on the same Olympic team."

Maddox would work out with Edwards after those early practices in Las Vegas, and it was just as much a unique experience for him and the rest of Edwards's crew as it was for Edwards himself. Maddox became friends with some of the players, and a lot of them were on a first-name basis with him by the end of it. Holland said he was that way with James.

"I was walking through breakfast one day and Bron was like, 'What's up, Just?'" Holland said. "Like, he gave me a nickname. . . . I went in there trying to, like, study the entourages. Like, how did they all do these things?"

According to Durant, there were probably about one hundred people in the whole Team USA party through the end of the Olympics. This meant a lot of dinners and social gatherings with groups within that hundred people. This is where Holland and Maddox were able to make connections.

"Little small gatherings, just playing cards and talking shit, talking shit about the season coming up," Maddox said. "All the guys were like, we come to Minnesota, Nick, we gonna call you."

While Edwards got to play with his favorite player growing up, Maddox got to meet one of his heroes, and someone he studied to learn about how he can best support Edwards—Randy Mims, a close friend of James.

"Dream come true for me," Maddox said.

There were a lot of surreal moments throughout the experience for Edwards and his closest friends. Maddox laughed as he recalled Edwards showing him the group text of Team USA introducing itself to each other. All the players used emojis.

"LeBron starts off with a crown. KD came back something with Slim Reaper. Curry coming with chef," Maddox said.

Maddox said he and Edwards were having lunch in Miami as the texts were coming in, and there was one that didn't come in yet, from Leonard, who ended up withdrawing from Team USA after a few practices because of a knee injury.

"That's who we were missing," Maddox said. "Then he was like, 'Claw.' The hand symbol. We died laughing. Then everybody got together, it was cool. I got to really be like amongst the greatest players to ever play the game . . . and my boy, my best friend, is literally not just sitting amongst them, playing with them, but telling them like, 'I'mma bust your ass.'"

There was one player in particular that Edwards made that clear to—Booker.

"The beef of him and Devin Booker—that was interesting," Maddox said.

Said Holland: "That relationship had always been kind of sketchy. . . . But you also realize y'all cut from the same cloth. Book's a dog. You really don't know people, it's what you see on TV, but once you're around them . . ."

Edwards and Booker's relationship changed for the better.

Early in Team USA practices, Edwards and Booker went at each other hard in drills and scrimmages. Edwards and the Wolves had just eliminated Booker and the Suns from the playoffs, and now there was a potential starting two-guard spot on the line during camp. Edwards wasn't backing down, especially not against Booker. Maddox said he was watching the two of them go at it in a shooting drill and he was on the sideline thinking to himself, Just make more shots than him.

"I loved the competition in camp," coach Steve Kerr said of them. "And then I loved the way it all shook out. . . . They compete during practice, but next thing you know they're sharing dinner together, they're on a flight next to each other and they're talking about their families. The bonding is amazing to watch."

Yes, there were some heated moments during that training camp in Las Vegas, high-intensity moments during drills and scrimmages where Edwards would let Booker know, loudly, what he was up against. But then one day Maddox got a phone call from Edwards that surprised him.

"'Hey, man, we finna go to the casino with D-Book,'" Maddox said Edwards told him. "I'm thinking, Oh y'all gonna go heads up versus each other or something? 'Nah, man, we just goin' to kick it.' 'Cause listen, I was getting in full military mode. I'm putting on my black bandana, black hoodie, black pants. I'm like, I wish one of his homeboys say anything because I can't wait to talk about the playoffs. I got all the stats in my head. Anything crazy, I'm goin' in.

"But we got in there and we were all just chillin'. Him and his homeboy Ben, me, and Ant playing blackjack."

Booker spent some of his formative years in Mississippi, and there was a southern sensibility that Edwards and Booker recognized in each other that helped them bond once they actually got to spend some time together. As Booker said in an interview, "That's the beauty of the Olympics." It can turn fierce rivals into friends.

"Everybody has a chance to break bread with each other," Booker said. "Get to know each other personally. Families get to know each other and that kid has a lot of personality. Me living in the South for my high school parts of my life, and him being from Atlanta, I know the language that he speaks."

There may still be an on-court rivalry moving forward—NBA general managers voted Edwards the top two-guard in the league in their 2024 annual preseason survey after Booker was the 2023 winner—but whatever personal animosity may have existed off the court ceased.

"We gambled together. We did pretty much everything together," Booker said. "We spent a lot of time. Also, the competitive edge is still there. It's going to be there for the rest of my career. He keeps raising the bar higher and higher and it's my job to return the favor to him and keep doing it."

As Edwards said in January 2025: "Our relationship wasn't the best before [Team] USA. But we got to know each other, we both like to do the same stuff. So we got super cool and was working out together. We got cooler, but every time we see each other, we know what it is, it's time to go at it. But I got respect for him, for sure."

Booker ended up being the starting two-guard, and Kerr had Edwards come off the bench. But Edwards was more than okay taking that bench spot considering who he would also get to play with on that second unit—Durant. After the Olympics, Kerr called Booker the "unsung hero" of the team given that he thrived in what his role called for him to do. He defended, he facilitated offense, and he did the little things that propelled Team USA to a gold medal. Booker's willingness to sacrifice his own numbers for the good of the team also caught Edwards's attention.

"He was huge. He turned into the utility guy," Holland said. "That's when he really gained Ant's respect. Because he didn't give a damn about the points. He wanted to win like everybody else. They swallowed their pride, and now they're cool. They play the game together and all that."

The ultimate sign that Edwards likes someone—when he hops on to play video games with you.

"Great" Energy

As Holland said, "there was a lot of shit-talking going on" the entire Olympics between everybody. The players themselves, the players and their respective crews, but it was a language that bonded everyone.

"Circle every game on the calendar [against each player]," Holland said. "Playing against Book? Playing against KD? Circle that game. They talk so much because they're still competitive, but it's still—I'll bust your ass when I see you."

Edwards was at the forefront of it, and his personality, authenticity, and bravado only endeared him to his teammates. The "first option" comment made that clear.

"The guys loved it," Kerr said. "Part of his appeal is his confidence and the way he approaches life—the joy, the smile, the laughter. You kind of take everything he says with a grain of salt anyway. I think the guys look at it that way. 'All right, young guy, he's coming in and he wants to be the man.' They respect that, and they enjoy the banter that comes with that."

This made for a few viral moments, like when Curry brought over the women's table tennis team to Edwards on the Team USA yacht during the opening ceremonies. Curry egged on Edwards, who told the team he could at least get a point against them. Edwards then sat in the stands for some of the women's table tennis matches later in the Olympics.

After the gold medal game, Edwards gave Curry flack for his shooting slump early in the tournament before he turned in a legendary performance against France with 24 points on eight threes, including several in the final minutes.

"My boy just showed up to Paris three days ago but we so glad he got here," Edwards said on Curry's Instagram Live video.

Said Curry: "First off, he talks trash nonstop. From my camp to playing against him, to getting to know him a lot better last summer, it's a very consistent personality. He talks, he yaps, he has fun. He cracks jokes. I was having fun with it too. I was just living in the moment."

Edwards was the right amount of energy for a team that featured some quieter players, Kerr said, like Jayson Tatum, Jrue Holiday, Derrick White, and Booker.

"You don't want twelve Ants, and you don't want twelve Derrick Whites," Kerr said. "If you have twelve Derrick Whites, nobody's saying a word. If you have twelve Ants, you can't hear anybody talk. So we really had a good mix, and Ant was just a breath of fresh air every day."

Edwards fit into the culture of the team, and he'd listen and learn from Curry, James, Durant, and others as much as he'd talk trash to them. Durant would teach him about the follow-through on his shot. He watched Curry's and James's workouts before and after practices and games. He observed how James would manipulate defenses late in games.

"He knew when to get to the hole. He knew when to take a three," Edwards said after a win over Denver in November 2024. "Just learning little shit like that man, it helped me a lot."

He incorporated part of James's pregame routine into his, and he surprised Hines when he came back to the Wolves that September when he was stretching before a shooting workout.

"Ant, what the hell are you doing stretching before shooting? I've never seen you do that," Hines said.

Edwards replied: "I saw LeBron doing it."

He watched how many shots Curry took during his workouts and incorporated some of that volume into his routines. The next season, Edwards's three-point percentage took a jump from just below 36 percent to the low forties. After practice was typically when the team would share tips and information.

"Those postpractice sessions, I saw a lot of it, just imitating moves," Kerr said. "They had a lot of different games going on, whether it was one-on-one or the shooting games that they played. You can see the banter and the interaction during those games, and there was a lot of good conversation where guys shared tricks of the trade, that sort of thing."

Said Durant: "We're not looking to give advice. We're just telling our experiences, and it's a give-and-take. You never know what these guys could take from listening to these stories and experiences. It was cool to see top-level guys just be vulnerable and open like that."

Durant and Edwards took to each other immediately when camp began. Durant was nursing a calf injury before the team got to Paris, and so when the games began, Kerr opted to have Durant come off the bench with Edwards. Even as players like Tatum and Joel Embiid cycled in and out of playing time throughout the Olympics, Edwards's role and minutes stayed fairly consistent in that bench role. Kerr said Edwards's physicality was a great fit for the FIBA style of play and the way international officials call games.

"Calls that you get in the NBA, you don't get in FIBA," Kerr said. "More than anybody, probably LeBron and Ant are the two guys who are most capable from that team of just driving right through contact, getting to the rim and finishing. . . . Then I think the fact that we brought Kevin off the bench to start, it made it more palatable for Ant to come off the bench. They just liked playing together so much better."

The team also liked Edwards's on-ball defense—he would hound opposing guards coming up the floor, and there were multiple times when he'd pick someone's pocket for an easy bucket going the other way.

"It's hard coming off the bench in FIBA and trying to be instant impact," Curry said. "But one, he played with great energy. He can get to his spots pretty much in any one-on-one type situation. . . . He played on-ball defense, kind of like what Book was for us in the starting lineup, he was that for the second unit. You just got to be as impactful as you can in your minutes. I think he proved that pretty much the whole time."

Edwards made his biggest impact in the group stage. Durant, coming off the calf injury, didn't play in any of the tune-up games prior to France, but he hit 8-for-9 for 23 points in the USA's blowout win over Serbia. The starting lineup was struggling to develop chemistry initially, but the bench unit created separation on the scoreboard through the group stage. Edwards's best game came against Puerto Rico, when he scored 26 points on 11-for-15 shooting. He also scored 17 in the quarterfinals victory over Brazil before Holland got a bad feeling prior to the semifinals rematch against Jokic and Serbia. Edwards said he wasn't worried about the game because "Bron, Steph, and KD and them ain't gonna let us lose."

"I said no, this ain't one of those situations. You got to be a part of this," Holland said. "I knew he was checked out."

Edwards came out "half-assed" in that game, Holland said. He had just two points in 13 minutes and was a minus-14. Edwards was right in the sense that those superstars didn't let the US lose. They were down 11 in the fourth quarter before storming back for the win behind 36 from Curry while Edwards watched from the bench.

"I was fucking pissed in the semifinals game, because I've never seen him become a fan during the game he's competing in," Holland said.

But afterward, Holland regained some perspective over just where Edwards was at this moment and just how far he had come.

"Man, this kid is literally playing on the court with his idols," Holland said. "These are the guys he watched his entire life."

In the finals against Gobert and France, Edwards only played nine minutes as Kerr leaned on the old guard of stars to deliver the gold medal. But there was a moment in that game that became an eternal one for Edwards, a moment that even little Ant Man growing up in Atlanta couldn't dream up and scribble on the walls of his grandparents' house, that's how impossible it once seemed.

A Kid and KD

In October 2024, prior to a Suns preseason game against Detroit, Durant sat at his locker for about fifteen minutes to talk about his experience playing with Edwards. Durant is a guardian of the game. He knows its history, he appreciates talent of all ages, all nationalities, and he wants to make sure the game is in good hands. A few years before 2024, Durant said he was watching an interview Edwards gave in which he mentioned Durant as his favorite player growing up. That was the start of a relationship that only grew over time and became a strong bond in the Olympics.

"He's just as advertised: authentic, real person who loves the game of basketball, loves his teammates, loves to play," Durant said. "That's somebody I usually gravitate towards."

He might not have known the depth of how much Edwards looked up to him. Yes, he wore the shoes, but he always played as Durant on *2K*, and his former AAU teammates used to tease him that he was KD's son. Well, he's not that, but Durant did compare him to another family member as he got to know him.

"I'm not trying to put him as a little bro, but it felt like that. When you wake up in the morning and your little bro got the most energy. That was Ant," Durant said. "It was a joy to be around him. Not just him, his whole crew was out there. . . . He has a family atmosphere around him, and he's big on family and his friends and his core people, and that's gonna take him a long way."

Off the court, the two were always talking, and Durant said they shared a lot of meals together. With the dozens of people in the traveling party, Durant said they would usually break off into small clusters for dinners or nights out. He and Edwards were often in those clusters together, especially when the team was in London prior to traveling to France. He smiled as he described how Edwards's voice would often ring in his head, even if Edwards would just send a text to him or the group chat.

"You can just hear the text," Durant said. "That's just that southern hospitality, that southern twang he got. He cares about family and community and relationships. That showed throughout our time here, because he's such a fan of everybody's. . . . He really appreciated that moment. It was cool to see, because it reminded me of myself when I was at my first Olympics."

He added: "I miss being around Ant every day."

Edwards will never forget a lot of things about his first Olympics, but specifically what happened in that gold medal game. Late in the third quarter, Anthony Davis got a steal, and he threw an outlet pass to Durant on the right side of the floor. Edwards raced down the left side. It was a two-on-one and both of them knew what was going to happen.

"I said, 'Oh they got to get this,'" Maddox said. "This would be nasty."

As he hit the left wing, Edwards chopped his feet to make sure he got the timing right on his dunk. Maddox said Edwards told him afterward he was anticipating Durant throwing the lob earlier. But Edwards got the timing right. Durant put a lot of touch on it over French defender Isaia Cordinier, and Edwards didn't try to do anything fancy. He got above the rim, caught it, and threw it down. Edwards has had more forceful dunks, but none more meaningful.

"It was an exciting moment for both of us," Durant said. "That's a high-flying connection. It's something that got people out their seats. I knew exactly how to throw the ball. Like our chemistry met—you seen our chemistry in that moment."

Edwards yelled and pointed at Durant as he made his way back down the floor. He seemed as if he was in delirium for a few seconds before he had to play defense again. In the arena and across the globe, Edwards's friends couldn't believe what they had just seen.

"It don't get no better than this," Maddox said. "Catching the alley-oop from your favorite player. . . . That moment right there was so surreal."

Said Sturdivant, his former AAU teammate and one of the people who used to tease him that he was Durant's son: "Life comes at you fast. One day you're playing 2K with that dude you look up to and next thing you look up and you're receiving and alley-oop from him. God is not only real but He's almighty. I looked into my brother's eyes, and I seen nothing but joy, because this road has been full of ups and downs, but we still became triumphant through it all."

Edwards was a gold medalist, and he accepted his medal standing between Curry and James. James later teased Edwards for not being able to open a bottle of champagne as the team celebrated afterward. Edwards will acquire that ability in due time, Durant said.

"He has the potential group to accomplish just about everything every great has accomplished," Durant said. "MVPs, finals, championships, all NBAs, max deals on top of max deals. Shoes. All of that stuff. It's there for him now, but it's going to get even bigger and better."

The kid from Oakland City who lost his mother, Yvette, and grandmother Shirley at thirteen, who could only look up to his idol through video games and highlights, now was getting an alley-oop in a gold medal game from his hero. The long odds of that becoming reality just don't compute. Durant doesn't know how Edwards did it.

"I can't fathom," Durant said. "My mom, my grandma, are my rocks. They're my support system. Everything to me. So to lose two important people in your life at an early age and still come out as a respectful, genuine human being—it takes a community to raise people, and he had a great community around him that kept him on the right track through tragedy like that."

So when Edwards leapt for that lob from Durant, he didn't do it on his own. So many from his past and present played a part in lifting him above that rim in Paris that day. So many people, so many families who made sure he was okay, made sure he had something to eat, a ride to school, to practice, to games. They provided the support, and Edwards found the drive within himself to use that support as his launching pad. Just imagine how Yvette and Shirley might have felt when Durant closed the interview by saying:

"It feels like he's part of my family."

Who knows how high he'll leap in the future?

ACKNOWLEDGMENTS

There are many people I'd like to thank for helping me get to this point in my career and for specifically helping this project get to the finish line. Apologies if I don't get them all. First, to Sean Desmond, for believing I could pull this off, and to my friend Joe Perry for setting this all up. This doesn't happen without that Zoom call in May 2024.

Thanks to Dana Watkins for the countless hours on the phone and in person for six weeks in Atlanta in August and September 2024. Thank you for introducing me to several people influential in Ant's life. I'll never forget hanging out in the Loews Hotel months before this project was on anybody's radar when you said I should write Ant's biography. Talk about speaking something into existence.

Thanks to Justin Holland for listening to my pitch in May 2024 and believing I could be the person to tell Ant's story. I know a lot of people came to you and asked if it was okay to talk to me for this project. Without your trust, this book doesn't get done. Thanks also to members of Ant's circle, like Drew Banks and Nick Maddox, for sharing your stories and memories.

Thanks to Rachel Little for inviting me to her home one day and telling stories she had never told anyone else about Holy Spirit. Thanks to Tom Crean and all those who crossed paths with Ant at Georgia for your time. Thanks to Chris and Mya Hinton, and Reign Watkins and Kyle Sturdivant, for your time and trust.

Thanks to the Timberwolves PR staff, including Sara Perez, Aaron Freeman, Derek Ahrnsbrak, and Patrick Rees, for their months of coordinating interviews for this project. Thank you also for being easy to work with during the course of long NBA seasons. Thanks to Tim Connelly and Matt Lloyd for their time and trust, and for thinking this project could be something special. Thanks to Chris Finch for always being a candid subject, for the multiple interviews you gave for this, along with allowing members of your staff to be interviewed. Thanks to Micah Nori and Chris Hines (no relation!) for their time. Thanks to all of Ant's teammates, past and present, for giving your time to make this project work and for your trust in me as a reporter to tell your stories over the years. Players like Naz Reid, Jordan McLaughlin, Mike Conley, Nickeil Alexander-Walker, Rudy Gobert, and Kyle Anderson. Thanks to Karl-Anthony Towns for doing our interview even after the trade.

Thanks to the PR staffs of the Suns, Warriors, Trail Blazers, and Knicks who helped arrange interviews. This wasn't about one of your players, but you helped anyway. Thank you to all the players and coaches around the league who spoke. The last chapter doesn't happen without Stephen Curry, Devin Booker, Steve Kerr, and Kevin Durant. Thanks to Gersson Rosas and Ryan Saunders for their perspective on the draft process and Ant's rookie year.

Personally, I'd like to thank my family for always being a source of positive support. Same for all my close friends from my time at Notre Dame, for all those who put up with me while I was sports editor and editor in chief at the school newspaper, *The Observer*, where I didn't know what I was doing. Thanks to all the people in the journalism department, like Matt Storin, Jack Colwell, Julia Keller, and Robert Schmuhl, who believed in me and helped kick-start my career. Thanks to Bill Dwyre and Laura Ornest for setting up the first internship of my career at the *Los Angeles Times*. Thanks to my best bud, Jake Burnett, for over fifteen years of friendship. Thank you for pushing me to have the courage to become an openly gay sportswriter.

Thanks to the people who brought me in for internships or mentored me during stops in Los Angeles and New York, people like Debbie Goffa, Randy Harvey, Mike James, Tom Jolly, Sandy Keenan, Naila-

Jean Meyers, and my good friend Jonathan Abrams, who has been a constant inspiration for my career.

Thanks to all the sports editors who hired me for a job or for whom I've worked: Mike Kellams, Tim Bannon, Joe Knowles, Glen Crevier, Chris Carr, and Ryan Kostecka. Thanks to my team leader, Chris Miller, at the *Minnesota Star Tribune*. You help make the job of NBA beat writer a lot less stressful. Thanks also to everyone at the *Star Tribune* for allowing me to do this project. Thanks to the reporters I've shared press boxes and many meals with during stops on beats at the University of Illinois, Notre Dame, the Chicago Blackhawks, and the Timberwolves. Thanks to the NHL writers in America and Canada for embracing me when I came out as a sportswriter while covering the Blackhawks in 2016. Your support and friendship meant the world at a delicate time in my life. Thank you to my colleagues around the NBA beat for your friendship and specifically to my friends on the Wolves beat, including Jon Krawczynski, Jace Frederick, Dane Moore, and Britt Robson.

Last but not least, thank you to Ant for opening the door to your world. Thank you for being open to this idea from the start and for giving the nod to those close to you on and off the court to speak. Thank you for trusting me to tell your story. It has been a privilege.

INDEX

ABOUT THE AUTHOR

A graduate of the University of Notre Dame and former staff writer for the *Chicago Tribune*, CHRIS HINE has covered the Timberwolves for the *Minnesota Star Tribune* since 2018. He was named Illinois Sportswriter of the Year in 2017 by the National Sports Media Association. He lives in Minneapolis.